Illustrated
Motor Cars of the World

Illustrated
Motor Cars of the World
REVISED AND ENLARGED EDITION

by
PIET OLYSLAGER

with an introduction by
JACK BRABHAM

PUBLISHERS - **GROSSET & DUNLAP** - NEW YORK

A National General Company

CONTENTS

ABBREVIATIONS

b.h.p.   Brake horsepower

d.o.h.c   Dual overhead camshafts

o.h.v.   Single overhead camshafts

s.v.   Side valves

F.head   Overhead intake, side exhaust valves

L-head   Side valves, all on the same side

T-head   Side valves, intake on one side of the block, exhaust on the other side

INTRODUCTION

No invention has revolutionized our way of living more then the automotive vehicle. But the motor car did not come into being in a flash of one man's inspiration. Rather, it was the product of an evolutionary process that started long before mankind ever dreamed of such a thing as an "auto age."

Automobile history can be traced to the Golden Age of the Roman Empire or even as far back as the discovery of the wheel. However, historians set 1769 as the year of the first self-propelled land vehicle — a cumbersome steam artillery tractor built by French Army Captain Nicolas Joseph Cugnot. The tractor's speed was about four miles an hour, about average walking gait. This vehicle also has to go on record as being involved in the first automotive traffic accident in history. Cugnot ran it into a stone wall and brought disaster and the police down upon him. He was jailed and his wrecked vehicle was impounded.

In 1801 an Englishman, Richard Trevithick, built a succesful steam carriage, and by 1830, England had several steam coaches operating on its roads. These vehicles climbed hills under their own power — a remarkable feat for their time — and carried as many as fourteen passengers at an average speed of about 15 to 20 miles an hour. But many people objected to those monsters of the road which frightened horses and children. The railroads and stagecoach lines also opposed steam carriages because they both were frightened of the competition. Because of this opposition, England passed in 1861 what is known as the Red Flag Law which required somebody to walk in front of a self-propelled vehicle with a red flag or a lantern at night, to warn of its coming. This all but ruled steam carriages off English roads until Parliament repealed the statute late in 1896.

But the mechanical evolution of the modern automobile really began to take form about 100 years ago when European inventors such as Jean Joseph Lenoir and Nikolaus August Otto developed the internal combustion engine. In 1864, Siegfried Marcus, an Austrian inventor, built a four-wheeled vehicle using a Lenoir-type engine. It ran, but somewhat crudely. For the next few years, Marcus worked on other engineering projects. But in 1875 he produced a true one-cylinder, four-wheeled machine with electrical ignition, jet carburetion, and a throttle. In spite of all other claims, this **could** be called the first automobile.

In 1885, Gottlieb Daimler built a two-wheeled motorcycle powered by a light, single-cylinder gasoline engine. The next year he installed a similar engine in a four-wheel vehicle. Karl Benz, working independently of Daimler, produced a three-wheel car with a water-cooled, single-cylinder gasoline engine in 1885. But it is not wise to rely completely on the dates. In the long view of history, a year one way or the other is not important, and it is only proper to consider both Benz and Daimler as the true fathers of the modern automobile.

Frenchmen established the present general design of cars. Emile Levassor and Rene Panhard, partners in a carriage firm, began building automobiles in the early 1890's, using Daimler engines. In the fashion of the French, romance determined the use of these engines. About 1886 Levassor was approached by a M. Sarazin with the idea of building Daimler engines in France. Sarazin had secured the French right for Daimler's engine patents, and Levassor agreed to build a few. When Sarazin died in 1887, his widow kept the license by a special arrangement with Gottlieb Daimler. On May 17, 1890, Emile Levassor married Louise Sarazin, and under French law, the Daimler patent license was transferred to him. **Maybe** they went off on their honeymoon in a Panhard-Levassor, powered by a Daimler engine.

Levassor was responsible for many design changes in the cars of that period. He placed the engine in the front, instead of trying to make the automobile look like a carriage. Power was transmitted to the rear wheels by a gear box. Another Frenchman, Louis Renault, was the first to develop a shaft drive. Until then, chains carried the power to the rear wheels. Early French leadership in the automotive industry also gave the English language such terms as chauffeur, chassis, garage, and even the coined word "automobile."

It has been **generally** recognized that the first succesful American car propelled by an internal combustion engine was the motorized buggy assembled by Charles and Frank Duryea in their Springfield, Massachusetts, machine shop and road-tested in 1893. The next year, Elwood G. Haynes designed a gasoline automobile which he had Elmer and Edgar Apperson and Jonathan Dixon Maxwell make for him. All four men later became prominent in the early automobile industry. Actually, by the turn of the century, building cars was big business. About 1903, people began to talk of an automobile industry. From an early lead, France has now been relegated in terms of production figures to a place behind Great Britain. The largest automobile producing countries today are the United States, West Germany, Great Britain, France, Japan, and Italy.

AMERICAN CARS

While the United States produces more cars than all the other countries of the world, it was not always that way. When the automobile appeared on the American scene it was somewhat like a ship on a desert. The United States was virtually a roadless land. A few carriage routes went beyond the cities and major towns, but in wet weather even these turned into winding rivers of mud. When dry, they were deeply rutted and dusty. Under any conditions, they offered little encouragement to pioneers of the dawning motor age.

The public was not too overly enthusiastic about the automobile, either. Vermont passed a "red flag law" of its own in 1894 that made it illegal for anyone to drive a car on a public road unless someone walked several hundred feet ahead to give warning. In Pennsylvania, the Farmers'

Anti-Automobile Society proposed the following measure to protect the terrified horses: "If a horse is unwilling to pass an automobile, the driver of the motorized vehicle should take the machine apart as rapidly as possible and conceal the parts in the bushes." Fortunately, the society never got its proposal enacted. In 1896, it was passed by both houses of the Pennsylvania legislature, but vetoed by the governor.

There were so few automobiles in the United States in 1896 that the Barnum & Bailey Circus displayed one as its main oddity. But that same year Henry Ford, Charles King, and Alexander Winton put their first cars on the road. By then it was obvious that America had the technical possibility of manufacturing cars, and at the turn of the century such makes as Oldsmobile, Haynes-Apperson, Stanley Steamer, Pope-Hartford, and Packard had appeared on the market. But as cars ceased to be a curiosity and began to fill numerous transportation needs, the factories were faced with the problem of catching up with the demand. There was only one solution — improved production methods.

The thought of mass production was no new idea, but the methods evolved by F. W. Taylor could not be applied in the auto industry before Henry M. Leland had perfected machine tools to a degree which permitted the assembly and replacement of parts without special fittings, and Ransom E. Olds had layed out an assembly-line. In the Olds plant, the framework of each auto was pushed on a wooden platform supported by rolling casters. The framework passed between lines of workmen who added parts until the car was completed. In 1901, the Olds Motor Vehicle Company built 425 cars. The next year, using mass-production methods, the company built over 2,500 Oldsmobiles.

Henry Ford greatly improved the mass-production technique by the introduction of conveyer belts. Ford had the bare frame, or chassis, of a car pulled along a conveyer. Workmen on each side added parts brought to them by other conveyers. Up to 1913, it required approximately a day and a half to assemble the famous Model T. But by using conveyer assembly line, the same model could be put together in 93 minutes, except for the body. The body was added a few minutes later.

As the production rate has increased and the American auto industry has grown in size, the numbers of makes has shrunk from over 1,500 to three giant concerns and one independent. Ford Motor Company builds Fords, Mercuries, and Lincolns. General Motors has five makes: Chevrolet, Pontiac, Oldsmobile, Buick, and Cadillac. The Chrysler Corporation makes the Plymouth, Dodge, Chrysler, and Imperial. American Motors is the only independent auto maker left.

The Ford Motor Company was incorporated in 1903 and in the first five years, Ford Models A, B, C, F, K, N, R, and S were built. In 1908, the Model T was introduced and was the Ford car for the next nineteen years. Thanks to mass production, Henry Ford was able to keep a promise he made when he conceived the Model T. That was to reduce the price each year of production. The Model T started at $ 950 in 1908. By 1912 it was down to $ 780, by 1913 to $ 600, by 1916 to

$ 440, and by 1917 to $ 360. It hit rock bottom at $ 290 in 1926. By the time the last Model T's were built and sold on May 31, 1927, a total of 15,456,868 of them had rolled from Ford assembly lines.

In 1927, the "Tin Lizzie," as the Model T was affectionately known, was replaced with the Model A. This car remained basically unchanged until 1932, when Ford brought out the "V-8" engine. The company acquired control of the Lincoln Motor Car Company in 1922. (Lincoln was founded by Henry M. Leland in 1917.) In 1938, the Ford Company introduced the Mercury line of cars. This new make was aimed for the medium price field. During the middle 1950's a "compact" line — Falcon and Comet (Mercury) — and sports car — Thunderbird — were added to the Ford family.

General Motors Corporation is the largest producer of automobiles in the world. William C. Durant was the creator of this colussus. A one-time partner in a cart and carriage factory, he got into the auto industry when took over the ailing Buick Motor Company in 1903, which had been formed the year before by David D. Buick). Five years after he acquired Buick, Durant organized General Motors with Buick, Oldsmobile, and Oakland as its initial units. (The latter became known as Pontiac in 1931.) Later Cadillac (founded by Henri M. Leland in 1903) and Durant's own Chevrolet Motor Company were added. In addition, Durant acquired dozens of other companies, including makers of parts as well as cars. Among the cars were such hazily remembered names as Cartercar, Rainier, Elmore, Welch-Detroit, Reliance, Rapid, and Randolph. It was Durant's fantastic dream to develop one gigantic company that would make virtually all the cars in the United States. But he ran out of credit and was forced out of General Motors in 1910. Five years later, however, Durant regained control of General Motors, and, as he had done before, immediately rushed into overexpansion. By 1920 he was bankrupt again. The corporation then came under Du Pont control and Alfred P. Sloan was appointed president. And it was Sloan who made General Motors big.

The Chrysler Corporation, with the Maxwell as its nucleus, was organized in 1925 by Walter P. Chrysler. The Maxwell make was one of the early lines of autos, being developed in 1903. But, in 1926, it became the Chrysler 50 and three years later it became known as the Plymouth. In 1928, the Chrysler Corporation purchased Dodge Brothers, Inc.

The Dodge organization was founded by the inseparable brothers, Horace E. and John F. Dodge, in 1914. John was a director and vice-president of the Ford Motor Company, while Horace was in charge of that company's engineering department. The brothers had a series of disagreements with Henry Ford and decided to start their firm. One industry chronicler, commenting on automobiles of the 1910-20 era remarked that whereas the Cadillacs "purred" and the Fords "rattled," the Dodges "chugged." But Dodge brothers seemed to be very happy with their chugging vehicles and tied it to the word "dependability" in their advertisements. Others believed in their slogan, too. The Dodge was chosen as the official staff-type car of the American Expeditionary Force in World War I. Before that, General John J. "Black Jack" Pershing used a

Dodge during the expedition against Pancho Villa in Mexico. Incidentally, Villa was so impressed that he used a Dodge as his official car and was chugging along in it when he met his violent death in 1923.

The Hudson Motor Car Company and Nash-Kelvinator Corporation were merged in 1954 to form American Motors. While the Hudson Motor Car Company was named after its principal source of money, Joseph L. Hudson, a Detroit department store owner, it was Roy D. Chapin who actually founded the organization. Chapin was one of the real pioneers of the auto industry, as was Charles W. Nash, founder of the Nash Corporation. American Motors discontinued production of both the Nash and Hudson models, concentrating its efforts on its Rambler, Ambassador, and American lines.

GERMAN CARS

Germany has an incontestable claim to being the cradle of the auto industry. After the early work of Otto, Daimler, and Benz, another type of engineer took over. A type who could look at the car as a whole, not as a power unit installed in some sort of a vehicle. The first of these engineers was Wilhelm Maybach, who created the lightweight "Stahlradwagen" in 1889. Two years later Theodor Bergmann and Joseph Vollmer brought out the Orient Express, and by 1893 had organized a small but steady output of these cars. Even the Benz organization began to produce the Benz Velo in 1893. But one of Germany's greatest auto achievements was its rise from utter ruin in 1945 to second greatest car producer in ten years.

Before World War II, five companies — Opel, Auto Union, Daimler-Benz, Adler, and Ford — produced 87 per cent of Germany's new cars. The situation is not so different today — but not all the names are the same. Volkswagen is the giant, having taken control of Auto Union (DKW and Audi). The next two biggest rivals are subsidiaries of American companies — Opel and Ford. The supporting cast of German producers is made up of BMW, Daimler-Benz, NSU, Porsche, and Glas.

The Volkswagen story began during the summer of 1934 when Dr. Ferdinand Porsche was summoned to the Hotel Kaiserhof in Berlin for a meeting with Adolph Hitler. Porsche, an Austrian, had been an outstanding car designer for Auto Union, Lohner, Maja, Daimler-Benz, Renault, Panhard, Cisitalia, and Steyr. At the time of the meeting, he had his own engineering consultant firm. In the private conference Hitler told Porsche that he wanted a car that would be small, perhaps a four-seater, have a good durable engine, get 35 to 40 miles to the gallon of gasoline, and be air-cooled since Germans did not have garages. Thus, in 1934, Hitler had described the modern Volkswagen. He even called it a Volkswagen — the people's car — and stipulated that it sell at a price below 1,000 marks (equivalent to about $ 250).

What Hitler did not know was that Porsche had already designed and built several small cars similar to what the dictator wanted. In partnership with Hans F. Neumayer of Zündapp Werke, he made his first small car prototype in 1931. The Zündapp-VW, as it was called, had a rear-mounted, five-cylinder radial engine with air-cooling, but it was not a success.

The following year, Porsche approached NSU with a revised design. The air-cooled, flat-four engine was rear mounted and it had a squared-off body, very much like the present VW. Even its name was similar — Volksauto. But NSU's motorcycle sales boomed in 1933, so the car design was shelved.

After the Hitler conference, Porsche resurrected the Volksauto and began to redesign it. It took time. He had established his workshop in his own private garage and, meticulous engineer that he was, refused to rush the project despite the relentless pressure of Hitler. Porsche even visited the United States to study the American production system. On returning, he informed Hitler that German private capital could never finance this kind of operation; it had to be done by the government. Der Führer agreed with him.

Finally in 1936 the three prototypes were ready. After severe road tests, Porsche was satisfied, and at the 1937 Automobile Show Hitler announced that production would soon start. But Volkswagens really never got rolling until after the war. Then, returned to private enterprise, the VW has become one of the most popular cars in the world.

Incidentally, Dr. Porsche was over 70 years old before his name appeared on a car. The first Porsche was produced in 1947 and exhibited to the public in 1949. It has been a success ever since.

Friedrich Lutzmann, an expert toolmaker, built his first Pfeil car in 1895, and built some sixty vehicles in less than three years before selling out, lock stock, and barrel, to Adam Opel. This company built a few cars under Lutzmann patents prior to 1900, but then acquired a license from Darracq (a French auto line) and expended their car business. In 1929, Opel became part of General Motors, Today, its Kadett is one of the more popular small cars.

Ford's activity in Germany began in 1926 with an assembly plant in Berlin. When the Model A was introduced, Ford started construction of a plant in Cologne. It began to produce cars in 1930. The first German-designed Ford came out in 1934. The first Taunus appeared in 1938. Since the war, the Cologne plant has been rebuilt and expanded in recent years to the point where Ford is the No. 3 auto producer in Germany.

The Mercedes-Benz, in terms of genealogical line, is the oldest car in automotive history. It stems directly from the first practical car made, the original Daimler of 1886. When Daimler needed financial backing to enter the auto business, he turned to Emile Jellinek, an early auto enthusiast. He agreed to raise the necessary money, under one stipulation — the new car must bear the name of his daughter, Mercedes. Daimler agreed, and the only great car to carry a girl's name was born.

The merger between Daimler and Benz Corporations was anticipated when the leaders entered an interest union in 1924. Two years later, the two formally merged. Under the name Daimler-Benz the new company had an undisputed claim to the earliest heritage of the automobile, an unbroken line from the first patents on. The cars were henceforth known as Mercedes-Benz. In the 1930's, the Daimler-Benz firm paid most of their attention to racing. Adolf Hitler, seeking to gain sporting prestige for his Nazi state, offered financial aid to the company to develop a championship racing car. From 1935 to 1938 the Mercedes ruled the auto racing world. But since the war, the firm has concentrated on roadsters, sedans, and sport cars.

BRITISH CARS

About 1904, the British auto industry became an organized part of the nation's economy. Many new makes appeared during the earliest years—Humber, Vauxhall, Rover, Sunbeam, Singer, Talbot, Standard, Austin, Lea-Francis, and Rolls-Royce. Several of the British constructors joined the continentals on the race tracks and established enviable traditions. After World War II, Great Britain has been extremely motor-sport conscious, and a number of small garages have grown into speed-equipment factories and racing establishments. Since 1957 Great Britain has had its own way in racing events of all types.

Such was the atmosphere when I arrived in England and added the Brabham name to the racing rosters and speed shops. But let us not forget the pioneers. I want to mention the Napier driven by S. F. Edge to victory in the Gordon Bennett Trophy race in 1902. Victor Rigal, in a Sunbeam, captured first place in the Coupe de l'Auto at Dieppe ten years later. Henry Segrave driving a later Sunbeam won the French Grand Prix at Tours in 1923. The next year, Bentley won the 24-hour race at Le Mans for the first time. Incidentally, Bentleys returned to win four consecutive races at Le Mans. Other cars with an outstanding competition record are ERA, MG, Talbot, AC, Riley, Aston Martin, and Singer. In recent history, the successes of such cars as Jaguar, Vanwall, Cooper, and Lotus are too numerous to count let alone mention.

Britain is still the producer of "The Best Car in the World" — the Rolls-Royce. And the manufacturer stands behind this slogan. A famous and perhaps slightly jealous American auto manufacturer once cracked that "the Rolls-Royce is the triumph of craftsmanship over design". While he meant this statement as no compliment, his quip high-lighted the reason for Rolls-Royce's success for more than sixty years. For every Rolls-Royce has been a triumph of craftsmanship, and if its design has often seemed behind the times, it is because the flashy mechanical tricks and gingerbread have always had to take second place to the homely virtues of smoothness, silence, durability, and the not-so-homely virtue of luxurious travel. The product of the firm founded by Charles S. Rolls and Henry Royce is a car that will run for a fantastic number of years and its classic elegance will never be dated. Some early models have become family heirlooms, passed down through several generations, and still in running order. Few will argue that RR's slogan is not justifiable.

The largest automotive combine in Britain is called BMC (British Motor Corporation). The makes owned by this concern are Austin, Riley, Morris, Wolseley, and MG. The latter initials, which are encased in an octagon, are derived in a round about way. In 1913, William R. Morris, a former bicycle builder, formed a company called Morris Motors Limited. This firm produced the Morris car. A short while later, he formed a subsidiary corporation to make another model. The new concern was named The Morris Garages and its product was called MG. But it was not until 1923 that the initials were placed on the radiator of the auto.

Morris (who later became Lord Nuffield in the 20's) purchased the ailing Wolseley Company in 1927, and took over the Riley in 1938. The Nuffield Organization, as BMC is often called, merged with Austin in 1952. The merger has led to simplification of the model lineup, spare parts organization, and large savings in manufacturing costs. In ten years, BMC did away with nine engine styles without reducing the number of car models. For commercial reasons, all nameplates of the merged companies are continued.

Another one of Britain's large auto combines is the Rootes Group (now under Chrysler Corporation control). William Rootes began as a Humber/Hillman dealer and grew to a point where, in 1928, he became the sole distributor and exporter of these cars. Four years later he acquired control of Humber and Hillman. In 1934 Talbot was added to his holdings; in 1935, Sunbeam. In 1938 the latter two were merged into Sunbeam-Talbot, but in 1954, the Talbot name was dropped from the nameplate. In 1956, Singer was added to the Rootes Group.

British Ford and General Motors' Vauxhall are two of the country's largest auto producers. Ford opened a factory in Manchester to build the Model T in 1911. Since that time, British Ford has pioneered many technical innovations including MacPherson front suspension on the Consul and Zephyr (1950), V-4 engines (1965), and V-6 engines and independent rear suspension (1966). General Motors' English division was founded in 1857 as Vauxhall Iron Works to build marine engines. The first Vauxhall car was made in 1903, and four years later, the firm's name was changed to Vauxhall Motors. The new company won a great sporting reputation with such vehicles as the Prince Henry in 1910 and the 30/98 in 1913. In the mid-20's, General Motors, shopping around for a factory in England, purchased Vauxhall, after failing to gain control of Wolseley. It proved to be a lucky move for GM, since their Vauxhall models have done well over the years.

Possibly the most forceful all-British elements in England's auto industry are the Leyland Group, Rover Motor Company, and Jaguar Cars. The Leyland Group includes Triumph; Jaguar Cars owns Daimler, Guy Truck, and Coventry Climax Engines; Rover builds Rover cars, Land-Rovers, and recently acquired Alvis Limited, makers of luxury cars and military vehicles, plus a range of aircraft engines.

The origins of Triumph go back to the formation of the Standard Motor Company in 1903. Standard's cars had few standout design features, but were well-known for the good service they gave. In 1945, Standard Motors took over Triumph's assets and the new line became known as Standard-Triumph. Triumph cars sprang from the Triumph Cycle Company, formed in 1885 by Schulte and Bettmann. In 1902 they began to manufacture motorcycles, and twenty years later acquired the plant of the Dawson Car Company and brought out the Triumph auto. Standard-Triumph became part of the Leyland Group in 1961. (Leyland is an important truck manufacturer, having built commercial vehicles since 1896). Ever since the original Standard-Triumph merger, the Triumph models have emerged as the best sellers. Thus, in 1963, the firm decided to discontinue the Standard (Vanguard) line.

Rover's beginning dates back to 1877 when J. K. Starley and W. Sutton built the first Rover bicycle. They built a motorcycle in 1903, but the following year decided to start making cars. The 12 h.p. Rover of 1911 established the make as a high-quality vehicle, and the company continues to enjoy this fine reputation. In 1950 Rover built the first gas-turbine-powered auto in the world, and in 1964 they entered a turbine-driven car in the 24-hour race at Le Mans for the first time. The Alvis branch of Rover has a glorious history, starting in 1920. During the 30's, their Speed 25 and Silver Crest were among the world's outstanding cars.

The Jaguar enterprises are founded on a business that William Lyons started in 1923 to build motorcycle sidecars. The firm expanded into the Swallow Sidecar and Coachbuilding Company, and it built car bodies for Austin and other manufacturers. In 1931, Lyons decided to enter the auto business and made arrangements with the Standard Motor Company to supply him with engines. Later that year the first SS (for Swallow Special) cars appeared. By 1933, the original Swallow Sidecar and Coachbuilding Company was only a small adjunct to the newly incorporated SS Cars Limited, and Lyons was finally a full member of Britain's auto industry.

In 1935, the SS Jaguar was introduced, and ten years later the SS name was dropped; all models were Jaguars. At the same time the corporation name was changed to Jaguar Cars Limited. The change was made for a very good psychological reason. While the initials SS were a dignified and meaningful title, it also stood for *Schutz-Staffel,* Hitler's Storm Troopers. Thus, with the memories of the dread SS troops in the minds of the world's people, Lyons felt that a continuing association with the now undesirable initials would hurt sales. Incidentally, William Lyons still holds the reins of the company and has guided it through a recent expansion era.

Since 1945, Britain has lost some of the smaller car manufacturers such as Lea-Francis, H. R. G., Frazer Nash, Alta, Jowett, and Lanchester. Healey survived by affiliating itself with Austin (now BMC). Aston Martin and Lagonda have survived under the eagis of David Brown, famous manufacturers of tractors and gears. Perhaps the future of the British auto trade may belong to such makes as Lotus, Lola, Marcas, Elva, McLaren, and, possibly, Brabham.

FRENCH CARS

France was once *the* country of automobiles. Motor racing began in France, and at the turn of the century, French cars were almost invincible in competition. Instead of Ferrari, Lotus, and Cooper, the winning makes were Darracq, Gobron-Brillié, Renault, Rochet-Schneider, Mors, Panhard-Levassor, Richard-Brasier, Peugeot, and Turcat-Méry. Even when Sunbeam, Duesenberg, Mercedes, Fiat, and Alfa Romeo threatened France's domination of the world's race tracks in the 1920's and '30's, French traditions were carried on by Ballot, Delage, Bugatti, and Talbot. But all these great names have left the French Automotive scene, except for that of Renault and Peugeot. And while these two companies produce some of the most roadworthy cars in the world, they do not race.

Actually Armand Peugeot, founder of the Peugeot line, was in at the very beginnings of the automobile. Like many of the early American pioneers, he started his automotive career as a bicycle maker. In 1889, he started experimenting with motor-driven vehicles and built a steam car that worked fairly well. When Daimler decided to sell his internal combustion engine to all buyers, Peugeot installed one in a specially designed vehicle. He employed a tubular steel chassis instead of a heavy frame and selected light bicycle wheels rather than the carriage type used by other car makers. Thus, even in 1890, Peugeot was establishing a formula of a light maneuverable car which the company still follows.

In 1894 Peugeot made a car that tied for first place with Panhard-Levassor in the Paris-to-Rouen race, one of the early reliability events. Then in 1895 Peugeot won the first place prize in the world's first organized road event — the Paris-to-Bordeaux race.

After this victory, Armand with his brother, Robert, decided to manufacture engines for their racers. With the help of Ernest Henri, the Peugeot factory developed the first light, fast power plant that won for the firm three Indianapolis and two Vanderbilt Cup contests. But it was not only in the field of racing that the Peugeot penchant for small, deft cars showed. In 1912 the company produced one of the first four-cylinder economy vehicles — the Bebe Peugeot. Because of the wide acceptance of this car, Peugeot stopped building racing machines and concentrated exclusively on the production of passenger vehicles and trucks. The solidly constructed, light and easy-to-handle cars that are now seen on the roads throughout the world demonstrate Peugeot's ideals in automotive construction.

Renault, France's largest automobile manufacturer, was established in 1899 by three brothers, Fernand, Louis, and Marcel Renault. But Marcel was killed in the Paris-to-Madrid auto race in 1903; Fernand also died at a young age. However, Louis Renault led the business until his death in 1944. He willed his factories to his employees, but the government nationalized the Renault plant in 1945.

As a matter of fact, the French government just after World War II had a plan to create six major auto manufacturer groups. Renault and Citroën (the second largest auto company in France) were considered large enough to form a group each on their own. The government plan grouped Peugeot with the Hotchkiss, the Latil, and the Saurer. The Berliet group comprised the Rochet-Schneider and the Isobloc. The Union Français de l'Automobile included the Panhard, the Somua, and the Willlème. The GFA (Groupement Français de l'Automobile) embraced the Bernard, the Delage, the Delahaye, the Laffly, the Unic, and the Simca. The plan never worked very well, although the individual factories managed to produce vehicles. By 1949, the government operation had completely collapsed. The auto makers were given full freedom, and mergers and agreements were allowed to form by natural process.

The resultant French auto picture differs considerably from the artificial government plan. For instance, Latil and Somua were taken over by Renault. The French Saurer plan merged with Unic, which in turn was absorbed by Simca. Panhard was taken over by Citroën.

The Citroën firm itself began operation in 1919 when Andre Citroën, a mechanical engineer who perfected the herringbone gear, decided to manufacture cars. He was determined to build the people's car of France. He succeeded because he introduced American mass production and assembly line techniques for the first time to the European auto industry. Because of this he has often been called the Henry Ford of France. Like Ford, Citroën resolved to design a basic model that could be produced for many years. In addition, he wanted a car that a purchaser could use for a long time, since the majority of French citizens could not afford to purchase cars periodically. His success on the latter can be pointed out by the fact that one of his 1934 Citroëns is still giving service after its original owner's claim of more than three million miles.

The other major French auto manufacturer, Simca, is controlled by an American firm. Simca, founded by Henri-Theodore Pigozzi, acquired a Fiat license in 1934 and, with Fiat's backing, built the Fiat 500 in France. It was not until 1951 that the first French-designed Simca appeared. But the biggest change in Simca evolution came in 1954 when the firm took over the modern Ford works at Poissy. (Ford of France had not met the same success that Ford enjoyed in England and Germany.) Simca continued the Ford models with Simca nameplates, but gradually developed hybrid models that lost the Ford flavor. In 1957, Chrysler Corporation started to buy into Simca and by 1962 had acquired the controlling interest. Thus, today Renault, Citroën, Peugeot, and Simca are the major representatives of the French automotive industry.

JAPANESE CARS

A few years ago, Japan displaced Italy as the fifth largest car-manufacturing country in the world. Japan has a long history of making cars, but it is only in recent years that production has reached significant figures and that the cars have been brought to world markets.

Actually, the man who did more than any other to get the Japanese auto industry off to a real start was an American industrialist, William R. Gorham. Without his help, Japanese factories would have been helplessly behind the times in terms of machine tools. In 1921, he built a three-wheeler for a disabled friend, and it received so much attention that he started a company to build more. The next year he manufactured four-wheel cars, and by 1926 the Gorham Company bought out DAT, the makers of the first gasoline-driven Japanese vehicles. The first DAT car was built in 1912 by Masujiro Hashimoto, an ambitious and hard-working engineer who had received his training in the United States.

In 1931, Japanese governmental pressure forced Gorham out of the country and local interests took over his factories. They brought out a series of light cars and trucks which they called Datsun. Three years later the Datsun was joined by a new line, the Nissan, and the firm was then renamed the Nissan Motor Company.

While several other auto makers — Ohta, Hino, Rokko, Isuzu, and Kyosan — started in the 1930's, no Japanese vehicle had world-wide acceptance and by 1941 all civilian production had ceased. Because of restrictions imposed by the United States occupation forces, auto factories were slow to restart. Even when manufacturing capacity existed, they had no new designs, no new tooling. Thus, license manufacture was the only solution.

Nissan started to build the Austin A-40 in 1953; simultaneously, Hino began making the Renault 4CU and Isuzu commenced manufacture of the Hillman Minx. These contracts expired in 1960, but many traces of Austin, Renault, and Hillman ancestry were evident in Japanese models for years beyond that date.

Today, the largest car maker in Japan is Toyota, with the Nissan/Datsun combine a close second. These two companies dominate the Japanese auto industry, while the supporting cast is made up of Prince, Isuzu, Hino, Mazda, Subaru, Mitsubishi, and Honda. Incidentally, the latter is the world's largest manufacturer of motorcycles. Soichiro Hondo got started by converting chain saw motors to cyclomotors, and the business evolved into a motorcycle factory. The first Honda car appeared in 1962 — an open sports model.

ITALIAN CARS

The birth of the Italian automobile industry came just before the turn of the century when Fiat, Bianchi and Isotta-Fraschini made their bow. The arrival of these Italian-designed autos was followed by the introduction of a number of makes produced in Italy under license. Such cars were the DeLuca (Daimler license), the Diatto (Clément), the Fides (Brasier), the Flag (Thornycroft), the Florentia (Rocket-Schneider), the Hisa (Hermès), the San Giorgio (Napier), the Victrix (Peugeot), and the Zust (Protos). Even the Italian-sounding corporation of Alfa Romeo had a French beginning early in the century.

Alexandre Darracq located a factory in Naples in 1906 as an assembly plant for his cars. He also established sales and service offices in other Italian cities and began to market the Darracq. However, the entire venture failed within three years and all the assets were purchased by a group of Italian financiers. They promptly had the Darracq redesigned to meet their own tastes and gave the new organization the imposing name of Amonima Lombarda Fabbrica Automobili. The firm, however, was quickly called by its initials, ALFA.

The new company just barely stayed in existence until a young engineer named Nicola Romeo took charge of it at the time of the beginning of World War I, added his name, and called the firm Alfa Romeo.

While the Alfa Romeos made racing history through the 1920's, the P3 model designed by Vittorio Jano in 1932 was one of the most famous racing vehicles ever constructed. For the next three years its invincibility made Italy the ruler of the racing world. Just as Adolf Hitler had helped finance Daimler-Benz organization, the Italian dictator, Benito, Mussolini, poured a great deal of his Fascist money into the Alfa Romeo operation. Both dictators desired prestige in the sporting world, but by 1935 the Nazis, with their Mercedes racers, pulled far ahead. It was not until after World War II that Alfa Romeo became the ruler of the race tracks again. But today its fine sports and touring cars are better known than its racing models.

Another Italian firm that used its initials for its name is the Fiat. Until 1906, this company's cars were called F. I. A. T. (for Fabbrica Italiana di Automobili, Torino). Then the firm was reorganized and its vehicles were simply called Fiat. From its beginning, this firm has had a wide range of models, from light touring cars to powerful racers. A 300-h.p. Fiat held the world speed record in 1911. The 1922 six-cylinder Grand Prix Fiat was virtually unchallenged on the racing circuits, and was copied by many others. There was even a Super-fiat with a twelve-cylinder engine in 1924 — sort of an Italian Rolls-Royce.

In Mussolini's time, Fiat brought out a true people's car — the Fiat 500. It was designed by Dante Giacosa, a young engineer in the truck department, who placed his drawings before the management. After a great deal of persuasion by Giacosa, the company agreed to build a prototype and test it. The car that he had designed proved far superior to all the other small autos then undergoing tests at Fiat. It became the famous Topolino (Mickey Mouse).

And Giacosa was to become technical director of the company with responsibility for all cars and trucks produced. Today, Fiat is Italy's leading motor vehicle producer.

One of Italy's newer auto manufacturers is also one of its best known, especially among sports car enthusiasts. As they will quickly state, a sports car, ideally, should be a de-tuned racing machine rather than warmed-over touring automobile. In addition, it must have a built-in feeling of excitement. The one maker in the world who builds cars that meet these requirements is the Commendatore Enzo Ferrari.

Ferrari was a racing driver for the Alfa Romeo firm before he established his own racing stable, Scuderia Ferrari, in 1929. He took over the factory team cars from Alfa Romeo and raced them with considerable success until 1936. In 1938, Alfa Romeo organized its own racing department, Alfa Corse, and Enzo Ferrari started toying with the idea of building his own cars. The first one was known as the Auto-Avio Type 815 and was raced just once before World War II. But in 1947 Ferrari had a new V-12 design and was ready to conquer the world. His cars have done just about that ever since.

While these are the leading Italian auto makers, there are several others — Maserati, Lamborghini, OSCA (Officine Specializzate di Costruzione Automobili), and Lancia — that you may see on the highways and byways of the world.

CARS BEHIND THE IRON CURTAIN

The recent automotive history of the Soviet Union is well documented, but its origins are nebulous. It seems that a Lieutenant J. V. Romanoff built an electrically driven carriage in about 1898. Prior to 1914, a car called the Russo-Baltic was assembled in Riga (Latvia), mainly from Fondu parts imported from Belgium.

When Lenin came to power he ordered that a genuinely Russian car be built, but no results were forthcoming until 1924. It was a light truck called the AMO-15, and it was almost an exact copy of a Fiat model. The first original design came on the scene in 1927 and was produced in the Spartak factory in Moscow from a design by Professor J. R. Brilling and his students at the Moscow Research Institute for Motors and Automobiles. NAMI, as the vehicle was called, had an air-cooled, two-cylinder engine that was capable of 18.5 horsepower.

Through the collaboration of Henry Ford and his company, the Soviet Union got its first full-fledged automobile factory in the town of Gorki in 1932. The products of the factory are called GAZ (Gorkovski Automobil Zavod). The GAZ A was a Model A Ford, while the GAZ M-1, which appeared in 1935, was a four-cylinder version of the 1934 Ford.

In 1933, the original AMO factory was reorganized and its vehicles carried the ZIS (Zavod Imenij Stalina) designation. The ZIS-101, for example, was a big luxury car with a straight-eight cylinder engine. The ZIS-110 was a copy of the 1940 Packard Eight. After the demise of Stalin, the ZIS works were renamed ZIL (L for Lichatjew, in honor of the minister of transport).

Another auto factory in Moscow, KIM, built a small car in 1940, just before the plant was transferred east of the Ural. When the Moscow plant was refurbished after the war, it was renamed MZMA (Moscow Works for Small Cars) and tooled up for the manufacture of the 1938 Opel Kadett. It was given the name Moskvitch, and gradually developed into an original and modern design.

The Soviet Union had no counterpart to the Volkswagen until 1959, when the technical staffs of NAMI and MZMA got together and created the Zaporozhets. The first version was a disaster, but the replacement of the flat-four cylinder engine with an ingenious V-4 in 1960 has improved the model greatly.

Of the other Iron Curtain countries, Czechoslovakia has two old-established automobile manufacturers still in business: Skoda and Tatra. The latter concern started in 1896 as the Nesselsdorfer Wagonfabrik and became quite famous in 1920 for the high degree of technical advance shown in chassis design. Skoda began to build cars in about 1920, and in 1924 took over Laurin-Klement, which had been building good cars since 1902.

Poland's small car industry produces the Syrena, the Smyk, and the Warszawa, while East Germany, in the former Auto Union, Stoewer, and BMW plants, makes a DKW copy called the Wartburg and small car named the Trabant.

OTHER EUROPEAN CARS

Of the other remaining European countries only the Scandinavian area is still producing passenger cars in any numbers. There the Volvo and Saab are making great headway.

The founders of Volvo were Assar Gabrielsson and Gustaf Larson. Both had been independently thinking about building a Swedish car. In 1927, they joined forces, obtained the necessary financial backing, and the first cars were produced. Volvo had a remarkable growth up to 1959, but then the expansion became almost explosive. The 500,000th Volvo was produced that year, and the millionth Volvo came off the line just four years later (1963).

Saab is a very young organization. It was established in 1937 as the Swedish Aeroplane Company. Deliveries of twin-engined bomber aircraft to the Swedish government began two years later. The early planes were made under Junkers license, or by arrangement with Northrop-Douglas or North American Aviation. Design work on all-Swedish planes in 1938 and the first flight took place in 1940. Following the decline in the military aircraft market at the end of World War II, Saab decided to establish an auto division. The prototype was completed in 1946 and the production model was shown to the press the next year. From then on, the expansion has been meteoric, and the Saab has acquired a reputation for aircraft quality.

Holland also has a small but prosperous auto business, thanks to the efforts of the brothers Wim and Hub van Doorne. They began to build trailer and truck bodies in 1928 and expanded to build complete trucks twenty years later. Then in 1956 they introduced a small economy car with several unique technical features, notably the Variomatic transmission with cone-and-belt drive. Both trucks and cars are sold under the DAF name.

While Belgium produced many famous makes such as Minerva, Excelsior, and Métallurgique in the early years, the country today is mainly a base for assembly plants for imported vehicles. This is also true of Spain, which never had a large auto industry, nevertheless gave birth to many famous cars — the Hispano-Suiza, the Elizalde, the Nacional Pescara, the Ricart-Espana, and the Pegaso. (The latter was once considered the most expensive car in the world.) But these cars are only a memory, as is the passenger auto industry in Spain. Danish, Swiss, and Austrian companies manufactured cars in the early days of automotive history, but they are just memories, too.

Notes on the Specifications

Bore and stroke indicate cylinder dimensions. The bore is the cylinder diameter and the stroke is the length of the cylinder swept by the piston. Displacement is measured in cubic centimeters (1,000 c.c. equal one liter) or cubic inches (61 cubic inches equal one liter). Compression ratio is decided by comparing the volume in each cylinder when the piston is at bottom dead center and when the piston is at top dead center. Horsepower cannot be calculated; it can only be arrived at by testing the engine. Test methods vary from country to country, and we have several kinds of horsepower. In America, engines are tested without air cleaners, generators, and other accessories, and the horsepower is called S.A.E. (Society of Automotive Engineers). In Germany, engines are tested with all accessories (as installed in the car), and the horsepower is called D.I.N. (Deutsche Industrie-Normen). The British and the Italians use test methods resembling but not identical to the D.I.N. formula. In this book no distinction has been made as to type of horsepower. We have accepted the figures given by the manufacturers, and it can be assumed that they conform to the standard used in the car's country of origin.

In conclusion I would like to express my gratitude to my associate, Jan P. Norbye, whose aid in research and fact-checking proved invaluable, and to Robert Scharff, who did the lion's share of the work in preparing this introduction.

Jack Brabham

CUGNOT   **FRANCE 1770**

Three-wheeler gun tractor. 2-cyl. (single-acting, cylinder bore 330 mm.) with front-wheel drive. Each stroke ¼ revolution of the front wheel. Max. speed 2.5 m.p.h. First steam-powered vehicle. Range of action 12 minutes.

GORDON   **GREAT BRITAIN 1824**

Steamer with iron legs (hoofs). 2-cyl. horizontal engine in front. Vehicle was very noisy, damaged road surface. Max. speed not satisfactory. Piston rods connected to "mechanical feet."

JAMES   **GREAT BRITAIN 1828**

18 pass. Steam diligence (6 pass. within, 12 pass. outside). 2 × 2-cyl. steam engines, each driving one rear wheel. 15-20 h.p. Max. speed 12 m.p.h. Weight approx. 6,600 lb. Superior to all other contemporary steam-driven vehicles.

CHURCH   **GREAT BRITAIN 1833**

3-wheeler steam diligence, 50 pass. Wheel spokes with spring action.
Intended for service between London and Birmingham, and did not come up to expectations. Built at Bramah's Yard.

L'OBEISSANTE   **FRANCE 1872**

Brake de chasse, 12 pass. steamcar. Max. h.p. 15. Max. speed 25 m.p.h. All-independent suspension. Weight 10,580 lb. Bollée's first vehicle, famous for its quietness. Did not startle horses.

MARCUS   **AUSTRIA 1875**

2/4 pass. 1-cyl. engine (horizontal). Bore and stroke 100 × 200 mm. Displacement 1,570 c.c. Max. b.h.p. ¼ at 500 r.p.m. Magneto ignition. Max. speed 5 m.p.h. First gasoline-driven car. Built but no proof it ran.

SELDEN   **U.S.A. 1879**

Car built in 1907 to designs supplied with George B. Selden's patent application of May 8, 1879. Built to furnish proof of the patent's validity, challenged by Henry Ford and other non-members of the Association of Licensed Automobile Manufacturers. A.L.A.M. members paid royalties to the Association on each car built. Suit started in 1903; a decision went against Ford in 1909. Ford appealed and won in 1911.

DE DION BOUTON   **FRANCE 1883**

First De Dion steamcar. 2-cyl. engine. Bore and stroke 70 × 100 mm. Front-wheel drive. Rear-wheel steering. Max. speed 25 m.p.h. First De Dion Bouton driven around Paris by Count De Dion.

BENZ   **GERMANY 1885**

2-seater three-wheeler. 1-cyl. horizontal s.v. engine. Bore and stroke 90 × 150 mm. Displacement 950 c.c. Max. h.p. $3/4$ at 450 r.p.m. Chain and belt drive. Max. speed 10 m.p.h. One forward speed; no reverse. First Benz.

DAIMLER   **GERMANY 1886**

1-cyl. 4-stroke engine. Bore and stroke 70 × 120 mm. Displacement 460 c.c. Max. h.p. 1.5 at 800 r.p.m. 2 speeds. Max. speed 11 m.p.h. First Daimler. Engine installed in horse-drawn vehicle.

SERPOLLET   **FRANCE 1890**

Three-wheeler. 2-cyl. engine beneath back seat. Average speed 8 m.p.h. Max. speed 16 m.p.h. 19-year-old Leon Serpollet built first car in 1877, second following year; in 1889 Peugeot built third to Serpollet's designs. All three-wheelers.

DURYEA   **U.S.A. 1893**

Buggy, 2-seater. 1-cyl. horizontal engine. Max. h.p. 4 at 500 r.p.m. 2 speeds. Weight ± 225 lbs. One of first American gasoline-driven cars. Won Chicago Times-Herald 1895 race with average speed of 7 m.p.h.

PANHARD LEVASSOR   **FRANCE 1895**

2-cyl. engine in line. Bore and stroke 80 × 120 mm. Displacement 1,220 c.c. Max. b.h.p. 4 at 800 r.p.m. 3 speeds. Max. speed approx. 19 m.p.h. First front-mounted engine. Winner of the first real automobile road race.

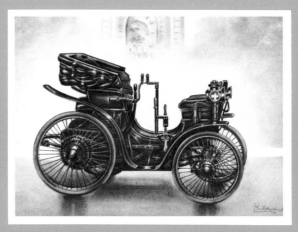

PEUGEOT   **FRANCE 1895**

Vis-à-Vis, 4 pass. (canopy). 2-cyl. engine (horizontal) (Daimler Phoenix). Bore and stroke 80 × 120 mm. Displacement 600 c.c. Max. b.h.p. 4 at 800 r.p.m. 2 speeds. Max. speed 10 m.p.h.

LANCHESTER   **GREAT BRITAIN 1895**

Phaëton, 6 pass. 2 cyl. air-cooled, horizontally-opposed engine. Two crankshafts, revolving in opposite directions. Max. b.h.p. 6. 3 pre-selective speeds. Max. speed 17 m.p.h. First Lanchester.

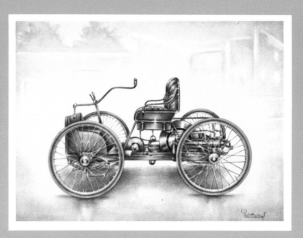

FORD   **U.S.A. 1896**

Quadricycle, Z-Seater. 2-cyl. horizontal s.v. engine in line. Bore and stroke 2.56 x 5.99 inches. Max. b.h.p. 10. 2 speeds, no reverse, no brakes. Chain-drive. Max. speed approx. 25 m.p.h. to get it out of the garage where is was built, Henry Ford knocked out the brick wall.

DE DION BOUTON FRANCE 1897

18 CV Brake, 6 pass. racing and touring car. 2-cyl. steam engine. Max. b.h.p. 30. 2 speeds. Max. speed 40 m.p.h. Weight 5,511 lb. Winner of Marseilles-Monte Carlo road race.

JEANTAUD FRANCE 1897

Electric carriage. Chain-driven. Position of driver's seat results in good passenger visibility. Intended for local taxi service. Award-winner in 1898 Paris Concours.

BOLLÉE FRANCE 1898

8 CV, 2-seater. 2-cyl. water-cooled engine; bore and stroke 110 x 160 mm. Finishing third in Paris-Amsterdam road race with average speed of 26 m.p.h., overall time of 37 hrs. and 8 min.

STANLEY U.S.A. 1898

Buggy, Z-seater, steam-driven 2-cyl. vertical engine. Bore and stroke 2.52 x 3.51 inches. Max. b.h.p. 12 at 400 r.p.m. Chain-drive. Max. speed approx. 25 m.p.h. Stanley Brothers sold out to Mobile and Locomobile, pledging to stay out of automobile business for two years.

HAUTIER   **FRANCE 1899**

"Modern Style Coupé". Position of driver's seat results in good passenger visibility.
65 x 99 mm. Displacement 679 c.c. Max. b.h.p. 3.54 at 400

JENATZY   **FRANCE 1899**

Jamais Contente. Weight 2,200 lb. Diameter of road wheels 25.6 in. Outstanding precise steering. Max. speed approx. 75 m.p.h. Electrically propelled. First built for record-breaking purposes. Achieved world speed record with speed of 65.8 m.p.h.

RENAULT   **FRANCE 1899**

Conduite Interieur, 2 pass. 1-cyl. $1^3/_4$ h.p. De Dion Bouton engine. Max. engine speed 1,500 r.p.m. 2 speeds. Max. speed approx. 12.5 m.p.h. The first car with shaft instead of chain drive and first all-enclosed car.

VALLEE   **FRANCE 1899**

La Pantoufle, 2-seater racing car. 4-cyl. 4-stroke horizontal engine. Bore and stroke 110 × 200 mm. Max. b.h.p. 16 at 600 r.p.m. Mean speed in events 26 m.p.h.

FIAT   **ITALY 1899**

3½ CV, 4 pass. 2-cyl. horizontal engine. Bore and stroke 65 x 99 mm. Displacement 679 c.c. Max. b.h.p. 3.54 at 400 r.p.m. 3 speeds. Max. speed 20 m.p.h. First Fiat.

PACKARD   **U.S.A. 1899**

A, 2-seater buggy. 1-cyl. horizontal water-cooled engine. Bore and stroke 5.52 x 5.99 inches. Displacement 81.7 cu.in. Max. b.h.p. 9 at 800 r.p.m. 2 speeds. Max. speed 19 m.p.h. Only Packard with Tiller Steering.

PIEPER   **BELGIUM 1900**

Electrique, 2-seater. Electrically-propelled car. Weight of batteries 550 lb. Range of action 45-50 miles. Max. speed 12 m.p.h. Good performance in mountainous areas.

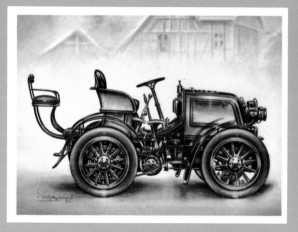

DAIMLER   **GERMANY 1900**

24 PS, 3 pass. sports-racing car. 4-cyl. engine. Water-cooled brakes. Max. speed 47 m.p.h. Honeycomb-type radiator. Forerunner of the Mercedes. Daimler died soon after finishing it.

NAPIER   **GREAT BRITAIN 1900**

16 HP, 2-seater sports. 4-cyl. s.v. engine in line. Bore and
stroke 102 × 152 mm. Displacement 4,940 c.c. Max. speed
unknown. Britain's most powerful car at the time.

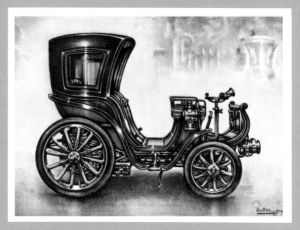

GEORGES RICHARD   **FRANCE 1901**

Victoria, 2-seater. 2-cyl. s.v. engine in line. Bore and stroke
110 × 110 mm. Max. b.h.p. 10 at 1,500 r.p.m. Fuel consumption 28$^1/_4$ m.p.g. 3 speeds. Max. speed 31 m.p.h. Developed
into Unic, now part of Simca.

OLDSMOBILE   **U.S.A. 1901**

Curved Dash, 2-seater runabout. 1-cyl. horizontal water-
cooled engine. Bore and stroke 4.49 x 5.99 inches. Swept
vol 112 cu. ins. Max. b.h.p. 7 at 700 r.p.m. Tiller Steering.
2 speeds. Max. speed 19 m.p.h. First Mass-production
automobile.

GARDNER-SERPOLLET   **FRANCE 1902**

F 1902, 4-pass. victoria steamcar. 4-cyl. engine. Bore and
stroke 56 × 93.5 mm. Max. b.h.p. 6. Chain drive. Kerosene.
Coachwork by Kellner in Paris.

30

SERPOLLET   FRANCE 1902

La Baleine, 2-seater steamcar. 1-cyl. engine. Displacement 397 c.c. In 1901 Flying Kilometre record; in 1902 world speed record with 77 m.p.h. Known as Easter Egg and Steam Shoe.

PANHARD LEVASSOR   FRANCE 1902

70, biposto racing car. 4-cyl. o.h.v. engine in line. Bore and stroke 160 × 170 mm. Displacement 13,700 c.c. Max. b.h.p. 70 at 1,200 r.p.m. 4 speeds. Max. speed approx. 75 m.p.h.

WHITE   U.S.A. 1902

White Elephant, 5 pass. steamcar. 10 h.p. compound engine. Range of action approx. 110 miles. Max. speed approx. 31 m.p.h. One of best-known American steamers. 1910 last year for White steamer.

MORS   FRANCE 1903

70, racing car. 4-cyl. F-head engine in line. Bore and stroke 145 × 175 mm. Displacement 11,200 c.c. Max. b.h.p. 70 at 1,200 r.p.m. 4 speeds. Max. speed 80 m.p.h. 4th place in 1903 Gordon Bennett Cup Race; driver, Gabriel.

31

RENAULT　　　　　　　　　　**FRANCE 1903**

30 CV, 2-seater racing car. 4-cyl. s.v. engine in line. Displacement 6,276 c.c. Max. b.h.p. 30. 4 speeds. Max. speed approx. 95 m.p.h. In 1903 Paris-Madrid road race.

STANDARD　　　　　　　**GREAT BRITAIN 1903**

6 HP, 4-seater. 1-cyl. engine. Bore and stroke 127 x 76 m.m. Cardan Shaft drive. 3 speeds. Max. speed approx. 25 m.b.h. First standard car. Production output six units in 1903.

WINTON　　　　　　　　　　**U.S.A. 1903**

Bullet II, racing car. 8-cyl. o.h.v. engine in line, horizontal. Bore and stroke 133 x 152 mm. Displacement 16,862 c.c. Max. b.h.p. 80 at 800 r.p.m. 2 speeds. Max. speed 84 m.p.h. Bullet I was a 4-cyl. engine in line. Bullet III horizontal 4-cyl.

DÜRKOPP　　　　　　　　　　**GERMANY 1914**

Knipper Dolling, 2-seater torpedo. Forerunner of the small economy car.(Further data not available.)Even after World War I, orders for the Knipper Dolling still arrived from U.S.A. Stopped manufacture of passenger cars in 1927.

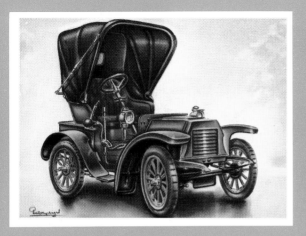

SIDDELEY　　　　　　　　　　GREAT BRITAIN 1904

6 HP, 2-seater. 1-cyl. engine. (Further data not available). Well-known small car especially in "light car events". Prototype of 1905 Wolseley.

NAPIER　　　　　　　　　　GREAT BRITAIN 1904

Tonneau, 4/5 pass. 6-cyl. F-head engine in line. Bore and stroke 102 × 102 m.m. Cylinders in blocks of two each. Max. b.h.p. 30 at 900 r.p.m. 3 speeds. Max. speed approx. 50 m.p.h. One of first production 6-cyl. engines.

SUNBEAM　　　　　　　　　　GREAT BRITAIN 1904

12 HP, 4/5 pass. tourer, 4 cyl. s.v. engine. Bore and stroke 84 × 120 mm. Max. b.h.p. 12 at 1,200 r.p.m. 4 speeds. Max. speed approx. 30 m.p.h. Engine designed by Berliet, built by Sunbeam.

WOLSELEY　　　　　　　　　　GREAT BRITAIN 1904

The Beetle, Gordon Bennett racing car. 4-cyl. o.h.v. horizontal, engine in line. Bore and stroke 181 × 152 mm. Displacement 15,600 c.c. Max. b.h.p. 96 at 1,300 r.p.m. 4 speeds. Max. speed approx. 80 m.p.h. Only three manufactured.

FIAT   **ITALY 1904**

Sport, 2-seater sports-racing car. 4-cyl. o.h.v. engine in line. Displacement 12,317 c.c. Max. b.h.p. 90. Chassis available with 75 h.p. and 110 h.p. 4-cyl. engines. Well-known car in road speed events.

OLDSMOBILE   **U.S.A. 1904**

6-C, 4 pass. light tonneau 1-cyl. s.v. horizontal water-cooled engine. Bore and stroke 5.52 x 5.99 inches. Displacement 260.4 cu. in. Max. b.h.p. 9 at 750 r.p.m. 2 speeds. Max. speed approx. 25 m.p.h. When 6-C was made. R. E. Olds had left Oldsmobile and started Reo.

PANHARD LEVASSOR   **FRANCE 1905**

50 CV, 4/5 pass. touring. 6-cyl. s.v. engine in line. Bore and stroke 160 × 175 mm. Displacement 21,100 c.c. Max. b.h.p. 50 at 900 r.p.m. 4 speeds. Max. speed 56 m.p.h. One of France's first production 6-cyl. engines.

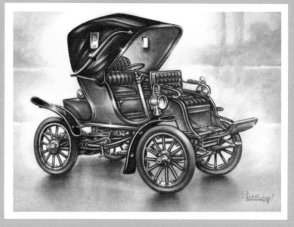

PIERCE STANHOPE   **U.S.A. 1905**

Motorette, 2-seater doctor's car. (De Dion Bouton) 1-cyl. vertical engine. Bore and stroke 3.55 x 4.31 inches. Displacement 52.5 cu. in. Max. b.h.p. 8 at 1,400 r.p.m. 2 speeds. Steering column gear change.

C.G.V. (CHARRON, GIRARDOT, VOIGT)   FRANCE 1906

30 CV, 4 pass. coupé-limousine. 4-cyl. s.v. engine in line. Displacement 5,560 c.c. Max. b.h.p. 30 at approx. 1,200 r.p.m. 4 speeds. Max. speed approx. 45 m.p.h. Dual ignition. Out of business by 1930.

RENAULT   FRANCE 1906

13 Liters, Grand Prix racing car. 4-cyl. s.v. engine in line. Bore and stroke 166 × 150 mm. Displacement 13,400 c.c. Max. b.h.p. 90 at 1,200 r.p.m. 4 speeds. Max. speed 93 m.p.h. Won first Grand Prix.

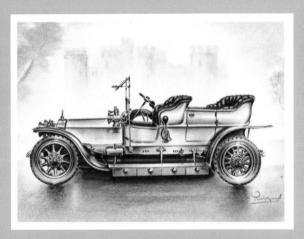

ROLLS-ROYCE   GREAT-BRITAIN 1906

Silver Ghost, 5/6 pass. tourer. 6-cyl. s.v. engine in line. Bore and stroke 114 × 114 mm. Displacement 7,046 c.c. Max. b.h.p. 48 at 1,200 r.p.m. 4 speeds. Max. speed approx. 80 m.p.h. Displacement raised to 7.4 liters in 1907.

FORD   U.S.A. 1906

K, 4 pass. touring. 6-cyl. s.v. engine. Bore and stroke 4.50 x 4.25 inches. Displacement 405.4 cu. in. Max. b.h.p. 40. 2 speeds. Max. speed 60 m.p.h. First big Ford.

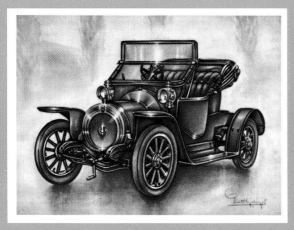

LE GUI   **FRANCE 1907**

10 CV, 2-seater torpedo. 4-cyl. s.v. engine in line. Bore and stroke 75 x 120 m.m. Displacement 2,131 c.c. Max. b.h.p. 10 at 1,500 r.p.m. 4 speeds. Max. speed approx. 40 m.p.h.

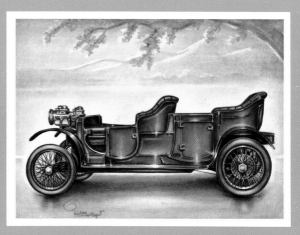

LANCHESTER   **GREAT BRITAIN 1907**

28 HP, 4/5 pass. tourer. 6-cyl. s.v. engine in line. Bore and stroke 102 x 76 m.m. Displacement 3,740 c.c. Max. b.h.p. 28 at 1,000 r.p.m. 3 speeds. Max. speed 56 m.p.h.

FRANKLIN   **U.S.A. 1907**

E, 2-seater runabout. 4-cyl. air-cooled engine in line. Displacement 1,763 c.c. Max. b.h.p. 12. 2 speeds. Max. speed approx. 45 m.p.h. Cardan shaft drive. Force-feed oilers on the dash.

ZEDEL   **FRANCE 1908**

10-12 CV, 3 pass. victoria. 4-cyl. s.v. engine. Bore and stroke 70 x 110 m.m. Displacement 1,680 c.c. Max. b.h.p. 15 at 1,200 r.p.m. 3 speeds. Max. speed 53 m.p.h. Zedel French pronunciation of Z & L (Zürcher & Luthi).

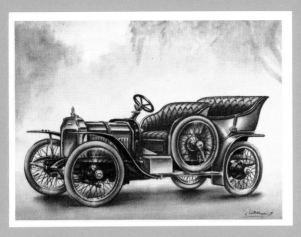

VAUXHALL   **GREAT BRITAIN 1908**

12/16, 4/5 pass. sports tourer. 4-cyl. engine in line. Bore and stroke 92 × 95 mm. Max. b.h.p. 20. 4 speeds. Max. speed approx. 70 m.p.h. Successful car in competitions.

STANLEY   **U.S.A. 1908**

F, 4/5 pass. touring. 2-cyl. engine. Displacement 70 cu. in. Max. b.h.p. 20. Range of action approx. 90 miles. Stanley Bros. returned to car manufacture in 1902, with 30 h.p. model with 26 in liquid fuel boiler.

BENZ   **GERMANY 1909**

4-cyl. o.h.v. engine in line. Bore and stroke 185 × 200 mm. Displacement 21,500 c.c. Max. b.h.p. 200 at 1,500 r.p.m. Max. speed approx. 135 m.p.h. 4 forward speeds and reverse. Leather cone clutch. World speed record car, 128 m.p.h.

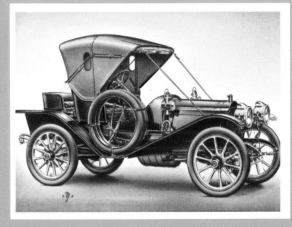

PACKARD   **U.S.A. 1909**

Thirty, runabout. 4-cyl. s.v. engine. Bore and stroke 127 × 139.7 mm. Displacement 7,086 c.c. Max. b.h.p. 40. 3 speeds. Max. speed 68 m.p.h. Introduced in 1904; replaced by 6-cyl. model in 1912.

BUGATTI FRANCE 1910

13, 2-seater sports-racing car. 4-cyl. s.o.h.c. engine in line. Bore and stroke 65 × 100 mm. Displacement 1,327 c.c. Max. b.h.p. 25 at 3,000 r.p.m. 4 speeds. Max. speed 62 m.p.h. In 1911 as fast as cars with 5 times more power.

GREGOIRE FRANCE 1910

Special, 4 pass. streamlined sports-saloon. 4-cyl. s.v. engine in line. Bore and stroke 80 × 160 mm. Displacement 3,220 c.c. Max. speed approx. 50 m.p.h. Body by Alin et Liotard.

SIZAIRE NAUDIN FRANCE 1910

1-cyl. F-head engine. Bore and stroke 120 × 140 mm. Displacement 1,584 c.c. Max. b.h.p. 9. 3 speeds. Max. speed 55 m.p.h. Independent front suspension.

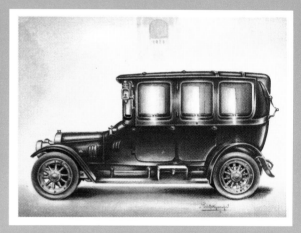

SPYKER (SPELLING) THE NETHERLANDS 1910

Thirty, runabout, 4-cyl. engine. Bore and stroke 5.0 x 5.5 inches. Displacement 432 cu. in. Max. b.h.p. 40. 3 speeds. Max. speed 70 m.p.h. Introduced in 1904 replaced by 6-cyl. model in 1912.

FIAT   **ITALY 1911**

300 CV, racing car. 4-cyl. o.h.v. engine in line. Bore and stroke 190 × 250 mm. Displacement 28,200 c.c. Max. b.h.p. 300 at 1,200 r.p.m. 4 speeds. Max. speed approx. 135 m.p.h. Built successfully to take world land speed record from Blitzen Benz.

LANCIA   **ITALY 1911**

Dialfa, 4/5 pass. tourer. 6-cyl. s.v. engine in line. Bore and stroke 90 × 100 mm. Displacement 3,820 c.c. Max. b.h.p. 30 at 1,500 r.p.m. 4 speeds. Max. speed approx. 70 m.p.h. Made from 1909 through 1913.

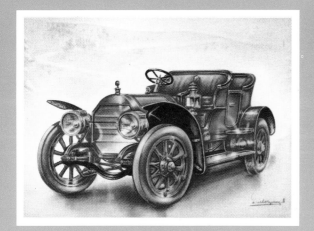

LOCOMOBILE   **U.S.A. 1911**

40, 4 pass. sports tourer. 4-cyl. o.h.v. engine. Max. b.h.p. 60. Dual chain drive. Well-known sports-racing car, winner of the Vanderbilt Cup. Price $ 4,500.

PEUGEOT   **FRANCE 1912**

7.6 Liter, racing car. 4-cyl. d.o.h.c. engine in line. Bore and stroke 110 × 200 mm. Displacement 7,600 c.c. Max. b.h.p. 130 at 2,200 r.p.m. 4 speeds. Max. speed 100 m.p.h. 4 valves per cyl.

KRUPP GERMANY 1912

Loreley, 4/5 pass. landaulet. 4-cyl. engine in line. (Further data not available.) Krupp Werke A.G. in Essen, large manufacturer of trucks from 1930's.

SPERBER GERMANY 1912

2-door torpedo. 4-cyl. s.v. engine. Bore and stroke 70.7 × 100 mm. Displacement 1,524 c.c. Max. b.h.p. 19.5 at 2,100 r.p.m. 4-speed by chain drive. Max. speed 34 m.p.h.

HISPANO SUIZA SPAIN 1912

Alfonso XIII, 2-seater sports. 4-cyl. s.v. engine in line. Bore and stroke 80 × 100 mm. Displacement 3,622 c.c. Max. b.h.p. 45 at 1,200 r.p.m. 4 speeds. Max. speed 80 m.p.h. Prototype built for Alphonso XIII of Spain.

GREGOIRE FRANCE 1913

Triple berline, 6 pass. 4-cyl. engine in line. Bore and stroke 80 × 160 mm. Displacement 3,246 c.c. 4 speeds. Not a regular production model.

MORRIS　　　　　　　　　　**GREAT BRITAIN 1913**

Oxford, 2-seater. 4-cyl. s.v. engine. (White & Poppe) Bore and stroke 60 × 90 mm. Displacement 1,018 c.c. Max. b.h.p. 10. 3 speeds. Max. speed approx. 45 m.p.h. First Morris price 175 pounds sterling ($ 490).

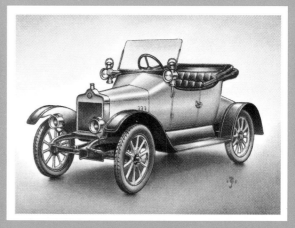

STANDARD　　　　　　　　**GREAT BRITAIN 1913**

S Rhyl, 2-seater. 4-cyl. s.v. engine. Bore and stroke 62 × 90 mm. Displacement 1,087 c.c. Max. h.p. 9.5. 3 speeds. Max. speed 44 m.p.h. 3-year warranty.

HUDSON　　　　　　　　　　**U.S.A. 1913**

54, 4 pass. 6-cyl. engine. Bore and stroke 4.12 x 5.25 inches. Displacement 421 cu. in. Max. b.h.p. 54 at 1,500 r.p.m. Max. speed 62 m.p.h. Weight 4,644 lbs. Hudson's First 6-cyl.; unchanged until 1916.

LOZIER　　　　　　　　　　**U.S.A. 1913**

Light six, 2-door sedan. 6-cyl. s.v. engine. Bore and stroke 4.63 x 5.50 inches. Displacement 556 cu. in. Max. b.h.p. 52. 4 speeds. Chassis on 127.5 in. wheelbase.

PEUGEOT　　　　　　　　　　　　**FRANCE 1914**

Bébé, 2 pass. conduite interieur. 4-cyl. s.v. engine in line.
Bore and stroke 55 × 90 mm. Displacement 855 c.c. 2/3
speeds. Very popular small car. Design by Ettore Bugatti.

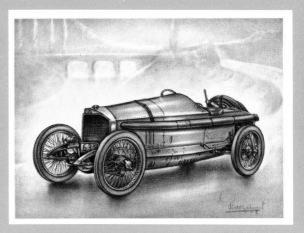

MERCEDES　　　　　　　　　　**GERMANY 1914**

4¹/₂ liter G.P., racing car. 4-cyl. s.o.h.c. engine in line. Bore
and stroke 93 × 165 mm. Displacement 4,483 c.c. Max. b.h.p.
115 at 2,800 r.p.m. 4 speeds. Max. speed 112 m.p.h. The
engine formed basis of power unit in WW I German
fighter planes.

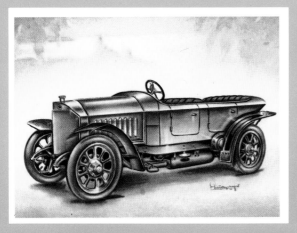

ISOTTA FRASCHINI　　　　　　　　**ITALY 1914**

125 H.P., 4/5 pass. tourer. 4-cyl. o.h.v. engine in line. Bore
and stroke 130 x 300 mm. Displacement 10, 620 c.c. Max.
b.h.p. 125. Max. speed 85 m.p.h.

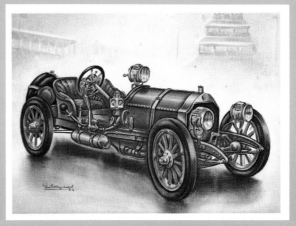

MERCER　　　　　　　　　　　　**U.S.A. 1914**

35-J Raceabout, 2-seater sportscar. 4-cyl. s.v. engine in
line. Bore and stroke 111 x 127 mm. Displacement
4,950 c.c. Max. b.h.p. 58 at 1,700 r.p.m. 4 speeds. Max.
speed approx. 70 m.p.h. Bosch ignition. T-head engine
camshafts ran on ball bearings.

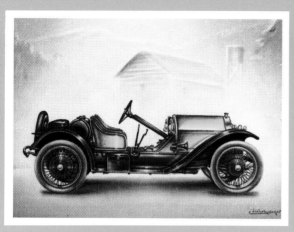

STUTZ　　　　　　　　　　　　　　**U.S.A. 1914**

E4 Bearcat, 2-seater sports roadster. 4-cyl. T-head engine
in line. Max. b.h.p. 60. Weight approx. 4,960 lb. Max. speed
approx. 80 m.p.h. Available with a 6-cyl. T-head engine.
Price $ 2.000.

EYSINK　　　　　　　　**THE NETHERLANDS 1915**

2-seater. 4-cyl. s.v. engine. Bore and stroke 60 × 80 mm.
Displacement 905 c.c. 3 speeds. Max. speed 37 m.p.h. Dutch
cars of the time: Altena, Brons, Econoom, Gelria, Omnia,
Simplex.

DODGE　　　　　　　　　　　　　**U.S.A. 1915**

2-door sedan. 4-cyl. s.v. engine. Bore and stroke 3.87 x
4.50 inches. Displacement 212.3 cu. in. Max. b.h.p. 35.
3 speeds. Max. speed 44 m.p.h. First Dodge Bros. car.
45,000 built in 1915.

PACKARD　　　　　　　　　　　　**U.S.A. 1915**

Twin six. coupe V-12 s.v. engine (60°). Bore and stroke
3.0 x 5.0 inches. Displacement 424 cu. in. Max. b.h.p. 85
at 3,000 r.p.m. 3 speeds. Max. speed 81 m.p.h. 10,645 sold
in 1916; 35,000 in 1921.

BRISCODE U.S.A. 1916

Standard, 5 pass. torpedo. 4-cyl. s.v. engine in line. Bore and stroke 3.11 x 5.12 inches. Displacement 156 cu. in. Max. b.h.p. 16 at 1,000 r.p.m. 3 speeds. Max. speed 50 m.p.h. One of America's First compact attemps.

BREWSTER U.S.A. 1917

Town Brougham, 4-cyl. sleeve valve engine (knight). Bore and stroke 4.00 x 5.50 inches. Displacement 277 cu. in. Max. b.h.p. 60. 3 speeds. Max. speed 45 m.p.h.

PATHFINDER U.S.A. 1918

Twin Six, 5 pass. sport torpedo. V-12 o.h.v. engine. (Weidely Engine Co.). Bore and stroke 2.96 x 4.96 inches. Displacement 386 cu. in. 3 speeds. Max. speed 75 m.p.h.

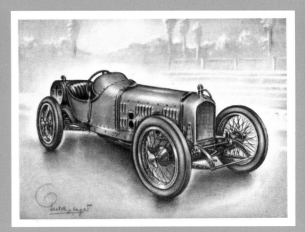

BALLOT FRANCE 1919

5 Liter G.P., racing car. 8-cyl. d.o.h.c. engine in line. Bore and stroke 74 × 140 mm. Displacement 4,900 c.c. Max. b.h.p. 140 at 3,000 r.p.m. 4 speeds. Max. speed 118 m.p.h. 4 valves per cyl.

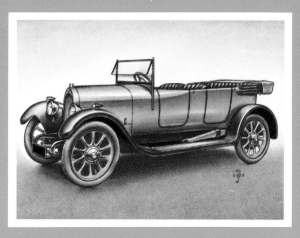

ARROL-JOHNSTON   GREAT BRITAIN 1919

Victory. 4-cyl. o.h.v. engine. Bore and stroke 80 x 120 mm. Displacement 2,412 c.c. Max. b.h.p. 22. 4 speeds. Converted to o.h.v. in 1928.

ENFIELD-ALLDAY   GREAT BRITAIN 1919

15 HP, 4/5 pass. touring. 6-cyl. o.h.v. engine in line. Bore and stroke 70 × 110 mm. Displacement 2,500 c.c. Max. b.h.p. 52 at 3,000 r.p.m. 4 speeds. Max. speed 62 m.p.h. Marque disappeared about 1927.

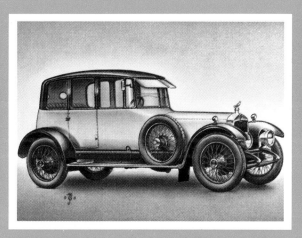

LANCHESTER   GREAT BRITAIN 1919

40 HP, saloon. 6-cyl. s.o.h.c. engine. Bore and stroke 101.6 × 127 mm. Displacement 6,178 c.c. Max. b.h.p. 80. Max. speed 78 m.p.h. 3-speed planetary transmission. Only model between 1919 and 1924.

RILEY   GREAT BRITAIN 1919

10.8 HP, family saloon. 4-cyl. s.v. engine in line. Bore and stroke 65.8 × 110 mm. Displacement 1,495 c.c. Max. b.h.p. 35. Engine enlarged in 1924. Developed into the 11/40 Redwing.

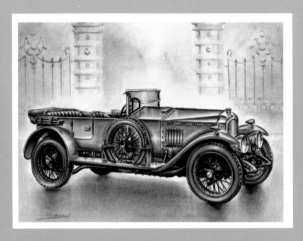

VAUXHALL   GREAT BRITAIN 1919

30/98, 4/5 pass. Sports torpedo. 4-cyl. s.v. engine in line.
Bore and stroke 98 x 150 mm. Displacement 4,540 c.c.
Max. b.h.p. 98 at 3,300 r.p.m. 4 speeds. Max. speed
approx. 85 m.p.h. 1922 engine redesigned with o.h.v.

MARMON   U.S.A. 1919

34, 4/5 pass. coupé de ville. 6-cyl. o.h.v. engine in line
(aluminium). Bore and stroke 95 x 130 mm. Displacement
5.721 c.c. Max. b.h.p. 74. 3 speeds. Max. speed approx. 70 m.p.h.

BENZ   GERMANY 1920

6/18 PS, roadster. 4-cyl. s.o.h.c. engine. Bore and stroke
68 × 108 mm. Displacement 1,570 c.c. Max. b.h.p. 45 at 3,200
r.p.m. 4 speeds. Max. speed 56 m.p.h. Foot brake on transmission shaft; hand brake on rear wheels.

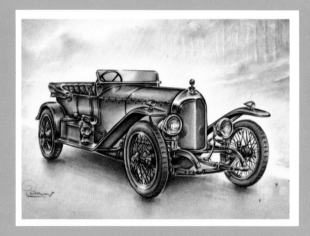

BENTLEY   GREAT BRITAIN 1920

3 Liter, 4/5 pass. tourer. 4-cyl. s.o.h.c. engine in line. Bore
and stroke 80 × 149 mm. Displacement 2,996 c.c. Max. b.h.p.
65 at 2,500 r.p.m. 4 speeds. Max. speed approx. 85 m.p.h.
No front brakes. First Bentley.

CALCOTT   **GREAT BRITAIN 1920**

Twelve, cabriolet. 4-cyl. s.v. engine. Bore and stroke 69 × 110 mm. Displacement 1,646 c.c. Max. b.h.p. 10.5. 3 speeds. Max. speed 47 m.p.h. Leather cone clutch.

JOWETT   **GREAT BRITAIN 1920**

7 HP, 2-seater roadster. 2-cyl. horizontally opposed o.h.v. engine. Bore and stroke 75 × 102 mm. Displacement 907 c.c. Max. b.h.p. 17 at 3,000 r.p.m. 3 speeds. Max. speed 43 m.p.h. 4-cyl. car in 1936.

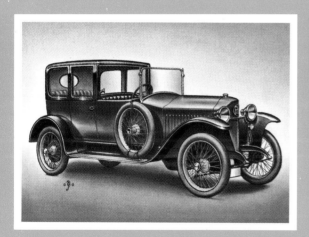

PIC PIC   **SWITZERLAND 1920**

16 HP, sedanca de ville. 4-cyl. sleeve valve engine. Bore and stroke 85 × 130 mm. Displacement 2,951 c.c. Max. b.h.p. 30. 4 speeds. Max. speed 50 m.p.h. Piccard-Pictet engine built under Argull license.

OLDSMOBILE   **U.S.A. 1920**

30, sedan. 6-cyl. s.v. engine. Bore and stroke 2.74 x 4.73 inches. Displacement 179 cu. in. Max. b.h.p. 44. 3 speeds. Max. speed 56 m.p.h. New York to Los Angeles in top gear in 12½ days.

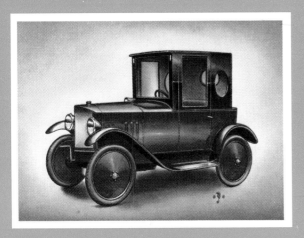

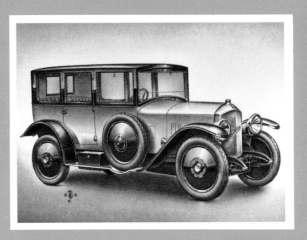

PERL   **AUSTRIA 1921**

3/15, coupé. 4-cyl. s.v. engine. Bore and stroke 57 × 88 mm.
Displacement 898 c.c. Max. b.h.p. 15 at 3,000 r.p.m. 3 speeds.
Max. speed 37 m.p.h. Wood frame.

LA BUIRE   **FRANCE 1921**

Sedan. 4-cyl. s.v. engine. Bore and stroke 75 × 150 mm.
Displacement 2,651 c.c. Max. b.h.p. 22. 4 speeds. Max. speed
50 m.p.h. Engine modified to o.h.v. in 1926.

UNIC   **FRANCE 1921**

Landaulet. 4-cyl. s.v. engine. Bore and stroke 80 × 130 mm.
Displacement 2,610 c.c. Max. b.h.p. 24. 4 speeds. Max. speed
50 m.p.h. 3-liter engine in 1925.

SZAWE   **GERMANY 1921**

10/38 PS, torpedo. 4-cyl. s.v. engine. Bore and stroke 83 ×
118 mm. Displacement 2,500 c.c. Max. b.h.p. 38 at 2,500 r.p.m.
4 speeds. Max. speed 56 m.p.h. Leather cone clutch.

LEYLAND   **GREAT BRITAIN 1921**

8, touring. 8-cyl. s.o.h.c. engine. Bore and stroke 89 ×146 mm. Displacement 7,266 c.c. Max. b.h.p. 120 at 2,500 r.p.m. 4 speeds. Max. speed 87 m.p.h. Discontinued in 1924. Leyland now a big truck manufacturer, owner of Triumph.

WOLSELEY   **GREAT BRITAIN 1921**

15 HP, 2 pass. coupé. 4-cyl. o.h.v. engine in line. Bore and stroke 80 × 130 mm. Displacement 2,652 c.c. Max. b.h.p. 15 at 2,000 r.p.m. 3 speeds. Max. speed approx. 70 m.p.h. 4-speed transmission available in 1923.

ANSALDO   **ITALY 1921**

12 HP, coach. 4-cyl. o.h.v. engine. Bore and stroke 70 × 120 mm. Max. b.h.p. 12. 3 speeds. In production until 1930.

DUSENBERG   **U.S.A. 1921**

3 Liter. racing car. 8-cyl. d.o.h.c. engine in line. Bore and stroke 2.50 x 4.61 inches. Displacement 179.9 cu. in. Max. b.h.p. 115 at 4,250 r.p.m. 3 speeds. Max. speed 115 m.p.h. First with hydraulic 4-wheel brakes.

PERRIS   U.S.A. 1921

60, phaeton. 6-cyl. s.v. engine. Bore and stroke 3.50 x 5.25 inches. Displacement 303 cu. in. Max. b.h.p. 60. 4 speeds. Max. speed 62 m.p.h.

HUPMOBILE   U.S.A. 1921

Series R, 4/5 pass. sedan 4-cyl. s.v. engine in line. Bore and stroke 3.27 x 5.52 inches. Displacement 182 cu. in. Max. b.h.p. 20 at 3000 r.p.m. Max. speed approx. 70 m.p.h. All-steel body supplied by Budd.

PIERCE ARROW   U.S.A. 1921

38 HP, 5/6 pass. touring. 6-cyl. s.v. engine in line. Bore and stroke 100 × 140 mm. Displacement 6,594 c.c. Max. b.h.p. 110 at 3,000 r.p.m. 3 speeds. Max. speed approx. 75 m.p.h. Price approx. $ 6,000.

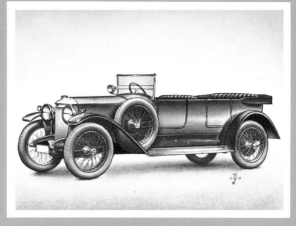

AUSTRO DAIMLER   AUSTRIA 1922

AD 617, phaeton. 6-cyl. s.o.h.c. engine. Bore and stroke 85 × 130 mm. Displacement 4,420 c.c. Max. b.h.p. 60 at 2,300 r.p.m. 4 speeds. Max. speed 68 m.p.h. Steel plate clutch in oil bath.

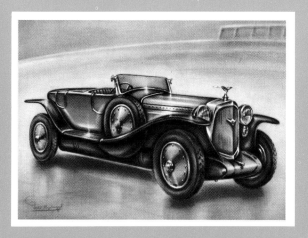

FARMAN FRANCE 1922

40 HP, A6A, 4 pass. grand sport torpedo. 6-cyl. s.o.h.c. engine in line (aluminum engine block). Bore and stroke 100 × 140 mm. Displacement 6,480 c.c. Dual ignition. 4 speeds. Max. speed approx. 93 m.p.h.

GEORGES IRAT FRANCE 1922

11 CV, 4/5 pass. transformable. 4-cyl. o.h.v. engine in line. Bore and stroke 69 × 130 mm. Displacement 1,950 c.c. Max. b.h.p. 40. 4 speeds. Max. speed 68 m.p.h. Dewandre power brakes.

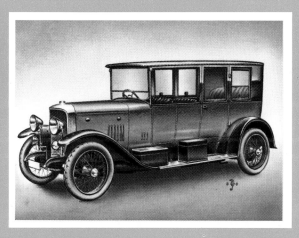

BERGMANN GERMANY 1922

10/30 PS, limousine. 4-cyl. s.v. engine. Bore and stroke 80 × 130 mm. Displacement 2,610 c.c. Max. b.h.p. 32 at 2,150 r.p.m. 4 speeds. Max. speed 50 m.p.h. No front wheel brakes. License from Metallurgique Belgium.

SIMSON SUPRA GERMANY 1922

Torpedo CO.4-cyl. F-head engine. Bore and stroke 80 × 130 mm. Displacement 2,595 c.c. Max. b.h.p. 40 at 1,900 r.p.m. 4 speeds. Max. speed 53 m.p.h. Metal cone clutch.

AUSTIN　　　　　　　　　　**GREAT BRITAIN** 1922

Seven, 2/4 pass. roadster. 4-cyl. s.v. engine in line. Bore and stroke 55 × 75 mm. Displacement 698 c.c. Max. b.h.p. 10 at 2,400 r.p.m. 3 speeds. Max. speed approx. 45 m.p.h. First really successful small car.

TROJAN　　　　　　　　　　**GREAT BRITAIN** 1922

Utility 4-pass. 2-cyl. 2-stroke engine (chain drive to rear axle without differential). Bore and stroke 64.5 × 120.7 mm. Displacement 1,557 c.c. Max. b.h.p. 10 at 1,200 r.p.m. 2 speeds. Max. speed 25 m.p.h. 28″ × 2″ solid rubber tires.

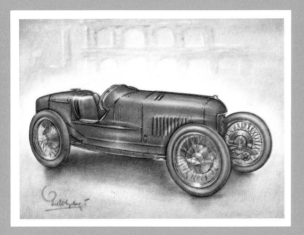

FIAT　　　　　　　　　　**ITALY** 1922

804, Grand Prix racing car. 6-cyl. d.o.h.c. engine in line. Bore and stroke 65 × 100 mm. Displacement 1,991 c.c. Max. b.h.p. 90 at 4,500 r.p.m. 4 speeds. Max. speed 106 m.p.h. No worthy competitor in 1922.

DANIELS　　　　　　　　　　**U.S.A.** 1922

Town Brougham. V-8 s.v. engine. Bore and stroke 3.50 x 5.25 inches. Displacement 404 cu. in. Max. b.h.p. 90. 3 speeds. Max. speed 56 m.p.h. No standard models: all cars made to order. 1,500 cars built between 1916 and 1922.

WILLS SAINTE CLAIRE　　　　　　　　**U.S.A. 1922**

A-68, 4/5 pass. touring V-8 s.o.h.c. engine (o.h.c.). Bore and stroke 3.47 x 3.98 inches. Displacement 267 cu. in. Max. b.h.p. 68 at 3,000 r.p.m. Max. speed 80 m.p.h. 2,464 cars in 1922.

PUCH　　　　　　　　**AUSTRIA 1923**

VII Alpenwagen, phaeton. 4-cyl. s.v. engine. Bore and stroke 90 × 140 mm. Displacement 3,560 c.c. Max. b.h.p. 40 at 2500 r.p.m. 4 speeds. Max. speed 56 m.p.h. Brakes on transmission shaft and rear wheels; none on front wheels.

TATRA　　　　　　　　**CZECHOSLOVAKIA 1923**

11, coach. 2-cyl. air cooled, horizontally opposed, o.h.v. engine. Bore and stroke 82 × 100 mm. Displacement 1,050 c.c. Max. b.h.p. 14 at 2,000 r.p.m. 4 speeds. Max. speed 47 m.p.h. Central tube "backbone" frame.

ARIES　　　　　　　　**FRANCE 1923**

15 HP, sedan de ville. 4-cyl. s.o.h.c. engine. Bore and stroke 85 × 140 mm. Displacement 3,178 c.c. 3/4 speeds. Max. speed 56 m.p.h. Discontinued in 1931.

PEUGEOT   **FRANCE 1923**

174-S, sport. 4-cyl. o.h.v. engine. Bore and stroke 95 × 135 mm. Displacement 3,828 c.c. Max. b.h.p. 70. 4 speeds. Max. speed 71 m.p.h. In production until 1929.

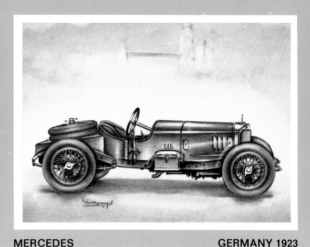

MERCEDES   **GERMANY 1923**

1.5 Liter, 2 pass. sports racing car. 4-cyl. s.o.h.c. engine in line with compressor. Bore and stroke 65 × 113 mm. Displacement 1,500 c.c. Max. b.h.p. 65 at 4,000 r.p.m. 4 speeds. Max. speed 84 m.p.h. First supercharged car.

OPEL   **GERMANY 1923**

Laubfrosch, 2 pass. roadster. 4-cyl. engine in line. Bore and stroke 60 × 90 mm. Displacement 1,010 c.c. Max. b.h.p. 12 at 2,750 r.p.m. 3 speeds. Max. speed 45 m.p.h. Direct copy of Citroën Trefle.

BEAN   **GREAT BRITAIN 1923**

Twelve, 4-pass. coupé. 4-cyl. s.v. engine. Bore and stroke 69 × 120 mm. Displacement 1,795 c.c. Max. b.h.p. 21 at 2,280 r.p.m. 4 speeds. Max. speed 47 m.p.h. In 1924 optional front wheel brakes.

SUNBEAM GREAT BRITAIN 1923

2 Liter, G.P., racing car. 6-cyl. d.o.h.c. engine in line. Bore and stroke 67 × 94 mm. Displacement 1,988 c.c. Max. b.h.p. 103 at 5,600 r.p.m. 4 speeds. Max. speed 110 m.p.h. Copy of 1922 Grand Prix Fiat.

SPIJKER THE NETHERLANDS 1923

Convertible. 6-cyl. s.v. engine (Maybach). Bore and stroke 95 × 135 mm. Displacement 5,800 c.c. Max. b.h.p. 72 at 2,200 r.p.m. 4 speeds. Max. speed 68 m.p.h.

CHEVROLET U.S.A. 1923

Superior, coupe. 4-cyl. air cooled o.h.v. engine. Bore and stroke 4.50 x 4.50 inches. Displacement 152 cu. in. Max. b.h.p. 22 at 1,750 r.p.m. 3 speeds. Max. speed 53 m.p.h. 759 "cooper-cooled" Chevrolets built; 100 sold, then re-called.

AMILCAR FRANCE 1924

CGS, 2-seater cabriolet. 4-cyl. s.v. engine in line. Bore and stroke 60 × 95 mm. Displacement 1,100 c.c. Max. b.h.p. 30 at 3,000 r.p.m. 3 speeds. Max. speed 55 m.p.h. Rear wheel brakes only.

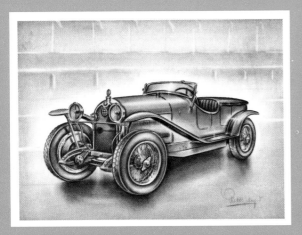

LORRAINE DIETRICH　　　　　　**FRANCE 1924**

Le Mans, sports 2-seater. 6-cyl. o.h.v. engine in line. Bore and stroke 75 × 130 mm. Displacement 3,440 c.c. Max. b.h.p. 70 at 3,000 r.p.m. 3 speeds. Max. speed 100 m.p.h. Won Le Mans 24-hour race in 1925 and 1926.

MAYBACH　　　　　　**GERMANY 1924**

W-3, sedan de ville. 6-cyl. s.v. engine. Bore and stroke 95 × 135 mm. Displacement 5,800 c.c. Max. b.h.p. 72 at 2,200 r.p.m. 2 speeds. Max. speed 68 m.p.h. Planetary transmission with pedal shift (like Model T Ford).

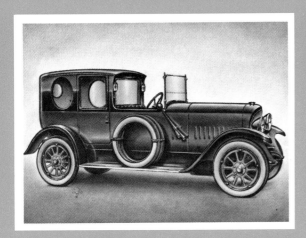

N.A.G.　　　　　　**GERMANY 1924**

D-4, sedan de ville. 4-cyl. o.h.v. engine. Bore and stroke 78 × 136 mm. Displacement 2,640 c.c. Max. b.h.p. 40 at 2,300 r.p.m. 4 speeds. Max. speed 56 m.p.h. Mechanical 4-wheel brakes.

RHEMAG　　　　　　**GERMANY 1924**

4/24 HP, sports roadster. 4-cyl. s.o.h.c. engine. Bore and stroke 62 × 86 mm. Displacement 1,065 c.c. Max. b.h.p. 24 at 3,000 r.p.m. 3 speeds. Max. speed 56 m.p.h. First Rhemag; discontinued in 1926.

AUSTIN GREAT BRITAIN 1924

Twelve, phaeton. 4-cyl. s.v. engine. Bore and stroke 72 × 102 mm. Displacement 1,660 c.c. Max. b.h.p. 20 at 2,000 r.p.m. Chassis had 100 in. wheelbase.

CALTHORPE GREAT BRITAIN 1924

12/20, 4-door convertible. 4-cyl. s.v. engine. Bore and stroke 69 × 100 mm. Displacement 1,496 c.c. Max. b.h.p. 20. 4 speeds. In production until 1931.

FIAT ITALY 1924

519, 4/5 pass. sports torpedo. 6-cyl. o.h.v. engine in line. Bore and stroke 85 × 140 mm. Displacement 4,750 c.c. Max. b.h.p. 80 at 2,500 r.p.m. 4 speeds. Max. speed 75 m.p.h. Weight 4,225 lbs.

CHRYSLER U.S.A. 1924

70, 4/5 pass. tourer. 6 cyl. engine in line. Bore and stroke 79 × 121 mm. Displacement 3,302 c.c. Max. b.h.p. 70 at 3.000 r.p.m. 3 speeds. Max. speed approx. 70 m.p.h. First Chrysler. One of first cars with hydraulic 4-wheel brakes.

MAXWELL U.S.A. 1924

25-C, Sport touring 4-cyl. s.v. engine. Bore and stroke 3.62 x 4.49 inches. Displacement 185 cu. in. Max. b.h.p. 38. 3 speeds. Last Maxwell; marque became Chrysler.

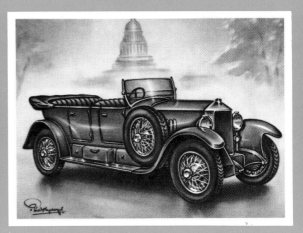

METALLURGIQUE BELGIUM 1925

Metal, 4/5 pass. torpedo. 4-cyl. s.o.h.c. engine in line. Bore and stroke 70 × 128 mm. Displacement 1,960 c.c. Max. b.h.p. 40 at 2,500 r.p.m. 4 speeds. Max. speed 68 m.p.h. Mechanical 4-wheel brakes.

BUGATTI FRANCE 1925

37 Grand Prix, 2-seater. 4-cyl. s.o.h.c. engine (3 valves per cylinder). Bore and stroke 69 × 100 mm. Displacement 1,496 c.c. 4 speeds. Max. speed 93 m.p.h.

CITROËN FRANCE 1925

B-12, 4 pass. torpedo. 4-cyl. s.v. engine in line. Bore and stroke 68 × 100 mm. Displacement 1,452 c.c. Max. b.h.p. 20 at 2,100 r.p.m. 3 speeds. Max. speed 47 m.p.h. Front-wheel brakes added in 1926.

PANHARD LEVASSOR   **FRANCE 1925**

8C Eyston record car. 8-cyl. sleeve valve engine in line.
Bore and stroke 95 × 140 mm. Displacement 7,897 c.c.
Max. b.h.p. 300 at 3,600 r.p.m. 4 speeds. Max. speed approx.
140 m.p.h. Broke speed records as late as 1932/33.

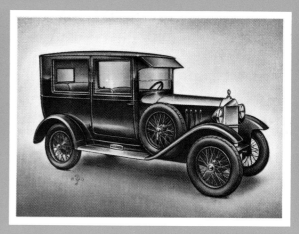

MAUSER   **GERMANY 1925**

M7, coach. 4-cyl. o.h.v. engine. Bore and stroke 68 × 108 mm.
Displacement 1,569 c.c. Max. b.h.p. 28 at 2,500 r.p.m. 3
speeds. Max. speed 50 m.p.h. Discontinued in 1927; company
now an arms manufacturer.

STOLLE   **GERMANY 1925**

6/40 HP, sports roadster. 4-cyl. s.o.h.c. engine. Bore and
stroke 69 × 100 mm. Displacement 1,500 c.c. Max. b.h.p.
40 at 3,500 r.p.m. 4 speeds. Max. speed 75 m.p.h. Optional
valveless engine.

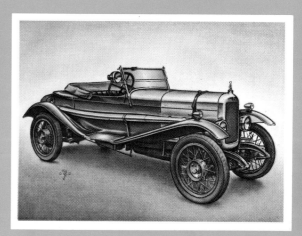

ALVIS   **GREAT BRITAIN 1925**

12/50 HP, super sport 4-cyl. o.h.v. engine. Bore and stroke
69 x 110 m.m. Displacement 1,645 c.c. Max. b.h.p. 50.
4 speeds. Max. speed 78 m.p.h.

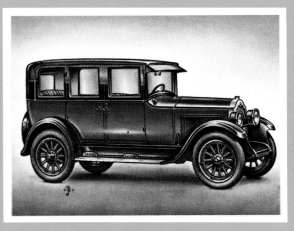

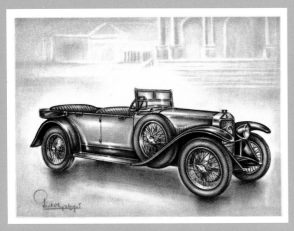

ITALA   **ITALY 1925**

61, 4/5 pass. torpedo. 6-cyl. o.h.v. engine in line. Bore and stroke 65 × 100 mm. Displacement 1,991 c.c. Max. b.h.p. 55 at 3,600 r.p.m. 4 speeds. Max. speed 62 m.p.h. Superseded by Tipo 65 with d.o.h.c. engine.

BUICK   **U.S.A. 1925**

27, Sedan. 6-cyl. o.h.v. engine. Bore and stroke 3.38 x 4.75 inches. Displacement 254 cu. in. Max. b.h.p. 70. 3 speeds. Max. speed 68 m.p.h. Buick 6-cyl. introduced in 1914.

STUDEBAKER   **U.S.A. 1925**

Standard Six, 4/5 pass. sedan 6-cyl. s.v. engine in line. Bore and stroke 86 x 114 mm. Displacement 3,971 c.c. Max. b.h.p. 50 at 2,200 r.p.m. 3 speeds. Max. speed 68 m.p.h. Body design by H. J. Bourgon.

GRÄF & STIFT   **AUSTRIA 1926**

VK2, landaulet. 4-cyl. o.h.v. engine. Bore and stroke 72 × 122 mm. Displacement 1,940 c.c. Max. b.h.p. 30 at 2,800 r.p.m. 4 speeds. Max. speed 56 m.p.h. Total weight only 1,540 lbs.

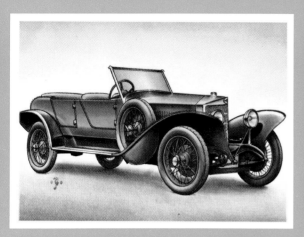

STEYR   AUSTRIA 1926

VI Sport, sporttourer. 6-cyl. s.o.h.c. engine. Bore and stroke 88 × 110 mm. Displacement 4,014 c.c. Max. b.h.p. 90 at 3,000 r.p.m. 4 speeds. Max. speed 84 m.p.h. Torque tube drive and cantilever rear springs.

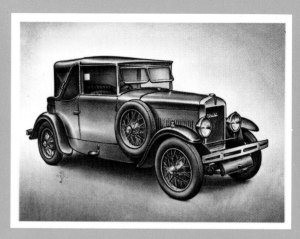

MAJOLA   FRANCE 1926

7 CV, Type F, cabriolet. 4-cyl. s.o.h.c. engine. Bore and stroke 62 × 90 mm. Displacement 1,088 c.c. 4 speeds. Later taken over by Georges Irat.

RENAULT   FRANCE 1926

40 CV (J.V.), 5/6 pass. conduite interieure. 6-cyl. s.v. engine in line. Bore and stroke 110 × 160 mm. Displacement 9,120 c.c. Max. b.h.p. 160 at 2,500 r.p.m. 4 speeds. Max. speed 93 m.p.h. Radiator behind the engine.

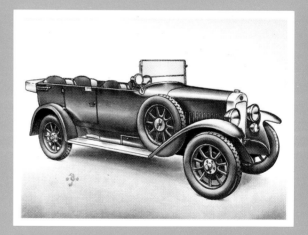

N.S.U.   GERMANY 1926

8/40 HP, phaeton. 4-cyl. s.v. engine. Bore and stroke 78 × 110 mm. Displacement 2,100 c.c. Max. b.h.p. 40 at 2,800 r.p.m. 4 speeds. Max. speed 56 m.p.h. Wet-type clutch with disks running in oil.

PHÄNOMEN   **GERMANY 1926**

412, sporttourer. 4-cyl. s.o.h.c. engine. Bore and stroke 85 × 138 mm. Displacement 3,128 c.c. Max. b.h.p. 50 at 2,100 r.p.m. 4 speeds. Max. speed 68 m.p.h. Light alloy rear axle casing.

ARMSTRONG-SIDDELEY   **GREAT BRITAIN 1926**

Short 18, sedan. 6-cyl. o.h.v. engine. Bore and stroke 73 × 114.3 mm. Displacement 2,872 c.c. 3 speeds. Became Short 20 in 1928.

CADILLAC   **U.S.A. 1926**

Coupe. V-8 s.v. engine. Bore and stroke 3.13 x 5.13 inches. Displacement 312 cu. in. Max. b.h.p. 80. 3 speeds. Counterweighted crankshaft and torsional vibration damper. Best balanced V-8 at the time.

FORD   **U.S.A. 1926**

Model T, 4/5 pass. touring 4-cyl. s.v. engine in line. Bore and stroke 3.75 x 4.00 inches. Displacement 176 cu. in. Max. b.h.p. 22 at 1,800 r.p.m. 2 speeds. Max. speed 45 m.p.h. 15 million model T's from 1908 to 1927.

LINCOLN   U.S.A. 1926

Series L, 4/5 pass. coupé de ville. V-8 s.v. engine. Bore and stroke 3.39 x 5.00 inches. Displacement 357 cu. in. Max. b.h.p. 85 at 2,800 r.p.m. 3 speeds. Max. speed 75 m.p.h. First Lincoln with balloon tires.

NASH   U.S.A. 1926

Advance 6, sedan 6-cyl. s.v. engine. Bore and stroke 3.14 x 5.00 inches. Displacement 277 cu. in. Max. b.h.p. 69 at 2,500 r.p.m. 3 speeds. Max. speed 52 m.p.h. chassis on 121 in wheelbase.

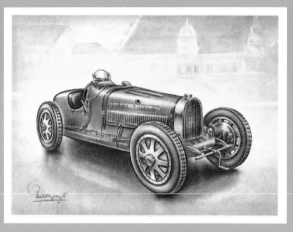

BUGATTI   FRANCE 1927

35 B, racing car. 8-cyl. s.o.h.c. engine in line with super-charger. Bore and stroke 60 × 100 mm. Displacement 2,261 c.c. Max. b.h.p. 140 at 5,500 r.p.m. 4 speeds. Max. speed approx. 130 m.p.h. Won 1,045 races in 2 years.

DELAGE   FRANCE 1927

1500 G.P., racing car. 8-cyl. d.o.h.c. engine in line with super-charger. Bore and stroke 56 × 76 mm. Displacement 1,488 c.c. Max. b.h.p. 170 at 8,000 r.p.m. 5 speeds. Max. speed 130 m.p.h. Still winning races in 1936.

DELAGE   FRANCE 1927

G.L., 4/5 pass. sports torpedo. 6-cyl. o.h.v. engine in line. Bore and stroke 95 × 140 mm. Displacement 5,954 c.c. Max. b.h.p. 50 at 3,500 r.p.m. 4 speeds. Max. speed 74 m.p.h. One of first Delages with spiral bevel final drive.

PRESTO   GERMANY 1927

F, phaeton. 6-cyl. o.h.v. engine. Bore and stroke 72 × 107 mm. Displacement 2,613 c.c. Max. b.h.p. 55 at 2,200 r.p.m. 3 speeds. Max. speed 56 m.p.h. Mechanical 4-wheel power brakes.

RILEY   GREAT BRITAIN 1927

9, Model Brooklands, 2-seater sports-racing car. 4 – cyl. o.h.v. engine in line. Bore and stroke 60 × 95 mm. Displacement 1,089 c.c. Max. b.h.p. 50 at 5,000 r.p.m. 4 speeds. Max. speed 90 m.p.h. Hemispherical combustion chambers in engine.

SUNBEAM   GREAT BRITAIN 1927

World speed record car. (203 m.p.h.). 2 12-cyl. engines. (Sunbeam Matabele). Bore and stroke 130 × 140 mm. Displacement (total) 44,888 c.c. Max. b.h.p. 1,000 at 2,000 r.p.m. Max. speed approx. 210 m.p.h. First car to top 200 m.p.h.

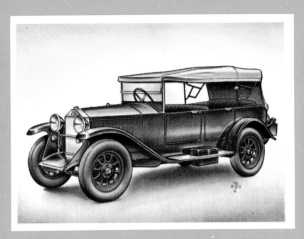

CEIRANO ITALY 1927

150S, phaeton. 4-cyl. o.h.v. engine. Bore and stroke 65 × 110 mm. Displacement 1,460 c.c. 4 speeds. Max. speed 68 m.p.h. Developed into 2.3 liter 250, last of the Ceiranos.

CHANDLER U.S.A. 1927

Big Six. 5/6 pass. metropolitan sedan de luxe. 6-cyl. s.v. engine in line. Bore and stroke 3.50 x 5.00 inches. Displacement 289 cu. in. Max. b.h.p. 55 at 2,100 r.p.m. 3 speeds. Max. speed 77 m.p.h. Body by Fisher in this period.

KISSEL U.S.A. 1927

Cabriolet. 8-cyl. s.v. engine (Lycoming). Bore and stroke 3.14 x 4.50 inches. Displacement 287.3 cu. in. Max. b.h.p. 71 at 3000 r.p.m. 3 speeds. Max. speed 68 m.p.h.

VELIE U.S.A. 1927

50, Sedan, 6-cyl. o.h.v. engine. Bore and stroke 3.13 x 4.25 inches. Displacement 195.8 cu. in. Max. b.h.p. 46 at 2600 r.p.m. 3 speeds. Discontinued in 1929.

EXCELSIOR   **BELGIUM 1928**

Albert I, 2-seater sports. 6-cyl. s.o.h.c. engine in line. Bore and stroke 90 × 140 mm. Displacement 5,350 c.c. Max. b.h.p. 125 at 3,000 r.p.m. 4 speeds. Max. speed 93 m.p.h. Power brakes standard equipment.

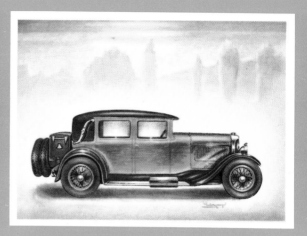

PANHARD LEVASSOR   **FRANCE 1928**

27 CV., 4/5 pass. conduite interieure (Weymann). 6-cyl. sleeve valve engine in line. Bore and stroke 85 × 103 mm. Displacement 3,440 c.c. Max. b.h.p. 60 at 3,500 r.p.m. 4 speeds. Max. speed 70 m.p.h. Fabric-covered wood bodywork.

HANOMAG   **GERMANY 1928**

Kommisbrot. 2 pass. coupé. 1-cyl. o.h.v. engine. Bore and stroke 80 × 100 mm. Displacement 502 c.c. Max. b.h.p. 10 at 2,800 r.p.m. 3 speeds. Max. speed 37 m.p.h.

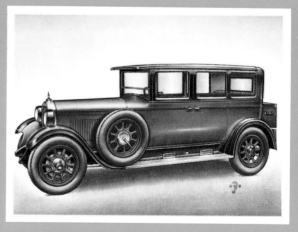

MANNESMANN   **GERMANY 1928**

M 8, sedan. 8-cyl. o.h.v. engine. Bore and stroke 63 × 94 mm. Displacement 2,395 c.c. Max. b.h.p. 55 at 3,400 r.p.m. 3 speeds. Max. speed 68 m.p.h. Finned light alloy brake drums, power brakes.

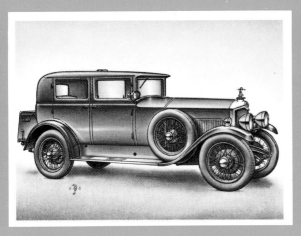

CROSSLEY   **GREAT BRITAIN 1928**

Super Six, limousine. 6-cyl. o.h.v. engine. Bore and stroke 75 × 120 mm. Displacement 3,198 c.c. 4 speeds. In production through 1934.

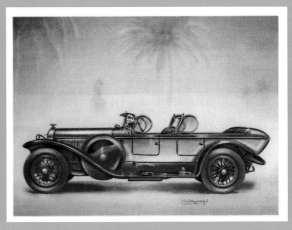

ISOTTA FRASCHINI   **ITALY 1928**

8-B, 4/5 pass. sports torpedo. 8-cyl. o.h.v. engine in line. Bore and stroke 95 × 130 mm. Displacement 7,372 c.c. Max. b.h.p. 100 at 2,500 r.p.m. 4 speeds. Max. speed 100 m.p.h. Carrozzeria Cesare Sala.

LANCIA   **ITALY 1928**

Lambda, 7th Series. 5/6 pass. tourer. V-4 o.h.v. engine (14°). Bore and stroke 79.37 mm. x 120 mm. Displacement 2,056 c.c. Max. b.h.p. 40 at 3,500 r.p.m. 4 speeds. Max. speed 75 m.p.h. 13,000 Lambdas between 1923 and 1930.

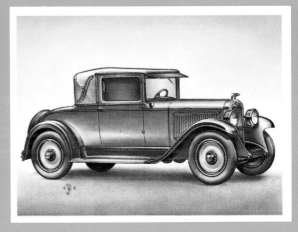

OAKLAND   **U.S.A. 1928**

Sport cabriolet. 6-cyl. engine. Bore and stroke 82,5 x 108 mm. Displacement 3,470 c.c. 3 speeds. Oakland replaced by Pontiac in 1931.

AUSTRO DAIMLER   AUSTRIA 1929

ADR, 4 pass. faux-cabriolet (hardtop). 6-cyl. s.o.h.c. engine
in line. Bore and stroke 82 × 115 mm. Displacement 3,614
c.c. Max. b.h.p. 120 at 3,500 r.p.m. 4 speeds. Max. speed 87
m.p.h. Central tube "backbone" frame chassis.

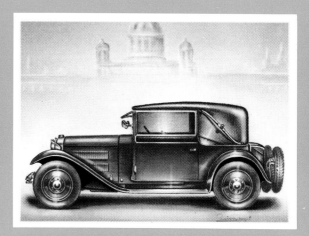

STEYR   AUSTRIA 1929

XX 8/40 ps, 4 pass. cabriolet. 6-cyl. o.h.v. engine in line.
Bore and stroke 65 × 104 mm. Displacement 2,056 c.c. Max.
b.h.p. 40 at 3,500 r.p.m. 4 speeds. Max. speed 62 m.p.h.
Swing-axle rear suspension.

DELAUNAY   FRANCE 1929

Belleville S-6, coupé de ville. 6-cyl. o.h.v. engine. Bore and
stroke 75 × 120 mm. Displacement 3,181 c.c. 4 speeds.
Power brakes acting on front wheels and transmission shaft.

BRENNABOR   GERMANY 1929

ASL, landaulet. 6-cyl. s.v. engine. Bore and stroke 77 × 111
mm. Displacement 3,080 c.c. Max. b.h.p. 45 at 2,400 r.p.m.
3 speeds. Max. speed 59 m.p.h. Mechanical 4-wheel brakes.

BENTLEY   **GREAT BRITAIN 1929**

$4^1/_2$ Liter Le Mans, sports. 4-cyl. s.o.h.c. engine in line with supercharger. Bore and stroke 100 × 140 mm. Displacement 4,486 c.c. Max. b.h.p. 240 at 4,200 r.p.m. 4 speeds. Max. speed 130 m.p.h. "Blower" created by independent racing stable, not a factory product.

ROLLS-ROYCE   **GREAT BRITAIN 1929**

Phantom II, 4/5 pass. continental saloon. 6-cyl. o.h.v. engine in line. Bore and stroke 108 × 140 mm. Displacement 7,668 c.c. Max. b.h.p. 150 at 4,000 r.p.m. 4 speeds. Max. speed 95 m.p.h. Servo (power) brakes standard.

MASERATI   **ITALY 1929**

4-liter GP, racecar. V-16 engine with compressor. Bore and stroke 67 × 82 mm. Displacement 3,960 c.c. Max. b.h.p. 260 at 5,500 r.p.m. 4 speeds. Max. speed 155 m.p.h. Engine united 2 straight-eight 2-liters.

DUESENBERG   **U.S.A. 1929**

J, 4/5 pass. touring. 8-cyl. d.o.h.c. engine in line. Bore and stroke 3.75 x 4.75 inches. Displacement 414.8 cu. in. Max. b.h.p. 265 at 4,200 r.p.m. 3 speeds. Max. speed 115 m.p.h. Body by Murphy.

HUDSON   U.S.A. 1929

Super six 5-pass. sedan. 6-cyl. o.h.v. engine. Bore and stroke 3.5 x 5.0 inches. Displacement 287 cu. in. Max. b.h.p. 92 at 3,500 r.p.m. 3 speeds. Max. speed 81 m.p.h. Replaced by a Straight-eight in 1930.

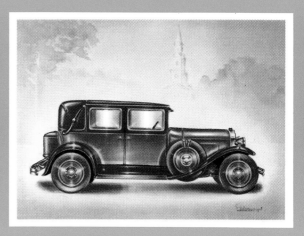

LA SALLE   U.S.A. 1929

Series 314, 5 pass. landau convertible (cabriolet) V-8 s.v. engine. Bore and stroke 3.21 x 4.92 inches. Displacement 339.7 cu. in. Max. b.h.p. 91 at 3,500 r.p.m. 3 speeds. Max. speed 80 m.p.h. Body design by Harley J. Earl.

OWEN-MAGNETIC   U.S.A. 1920

MM, convertible. 8-cyl. o.h.v. engine. Bore and stroke 90 × 150 mm. Displacement 7,634 c.c. Max. b.h.p. 80. Max. speed 75 m.p.h. No conventional gearbox; drive by means of magnetic clutch.

RUXTON   U.S.A. 1929

85 HP, 2/4 pass. roadster. 8-cyl. s.v. engine in line. (Continental Motors Corp.) Displacement 274.6 cu. in. Max. b.h.p. 85 at 3000 r.p.m. 3 speeds. Max. speed 80 m.p.h. front wheel drive.

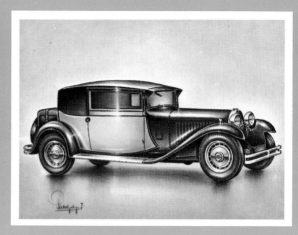

MINERVA BELGIUM 1930

40 CV, 4/5 pass. limousine de ville. 8-cyl. sleeve valve engine in line. Bore and stroke 90 × 130 mm. Displacement 6,616 c.c. Max. b.h.p. 140 at 4,000 r.p.m. 4 speeds. Max. speed 93 m.p.h. "The Car of Kings and Queen of Cars."

BUGATTI FRANCE 1930

50, 4-pass. faux-cabriolet. 8-cyl. d.o.h.c. engine with super-charger. Bore and stroke 86 × 107 mm. Displacement 4,840 c.c. Max. b.h.p. 200 at 4,000 r.p.m. 3 speeds. Max. speed 124 m.p.h. Weight ± 1,700 kg. Fuel consumption 1:6.

BUGATTI FRANCE 1930

41 La Royale, 5/6 pass. limousine. 8-cyl. s.o.h.c. engine in line. Bore and stroke 125 × 130 mm. Displacement 12,760 c.c. Max. b.h.p. 200 at 2,000 r.p.m. 3 speeds. Max. speed 125 m.p.h. 7 built, none with identical coach work.

HOTCHKISS FRANCE 1930

617, 4 pass. roadster. 6-cyl. o.h.v. engine in line. Bore and stroke 80 × 100 mm. Displacement 3,016 c.c. Max. b.h.p. 60 at 3,800 r.p.m. 4 speeds. Max. speed 70 m.p.h. Torque tube instead of Hotchkiss drive.

ADLER   **GERMANY 1930**

Standard 8, 5/6 pass. pullman limousine. 8-cyl. s.v. engine in line. Bore and stroke 75 × 110 mm. Displacement 3,861 c.c. Max. b.h.p. 80 at 3,300 r.p.m. 3 speeds. Max. speed 62 m.p.h. Engine patterned on 8-cyl. Chrysler.

INVICTA   **GREAT BRITAIN 1930**

4.5 Liter, 4 pass. sports. 6-cyl. o.h.v. engine in line. Bore and stroke 88.5 × 121 mm. Displacement 4,467 c.c. Max. b.h.p. 110 at 3,500 r.p.m. 4 speeds. Max. speed 100 m.p.h. Engine supplied by Henry Meadows.

MORRIS   **GREAT BRITAIN 1930**

8 HP Minor, 4 pass. saloon. 4-cyl. s.o.h.c. engine in line. Bore and stroke 57 × 83 mm. Displacement 847 c.c. Max. b.h.p. 12 at 4,500 r.p.m. 3 speeds. Max. speed 50 m.p.h. Morris' answer to the Austin Seven.

BIANCHI   **ITALY 1930**

S-8, 4/5 pass. sports torpedo. 8-cyl. o.h.v. engine in line. Bore and stroke 68 × 100 mm. Displacement 2,906 c.c. Max. b.h.p. 78 at 4,000 r.p.m. 4 speeds. Max. speed 71 m.p.h. Engine: 2 S-5 4-cyl. blocks.

CORD   U.S.A. 1930

L-29, 2/3 pass. convertible (cabriolet). 8-cyl. s.v. engine in
line. Bore and stroke 3.25 x 4.50 inches. Displacement
384.8 cu. in. Max. b.h.p. 125 at 3400 r.p.m. 3 speeds. Max.
speed 90 m.p.h. Front wheel drive. Body design by Al
Leamy.

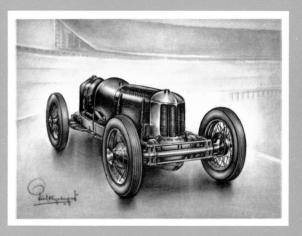

MILLER   U.S.A. 1930

F W D, racing car. 8-cyl. o.h.v. engine in line with Supercharger, Front-wheel drive. Bore and stroke 2.21 x 2.99
inches. Displacement 89.3 cu. in. Max. b.h.p. 200 at 7,200
r.p.m. 3 speeds. Max. speed approx. 150 m.p.h. Won Indianapolis 500 from 1928 through 1936.

PACKARD   U.S.A. 1930

833, 5/6 pass. Sedan. 8-cyl. s.v. engine in line. Bore and
stroke 3.18 x 5.00 inches. Displacement 320 cu. in. Max.
b.h.p. 100 at 3,200 r.p.m. 3 speeds. Max. speed 80 m.p.h.
28,177 built in 1930.

DE DION BOUTON   FRANCE 1931

LA 14/40, convertible. 4-cyl. o.h.v. engine in line. Bore and
stroke 72.5 × 120 mm. Displacement 1,982 c.c. 4 speeds.
Mechanically unchanged from 1928.

HISPANO SUIZA   **FRANCE 1931**

H6C, 4/5 pass. million guiet sedan. 6-cyl. o.h.v. engine in line. Bore and stroke 110 × 140 mm. Displacement 7,983 c.c. Max. b.h.p. 180 at 2,500 r.p.m. 4 speeds. Max. speed 100 m.p.h. Power brakes standard equipment.

VOISIN   **FRANCE 1931**

Surbaissé, 4 pass. coupé. 6-cyl. sleeve valve engine in line. Bore and stroke 94 × 130 mm. Displacement 5,830 c.c. Max. b.h.p. 140 at 4,000 r.p.m. 4 speeds. Max. speed 100 m.p.h. V-12 available.

BENTLEY   **GREAT BRITAIN 1931**

8 Liter, 4/5 pass. saloon. 6-cyl. s.o.h.c. engine in line. Bore and stroke 110 × 140 mm. Displacement 7,983 c.c. Max. b.h.p. 240 at 3,500 r.p.m. 4 speeds. Max. speed 112 m.p.h. Last production Bentley before Rolls-Royce take over.

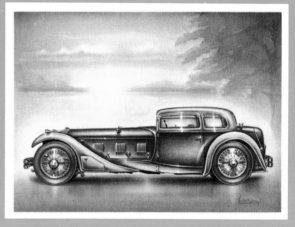

DAIMLER   **GREAT BRITAIN 1931**

Double Six, 4 pass. sport coupé. V-12 sleeve valve engine. Bore and stroke 73 × 104 mm. Displacement 5,296 c.c. Max. b.h.p. 150 at 4,000 r.p.m. 4 speeds. Max. speed 93 m.p.h. Fluid flywheel transmission. Body by Corsica.

AUBURN   U.S.A. 1931

8-98 2/3 pass. convertible (cabriolet). 8-cyl. s.v. engine in line (Lycoming). Bore and stroke 3.0 x 4.7 inches. Displacement 286.6 cu. in. Max. b.h.p. 98 at 3400 r.p.m. 3 speeds. Max. speed 87 m.p.h.

CHRYSLER   U.S.A. 1931

CG, 6 pass. Imperial custom Eight phaeton. 8-cyl. s.v. engine in line. Bore and stroke 3.5 x 5.0 inches. Displacement 384.8 cu. in. Max. b.h.p. 125 at 3200 r.p.m. 3 speeds. Max. speed 87 m.p.h. Body design by LeBaron; built by Briggs.

DOBLE   U.S.A. 1931

F-30, 2/3 pass. convertible (cabriolet). 4-cyl. cross-compound. Piston-type valves with Stephenson control. Bore and stroke 4.49 x 5.00 inches. Max. speed 77 m.p.h. Last series-production steam car.

MARMON   U.S.A. 1931

V-16, 4/5 pass. club sedan. V-16 o.h.v. engine. Bore and stroke 3.1 x 4.0 inches. Displacement 490 cu. in. Max. b.h.p. 200 at 3400 r.p.m. 3 speeds. Max. speed approx. 105 m.p.h. Body design by Walter Dorwin Teague.

PLYMOUTH   U.S.A. 1931

Phaeton. 4-cyl. s.v. engine. Bore and stroke 3.06 x 4.75 inches. Displacement 196.09 cu. in. Max. b.h.p. 48 at 2800 r.p.m. 3 speeds. Max. speed 71 m.p.h. Coast-to-coast round trip record (132 hrs. and a min.).

AMILCAR   FRANCE 1932

M 3, 2 CV, cabriolet. 4-cyl. s.v. engine. Bore and stroke 60 × 110 mm. Displacement 1,240 c.c. 4 speeds. Overall length 145 in.

BUCCIALI   FRANCE 1932

V-16, 4 pass. coupé. V-16 o.h.v. engine. Front wheel drive. Max. b.h.p. 165. 4 speeds. Max. speed 125 m.p.h. Few Buccialis made but new models presented at every automobile show.

BUGATTI   FRANCE 1932

55, 2 pass. super sports-roadster. 8-cyl. d.o.h.c. engine in line, with compressor. Bore and stroke 60 × 100 mm. Displacement 2,270 c.c. Max. b.h.p. 140 at 5,500 r.p.m. 4 speeds. Max. speed 112 m.p.h. 51 engine with 50 chassis and new sports body.

LORRAINE FRANCE 1932

Dietrich 20 CV. 6-cyl. s.v. engine. Bore and stroke 85 × 120 mm. Displacement 4,086 c.c. 4 speeds. Reverted from o.h.v. to s.v. with this model.

BLUE BIRD GREAT BRITAIN 1932

Blue Bird, World speed record car. V-12 engine with super-charger (Napier Lion aircraft). Bore and stroke 140 × 130 mm. Displacement 23,936 c.c. Max. b.h.p. 1,450 at 3,500 r.p.m. Max. speed approx. 246 m.p.h. Built by Thompson & Taylor for Malcolm Campbell.

LEA FRANCIS GREAT BRITAIN 1932

16/70 H.P., de luxe Saloon. 6-cyl. s.o.h.c. engine. Bore and stroke 65 x 100 m.m. Displacement 1,991 c.c. 4 speeds. Max. speed 75 m.p.h. Developed from the 1928 16/60.

ALFA ROMEO ITALY 1932

8C 2300 Mille Miglia, Gran Sport 2-seater. 8-cyl. d.o.h.c. engine in line with supercharger. Bore and stroke 65 × 88 mm. Displacement 2,336 c.c. Max. b.h.p. 140 at 5,200 r.p.m. 4 speeds. Max. speed 105 m.p.h. First 7 places in 1932 Mille Miglia.

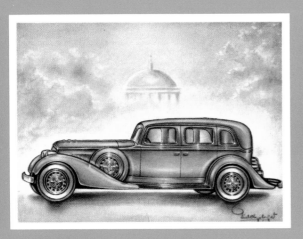

GRAHAM PAIGE U.S.A. 1932

Blue Streak, 5 pass. sedan. 8-cyl. s.v. engine in line. Bore and stroke 3.11 x 4.00 inches. Displacement 245.4 cu. in. Max. b.h.p. 95 at 3400 r.p.m. 3 speeds. Max. speed approx. 80 m.p.h. Paige dropped in 1934; car continued as Graham.

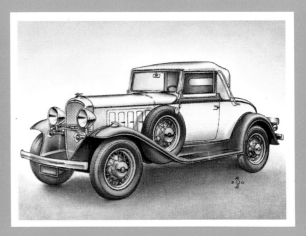

OLDSMOBILE U.S.A. 1932

Cabriolet. 6-cyl. s.v. engine. Bore and stroke 3.37 x 4.11 inches. Displacement 221.4 cu. in. Max. b.h.p. 80 at 3200 r.p.m. 3 speeds. Max. speed 84 m.p.h. Straight-eight available.

CITROËN FRANCE 1933

15, sedan. 6-cyl. s.v. engine in line. Bore and stroke 75 × 100 mm. Displacement 2,650 c.c. Max. b.h.p. 53 at 3,200 r.p.m. 3 speeds. Max. speed 70 m.p.h. One of last rear-drive Citroëns.

RENAULT FRANCE 1933

Reinasport. 8-cyl. s.v. engine in line. Bore and stroke 90 × 140 mm. Displacement 7,122 c.c. 3/4 speeds. Engine new in 1928.

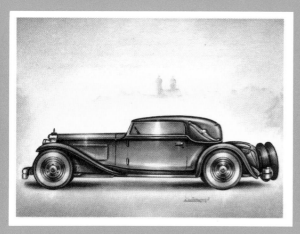

MAYBACH GERMANY 1933

Zeppelin, 4/5 pass. faux-cabriolet (hardtop). V-12 o.h.v. engine. Bore and stroke 92 × 100 mm. Displacement 7,977 c.c. Max. b.h.p. 200 at 3,200 r.p.m. 4 speeds. Max. speed 103 m.p.h. 8-speed transmission.

MERCEDES-BENZ GERMANY 1933

SSK, super sports 2-seater. 6-cyl. s.o.h.c. engine in line with supercharger. Bore and stroke 100 × 150 mm. Displacement 7,020 c.c. Max. b.h.p. 200 at 3,200 r.p.m. 4 speeds. Max. speed 125 m.p.h. K stands for Kurz (short); original SS was 4-seater.

N.A.G. GERMANY 1933

218, cabriolet. V-8 o.h.v. engine. Bore and stroke 85 × 100 mm. Displacement 4,500 c.c. Max. b.h.p. 100 at 3,100 r.p.m. 4 speeds. Max. speed 75 m.p.h. Front wheel drive.

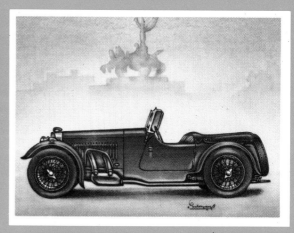

ASTON MARTIN GREAT BRITAIN 1933

Le Mans, 4 pass. sports. 4-cyl. s.o.h.c. engine in line. Bore and stroke 69 × 99 mm. Displacement 1,495 c.c. Max. b.h.p. 70 at 4,750 r.p.m. 4 speeds. Max. speed 87 m.p.h. Only 57 built in 1933.

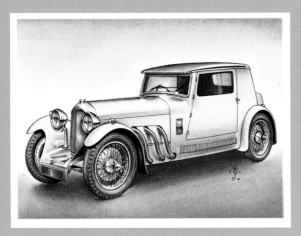

MARENDAZ   GREAT BRITAIN 1933

Special 12.8 HP, coupe. 6-cyl. s.v. engine. Bore and stroke 59 x 114 m.m. Displacement 1,869 c.c. 4 speeds. Max. speed 80 m.p.h. Low-volume production car, fast and durable, with Marendaz engines exclusively.

SS   GREAT BRITAIN 1933

SS-I, 4 pass. coupé. 6-cyl. s.v. engine. Bore and stroke 73 × 101.6 mm. Displacement 2,552 c.c. 4 speeds. Max. speed 75 m.p.h. Weight ± 1,250 kg. Fuel consumption 1:6. Predecessor of Jaguar.

WOLSELEY   GREAT BRITAIN 1933

Hornet, 4 pass. saloon. 6-cyl. s.o.h.c. engine in line. Bore and stroke 57 × 83 mm. Displacement 1,271 c.c. Max. b.h.p. 30 at 4,000 r.p.m. 4 speeds. Max. speed 62 m.p.h. Engine mounted unusually far forward.

BRIGGS   U.S.A. 1933

Dream car. Designed with rear-mounted engine. Wooden mock-up prototype. Built to explore airflow by Briggs Mfg. Co. (now Briggs Body Division of Chrysler Corp.).

DODGE   U.S.A. 1933

Dynamic Six. 2/3 pass. coupe 6-cyl. s.v. engine in line. Bore and stroke 3.11 x 4.37 inches. Displacement 201.3 cu. in. Max. b.h.p. 75 at 3600 r.p.m. 3 speeds. Max. speed 77 m.p.h. First Dodge with independent front suspension.

DUSENBERG   U.S.A. 1933

S. J. Twenty Grand. 8-cyl. d.o.h.c. supercharged engine in line. Bore and stroke 3.75 x 4.75 inches. Displacement 4.20 cu. in. Max. b.h.p. 320 at 4750 r.p.m. 3 speeds. Max. speed 130 m.p.h. Body by Rollston.

NASH   U.S.A. 1933

Ambassador Eight, 2/3 pass. convertible roadster. 8-cyl. o.h.v. engine in line. Bore and stroke 3.07 x 4.50 inches. Displacement 322 cu. in. Max. b.h.p. 125 at 3600 r.p.m. 3 speeds. Max. speed 87 m.p.h. 2 Spark plugs per cylinder.

PIERCE ARROW   U.S.A. 1933

Silver Arrow, 5 pass. sedan. V-12 s.v. engine. Bore and stroke 3.5 x 4.0 inches. Displacement 462 cu. in. Max. b.h.p. 175 at 3000 r.p.m. 3 speeds. Max. speed 112 m.p.h. Only 5 built.

STUDEBAKER U.S.A. 1933

President St. Regis, 5 pass. brougham. 8-cyl. s.v. engine in line. Bore and stroke 3.06 x 4.25 inches. Displacement 250.4 cu. in. Max. b.h.p. 110 at 3800 r.p.m. 3 speeds. Max. speed 90 m.p.h. weight. 3,490 lbs. Engine unchanged until 1941.

STEYR AUSTRIA 1934

120 S, cabriolet. 6-cyl. o.h.v. engine. Bore and stroke 68.5 × 90 mm. Displacement 1,990 c.c. Max. b.h.p. 50 at 3,800 r.p.m. 4 speeds. Max. speed 75 m.p.h. Swing axle independent rear suspension.

BUGATTI FRANCE 1934

59, 2-seater sports-racing car. 8-cyl. d.o.h.c. engine in line with supercharger. Bore and stroke 72 × 100 mm. Displacement 3,255 c.c. Max. b.h.p. 275 at 5,000 r.p.m. 4 speeds. Max. speed approx. 155 m.p.h. G.P. racing car, later converted to road use by Rodney Clarke.

PEUGEOT FRANCE 1934

301, roadster. 4-cyl. s.v. engine. Bore and stroke 72 × 90 mm. Displacement 1,465 c.c. Max. b.h.p. 34. 3 speeds. Introduced in 1932; 45,000 by 1935.

WANDERER   **GERMANY 1934**

W 35, sedan. 6-cyl. o.h.v. engine. Bore and stroke 65 × 85 mm. Displacement 1,692 c.c. Max. b.h.p. 35 at 3,500 r.p.m. 4 speeds. Independent rear suspension with swing axles and a cross-spring.

M.G.   **GREAT BRITAIN 1934**

Magnette N, 4-door saloon. 6-cyl. s.o.h.c. engine (2 carburetors). Bore and stroke 57 × 84 mm. Displacement 1,287 c.c. 4 speeds. Max. speed 82 m.p.h. Replaced the Magna L.

ALFA ROMEO   **ITALY 1934**

P-3, Monoposto racing car. 8-cyl. d.o.h.c. engine in line with supercharger. Bore and stroke 65 × 100 mm. Displacement 2,654 c.c. Max. b.h.p. 198 at 5,400 r.p.m. 4 speeds. Max. speed 135 m.p.h. A separate drive shaft from the gearbox led diagonally to each rear wheel.

FIAT   **ITALY 1934**

518-C Ardita, 5 pass. torpedo. 4-cyl. s.v. engine in line. Bore and stroke 82 × 92 mm. Displacement 1,944 c.c. Max. b.h.p. 45 at 3,600 r.p.m. 4 speeds. Max. speed 68 m.p.h. Followed by 6-cyl. 2^1/$_2$-liter Ardita.

BUICK U.S.A. 1934

61, club sedan. 8-cyl. o.h.v. engine in line. Bore and stroke 3.00 x 4.06 inches. Displacement 278.1 cu. in. Max. b.h.p. 100 at 3200 r.p.m. 3 speeds. First Buick with independent front suspension.

FORD U.S.A. 1934

V-8, 2/3 pass. roadster de grand luxe. V-8 s.v. engine. Bore and stroke 3.06 x 3.75 inches. Displacement 220 cu. in. Max. b.h.p. 85 at 3800 r.p.m. 3 speeds. Max. speed 85 m.p.h. still equipped with mechanical brakes.

BERLIET FRANCE 1935

11 CV Dauphine, 4/5 pass. convertible. 4-cyl. o.h.v. engine in line. Bore and stroke 80 x 100 mm. Displacement 2,000 c.c. 4 speeds. One of last Berliet passenger-models; now big truck manufacturer.

RENAULT FRANCE 1935

Momaquatre, convertible. 4-cyl. s.v. engine in line. Bore and stroke 70 × 95 mm. Displacement 1,463 c.c. 3 speeds. Max. speed 65 m.p.h. Still equipped with mechanical brakes.

ADLER GERMANY 1935

Diplomat, 4/5 pass. convertible. 6-cyl. s.v. engine in line. Bore and stroke 75 × 110 mm. Displacement 2,914 c.c. Max. b.h.p. 65 at 3,200 r.p.m. 4 speeds. Max. speed 65 m.p.h. Adler's only rear-drive for many years.

MERCEDES-BENZ GERMANY 1935

130, 4 pass. limousine. 4-cyl. s.v. engine in line (at rear). Bore and stroke 70 × 85 mm. Displacement 1,299 c.c. Max. b.h.p. 26 at 4,000 r.p.m. 4 speeds. Max. speed 65 m.p.h. NSU, Zündapp, Adler, Ardie and Porsche also experimenting with rear engines.

STANDARD GREAT BRITAIN 1935

10/12 HP Avon, coupé. 4-cyl. s.v. engine in line. Bore and stroke 69.5 × 106 mm. Displacement 1,608 c.c. Max. b.h.p. 32.5. 4 speeds with freewheel. Max. speed ± 65 m.p.h.

E.R.A. GREAT BRITAIN 1935

1500A, racing car. 6-cyl. d.o.h.c. engine in line with supercharger. Bore and stroke 57.5 × 95 mm. Displacement 1,488 c.c. Max. b.h.p. 165 at 6,500 r.p.m. 4 speeds. Max. speed approx. 135 m.p.h. Engine design based on Riley.

RAILTON　　　　　　　　　　**GREAT BRITAIN 1935**

Straight Eight, 4 pass. sports tourer. 8-cyl. s.v. engine in line (Hudson). Bore and stroke 76 × 114 mm. Displacement 4,168 c.c. Max. b.h.p. 113 at 3,800 r.p.m. 3 speeds. Max. speed approx. 95 m.p.h.

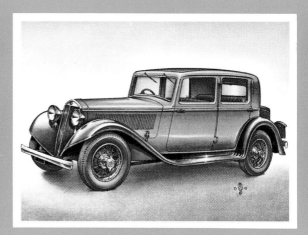

LANCIA　　　　　　　　　　**ITALY 1935**

2330 Astura, sedan. V-8 s.o.h.c. engine. Bore and stroke 74.6 × 85 mm. Displacement 2,972 c.c. Max. b.h.p. 82 at 4,000 r.p.m. 4 speeds. Max. speed 80 m.p.h. Narrow angle between cylinders gave extremely compact engine block.

CHEVROLET　　　　　　　　　　**U.S.A. 1935**

Master Touring, Sedan. 6-cyl. o.h.v. engine in line. Bore and stroke 3.31 x 4.00 inches. Displacement 206.8 cu. in. Max. b.h.p. 74 at 3200 r.p.m. 3 speeds. Max. speed 80 m.p.h. Optional Independent Front Suspension.

PONTIAC　　　　　　　　　　**U.S.A. 1935**

Business coupé 8-cyl. s.v. engine in line. Bore and stroke 3.81 x 3.50 inches. Displacement 223.4 cu. in. Max. b.h.p. 84 at 3400 r.p.m. 3 speeds. Max. speed 80 m.p.h. Optional independent Front Suspension.

BUGATTI   **FRANCE 1936**

57S, 2 seater Atlantic coupé. 8-cyl. s.o.h.c. engine in line.
Bore and stroke 72 × 100 mm. Displacement 3,255 c.c. Max.
b.h.p. 175 at 5,500 r.p.m. 4 speeds. Max. speed 125 m.p.h.
Engine bolted direct to frame of early models.

HANSA   **GERMANY 1936**

1100, limousine (coach). 4-cyl. o.h.v. engine. Bore and stroke
65 × 82 mm. Displacement 1,088 c.c. Max. b.h.p. 28 at 3,200
r.p.m. 4 speeds. Max. speed 59 m.p.h. Swing axle independent rear suspension.

OPEL   **GERMANY 1936**

2-liter, cabriolet. 6-cyl. s.v. engine. Bore and stroke 67.5 x
90 m.m. Displacement 1,920 c.c. Max. b.h.p. 36 at 3,300
r.p.m. 4 speeds. Max. speed 65 m.p.h.

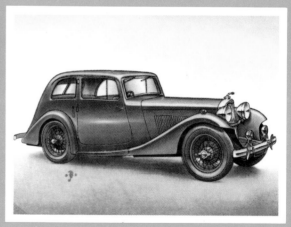

A.C.   **GREAT BRITAIN 1936**

Aero, saloon. 6-cyl. s.o.h.c. engine (3 carburetors). Bore
and stroke 65 × 100 mm. Displacement 1,991 c.c. 4 speeds.
Max. speed 81 m.p.h. Frame underslung (below rear axle).

AUSTIN   **GREAT BRITAIN 1936**

750, supercharged racing car. 4-cyl. d.o.h.c. engine in line. Bore and stroke 60 × 65 mm. Displacement 744 c.c. Max. b.h.p. 116 at 9,000 r.p.m. 4 speeds. Max. speed approx. 125 m.p.h. Mechanical brakes. Front axle with cross-spring.

MORRIS   **GREAT BRITAIN 1936**

16/6, coupé. 6-cyl. s.v. engine. Bore and stroke 65.5 × 102 mm. Displacement 2,062 c.c. 3 speeds. Max. speed 68 m.p.h. Replaced 6-cyl. Oxford.

AUBURN   **U.S.A. 1936**

Speedster, 2 Seater roadster. 8-cyl. s.v. engine in line with Supercharger. Bore and stroke 3.06 x 4.75 inches. Displacement 279.9 cu. in. Max. b.h.p. 150 at 4000 r.p.m. 3 speeds. Max. speed 100 m.p.h. Body Design by Harold Ames and Gordon Buehrig.

CHRYSLER   **U.S.A. 1936**

Airflow Eight, 5/6 pass. imperial coupé. 8-cyl. s.v. engine in line. Bore and stroke 3.25 x 3.87 inches. Displacement 323.5 cu. in. Max. b.h.p. 130 at 3400 r.p.m. 3 speeds. Max. speed 90 m.p.h. 29,918 Airflows built between 1934 and 1938.

CORD   U.S.A. 1936

810, 4/5 pass. Sedan. V-8 s.v. engine. Bore and stroke 3.50 x 3.75 inches. Displacement 288.6 cu. in. Max. b.h.p. 125 at 3500 r.p.m. 4 speeds. Max. speed 90 m.p.h. Front wheel drive. Body design by Gordon Buehrig.

PACKARD   U.S.A. 1936

Twelve, 4 pass. phaeton. V-12 s.v. engine. Bore and stroke 3.43 x 4.25 inches. Displacement 473 cu. in. Max. b.h.p. 175 at 3200 r.p.m. 3 speeds. Max. speed 90 m.p.h. 7.50 x 17 tires.

CITROËN   FRANCE 1937

7 CV, 4 pass. sedan. 4-cyl. o.h.v. engine in line. Bore and stroke 72 × 100 mm. Displacement 1,628 c.c. Max. b.h.p. 35 at 3,200 r.p.m. 3 speeds. Max. speed 62 m.p.h. Front wheel drive. First modern unit-construction body.

B.M.W.   GERMANY 1937

328, 2 pass. sports-roadster. 6-cyl. o.h.v. engine in line. Bore and stroke 66 × 96 mm. Displacement 1,971 c.c. Max. b.h.p. 80 at 4,500 r.p.m. 4 speeds. Max. speed 100 m.p.h. Won 125 races in its first year.

D.K.W.   GERMANY 1937

Meisterklasse, 4 pass. limousine. 2-cyl. 2-stroke engine in
line. Bore and stroke 76 × 76 mm. Displacement 684 c.c.
Max. b.h.p. 20 at 3,500 r.p.m. 3 speeds. Max. speed 55 m.p.h.
Front wheel drive. Fabric-covered plywood doors and body
side panels.

HORCH   GERMANY 1937

5 Liter, 4/5 pass. sports convertible (cabriolet). 8-cyl. s.o.h.c.
engine in line. Bore and stroke 87 × 104 mm. Displacement
4,944 c.c. Max. b.h.p. 100 at 3,800 r.p.m. 4 speeds. Max. speed
87 m.p.h. Auto-Union's rival of Mercedes-Benz 540-K.

MERCEDES-BENZ   GERMANY 1937

W 125, racing car. 8-cyl. d.o.h.c. engine in line with supercharger. Bore and stroke 94 × 102 mm. Displacement 5,660
c.c. Max. b.h.p. 646 at 5,800 r.p.m. 4 speeds. Max. speed 200
m.p.h. Independent suspension for all wheels.

MERCEDES-BENZ   GERMANY 1937

540K, 2-seater roadster. 8-cyl. o.h.v. engine in line with
supercharger. Bore and stroke 88 × 111 mm. Displacement
5,401 c.c. Max. b.h.p. 180 at 3,500 r.p.m. 4 speeds. Max. speed
120 m.p.h. K stands for Kompressor (supercharger), (auto-
matically engaged for acceleration).

90

WANDERER   GERMANY 1937

W25K, 2 seater sports-cabriolet. 6-cyl. o.h.v. engine in line
with supercharger. Bore and stroke 70 × 85 mm. Displacement 1,963 c.c. Max. b.h.p. 85 at 4,000 r.p.m. 4 speeds. Max.
speed approx. 95 m.p.h. Reverted from swing axles to rigid
rear axle.

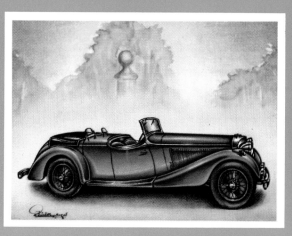

JENSEN   GREAT BRITAIN 1937

3$^1/_2$ Liter, 4/5 pass. tourer. V-8 s.v. engine (Ford V-8). Bore
and stroke 78 × 95 mm. Displacement 3,622 c.c. Max. b.h.p.
90 at 4,000 r.p.m. 3 speeds. Max. speed 90 m.p.h. Mechanical
4-wheel brakes.

M.G.   GREAT BRITAIN 1937

T Midget, 2-seater sports roadster. 4-cyl. o.h.v. engine in
line. Bore and stroke 63.5 × 102 mm. Displacement 1,292
c.c. Max. b.h.p. 50 at 4,500 r.p.m. 4 speeds. Max. speed 80
m.p.h. Era of non-racing MGs began with T Midget.

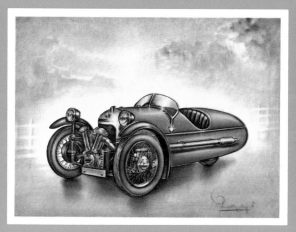

MORGAN   GREAT BRITAIN 1937

Super Sport, 2 seater. V-2 o.h.v. air-cooled engine. Bore
and stroke 85.5 × 85.5 mm. Displacement 990 c.c. Max.
b.h.p. 30 at 4,500 r.p.m. 3 speeds. Max. speed approx. 75
m.p.h. Design practically unchanged from 1909.

ROLLS-ROYCE   GREAT BRITAIN 1937

40/50 Phantom III, 4/5 pass. sedanca de ville. V-12 o.h.v. engine. Bore and stroke 82.5 × 114 mm. Displacement 7,340 c.c. Max. b.h.p. 160 at 4,500 r.p.m. 4 speeds. Max. speed 100 m.p.h. First Rolls-Royce with independent front suspension.

THUNDERBOLT   GREAT BRITAIN 1937

Thunderbolt, world speed record car. 2 12-cyl. engines with superchargers (Rolls-Royce aircraft). Bore and stroke 152 × 167 mm. Displacement (total) 73,164 c.c. Max. b.h.p. 4,700 at 4,000 r.p.m. Max. speed approx. 323 m.p.h. Speed record 311.3 m.p.h.

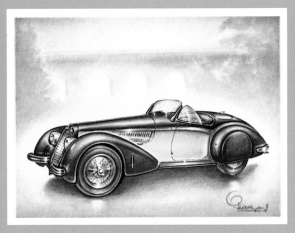

ALFA ROMEO   ITALY 1937

8C-2900/B, 2-seater sports-spider (Turinga). 8-cyl. d.o.h.c. engine in line with supercharger. Bore and stroke 68 × 100 mm. Displacement 2,905 c.c. Max. b.h.p. 180 at 5,000 r.p.m. 4 speeds. Max. speed 115 m.p.h. Production model created from leftover racing engines.

FIAT   ITALY 1937

500 Topolino, 2 pass. coupé. 4-cyl. s.v. engine in line. Bore and stroke 52 × 67 mm. Displacement 570 c.c. Max. b.h.p. 13 at 4,000 r.p.m. 4 speeds. Max. speed 55 m.p.h. Engine placed ahead of front wheel centers.

DELAHAYE FRANCE 1938

135 Sport, 2/3 pass. roadster. 6-cyl. o.h.v. engine in line. Bore and stroke 84 × 107 mm. Displacement 3,557 c.c. Max. b.h.p. 120 at 4,500 r.p.m. 4 speeds. Max. speed 100 m.p.h. Optional Cotal preselector transmission. Body by Carosserie Henri Chapron.

HOTCHKISS FRANCE 1938

Sedan. 6-cyl. o.h.v. engine. Bore and stroke 86 × 100 mm. Displacement 3,485 c.c. 4 speeds. Max. speed 85 m.p.h. Lockheed hydraulic brakes from 1936.

AUTO UNION GERMANY 1938

D, Grand-Prix racing car. V-12 o.h.v. engine with supercharger. Bore and stroke 65 × 75 mm. Displacement 2,909 c.c. Max. b.h.p. 500 at 7,000 r.p.m. 5 speeds. Max. speed 185 m.p.h. Engine behind driver, in front of rear wheels.

MAYBACH GERMANY 1938

Zeppelin V-12, cabriolet sports roadster. V-12 o.h.v. engine. Bore and stroke 92 × 100 mm. Displacement 7,977 c.c. Max. b.h.p. 200 at 3,000 r.p.m. 8 speeds. Max. speed 99 m.p.h. Mechanical 4-wheel brakes with vacuum Servo (power brakes).

OPEL   **GERMANY 1938**

Olympia, 4 pass. limousine. 4-cyl. o.h.v. engine in line. Bore and stroke 80 x 74 m.m. Displacement 1,488 c.c. Max. b.h.p. 43 at 3400 r.p.m. 3 Speeds. Max. speed 68 m.p.h.

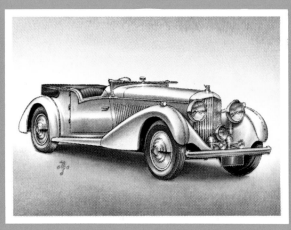

BENTLEY   **GREAT BRITAIN 1938**

Sports roadster. 6-cyl. o.h.v. engine (2 carburetors). Bore and stroke 88 x 114 m.m. Displacement 4,257 c.c. Max. b.h.p. 125. 4 speeds. Max. speed 91 m.p.h.

DAIMLER   **GREAT BRITAIN 1938**

4 Liter Straight Eight, 4/5 pass. saloon. 8-cyl. o.h.v. engine in line. Bore and stroke 77 × 105 mm. Displacement 3,960 c.c. Max. b.h.p. 95 at 3,600 r.p.m. 4 speeds. Max. speed 87 m.p.h. Last Daimler without independent front suspension.

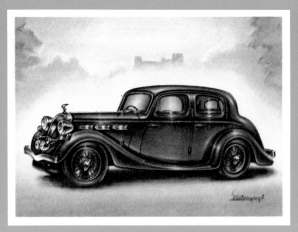

TRIUMPH   **GREAT BRITAIN 1938**

14/60 Dolomite, 4/5 pass. saloon. 4-cyl. o.h.v. engine in line. Bore and stroke 75 × 100 mm. Displacement 1,767 c.c. Max. b.h.p. 70 at 4,500 r.p.m. 4 speeds. Max. speed 77 m.p.h. Dual brake master cylinders.

BUICK U.S.A. 1938

Experimental Y, 2 pass. cabriolet. Height 1.37 m. Headlamps integral with fenders, electrically operated. Body design by Harley J. Earl.

GRAHAM U.S.A. 1938

Super Custom, 5 pass. Sedan de luxe. 6-cyl. s.v. engine in line with Supercharger. Bore and stroke 3.25 x 4.37 inches. Displacement 217.8 cu. in. Max. b.h.p. 116 at 4000 r.p.m. 3 speeds. Max. speed 90 m.p.h. Body design by Amos Northup.

OLDSMOBILE U.S.A. 1938

Six, 2/3 pass. sports coupé. 6-cyl. s.v. engine in line. Bore and stroke 3.43 x 4.11 inches. Displacement 229.7 cu. in. Max. b.h.p. 95 at 3400 r.p.m. 3 speeds. Max. speed 85 m.p.h. Semi-automatic transmission available.

BUGATTI FRANCE 1939

57 SC, 2-seater Le Mans super sports. 8-cyl. d.o.h.c. engine in line with supercharger. Bore and stroke 72 × 100 mm. Displacement 3,255 c.c. Max. b.h.p. 200 at 5,500 r.p.m. Max. speed 168 m.p.h. Won Le Mans 24-hr. race in 1939.

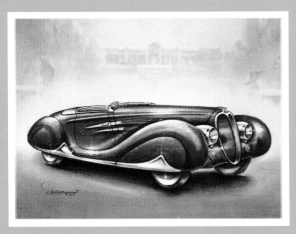

DELAHAYE FRANCE 1939

165, 2-seater sports-roadster. V-12 o.h.v. engine. Bore and stroke 75 × 85 mm. Displacement 4,500 c.c. Max. b.h.p. 160 at 4,500 r.p.m. 4 speeds. Max. speed 100 m.p.h. Body by Figoni & Falaschi. V-12 engine tamed version of Delahaye's last racing engine.

B.M.W. GERMANY 1939

327, 2/4 pass. sports-cabriolet. 6-cyl. o.h.v. engine in line. Bore and stroke 66 × 96 mm. Displacement 1,971 c.c. Max. b.h.p. 80 at 4,500 r.p.m. 4 speeds. Max. speed 93 m.p.h. Eisenach (East Germany) plant still producing this car in 1949.

D.K.W. GERMANY 1939

Meisterklasse, 4 pass. cabriolet de luxe. 2-cyl. 2-stroke engine in line. Bore and stroke 76 × 76 mm. Displacement 684 c.c. Max. b.h.p. 20 at 4,000 r.p.m. 3 speeds. Max. speed 59 m.p.h. Almost 100,000 D.K.W.s built in 1939.

MERCEDES-BENZ GERMANY 1939

W 163, single seater racing car. V-12 d.o.h.c. engine with supercharger. Bore and stroke 67 × 70 mm. Displacement 2,960 c.c. Max. b.h.p. 483 at 7,800 r.p.m. 5 speeds. Max. speed 193 m.p.h. Won the Yugoslav G.P. the day Hitler marched on Poland.

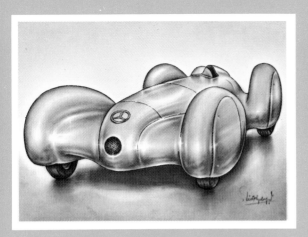

MERCEDES-BENZ   **GERMANY 1939**

Recordcar class D (2-3 ltr.) records with standing start. V-12 engine, with compressor. Bore and stroke 67 x 70 mm. Displacement 2,960 c.c. Max. b.h.p. 483 at 7800 r.p.m. 5-speeds. Max. speed 310 km/193 m.p.h.

ALVIS   **GREAT BRITAIN 1939**

4.3 Liter, 4/5 pass. drophead coupé. 6-cyl. o.h.v. engine in line. Bore and stroke 92 × 110 mm. Displacement 4,387 c.c. Max. b.h.p. 137 at 3,600 r.p.m. 4 speeds. Max. speed 105 m.p.h. One of first English sports cars with independent front suspension.

JAGUAR   **GREAT BRITAIN 1939**

SS 100, 2-seater coupé. 6-cyl. o.h.v. engine in line. Bore and stroke 82 × 110 mm. Displacement 3,485 c.c. Max. b.h.p. 130 at 4,800 r.p.m. 4 speeds. Max. speed 100 m.p.h. This body not in regular production.

JAGUAR   **GREAT BRITAIN 1939**

Type SS 100, 2-seater sports-roadster. 6-cyl. o.h.v. engine in line (modified Standard). Bore and stroke 82 × 110 mm. Displacement 3,486 c.c. Max. b.h.p. 130 at 4,800 r.p.m. 4 speeds. Max. speed 100 m.p.h.

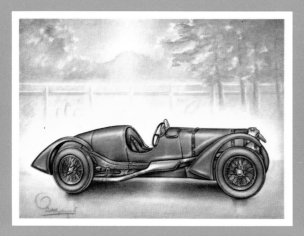

LAGONDA   **GREAT BRITAIN 1939**

Le Mans, sports 2-seater. V-12 s.o.h.c. engine. Bore and
stroke 75 × 85 mm. Displacement 4,480 c.c. Max. b.h.p. 220
at 6,000 r.p.m. 4 speeds. Max. speed 136 m.p.h. Torsion-bar
independent front suspension.

LAGONDA   **GREAT BRITAIN 1939**

Rapide, 4/5 pass. drophead coupé. V-12 s.o.h.c. engine.
Bore and stroke 75 × 84.5 mm. Displacement 4,480 c.c.
Max. b.h.p. 180 at 5,500 r.p.m. 4 speeds. Max. speed 103 m.p.h.
Lockheed hydraulic 4-wheel brakes.

SINGER   **GREAT BRITAIN 1939**

9 HP, 4 pass. sports roadster. 4-cyl. s.o.h.c. engine in line.
Bore and stroke 60 x 95 mm. Displacement 1,074 c.c. Max.
b.h.p. 36 at 5000 r.p.m. 3 speeds. Max. speed 70 m.p.h.

ALFA ROMEO   **ITALY 1939**

158, Monoposto racing car. 8-cyl. d.o.h.c. engine in line with
supercharger. Bore and stroke 58 × 70 mm. Displacement
1,479 c.c. Max. b.h.p. 225 at 7,500 r.p.m. 4 speeds. Max. speed
approx. 185 m.p.h. Won races with 405 h.p. engine as late
as 1951.

LANCIA　　　　　　　　　　　　**ITALY 1939**

Aprilia 2nd series, 4 pass. berlina. V-4 engine. Bore and stroke 74.61 × 85 mm. Displacement 1,486 c.c. Max. b.h.p. 48 at 4,300 r.p.m. 4 speeds. Max. speed 80 m.p.h. Unit-construction body.

LINCOLN　　　　　　　　　　　　**U.S.A. 1939**

Zephyr, 5/6 pass. Sedan. V-12 s.v. engine. Bore and stroke 2.75 x 3.75 inches. Displacement 267.3 cu. in. Max. b.h.p. 110 at 3900 r.p.m. 3 speeds. Max. speed 95 m.p.h. Fords first unit-construction.

MERCURY　　　　　　　　　　　　**U.S.A. 1939**

Eight, 4/5 pass. club cabriolet (convertible) V-8 s.v. engine. Bore and stroke 3.81 x 3.75 inches. Displacement 239 cu.in. Max. b.h.p. 95 at 3800 r.p.m. 3 speeds. Max. speed 90 m.p.h. Created as a medium-price model between Ford and Lincoln.

NASH　　　　　　　　　　　　**U.S.A. 1940**

Ambassador Six, 6 pass. 6-cyl. o.h.v. engine in line. Bore and stroke 3.37 x 4.37 inches. Displacement 234.8 cu. in. Max. b.h.p. 105 at 3400 r.p.m. 3 speeds. Max. speed 85 m.p.h. Body design by George W. Walker.

STUDEBAKER   U.S.A. 1941

President, 6pass. cruising sedan. 8-cyl. s.v. in line engine.
Bore and stroke 3.06 x 4.25 inches. Displacement
250.4 cu. in. Max. b.h.p. 117 at 4000 r.p.m. 3 speeds. Max.
speed 90 m.p.h. Body design by Raymond Loewy.

CADILLAC   U.S.A. 1942

Sixty Special, 5 pass. Fleetwood sedan. V-8 s.v. engine.
Bore and stroke 3.5 x 4.5 inches. Displacement 346 cu. in.
Max. b.h.p. 150 at 3400 r.p.m. 3 speeds. Max. speed 90
m.p.h. Hydra-Matic transmission available.

CHRYSLER   U.S.A. 1942

Windsor, 6 pass. convertible coupé. 6-cyl. s.v. engine in
line. Bore and stroke 3.43 x 4.50 inches. Displacement
250.6 cu. in. Max. b.h.p. 120 at 3800 r.p.m. Max. speed
90 m.p.h. Fluid Drive semi-automatic transmission.

HUDSON   U.S.A. 1942

Commodore, 5 pass. club coupé. 8-cyl. s.v. engine in line.
Bore and stroke 3.0 x 4.5 inches. Displacement 254 cu. in.
Max. b.h.p. 128 at 4200 r.p.m. 3 speeds. Max. speed
95 m.p.h. Electric gearshift available.

PACKARD　　　　　　　　　　　　　**U.S.A. 1942**

180 Clipper, 6 pass. 8-cyl. s.v. engine in line. Bore and stroke 3.25 x 4.25 inches. Displacement 282 cu. in. Max. b.h.p. 125 at 3600 r.p.m. 3 speeds. Max. speed 85 m.p.h. Basically 1923 engine.

PLYMOUTH　　　　　　　　　　　　**U.S.A. 1942**

Special De Luxe, 5/6 pass. 2-door sedan. 6-cyl. s.v. engine in line. Bore and stroke 3.25 x 4.37 inches. Displacement 217.8 cu. in. Max. b.h.p. 95 at 3400 r.p.m. 3 speeds. Max. speed 85 m.p.h. America's third best-selling make.

MATHIS　　　　　　　　　　　　　**FRANCE 1945**

VL 333, 3 pass. coupé. 2-cyl. o.h.v. horizontally-opposed engine. Bore and stroke 75 x 80 mm. Displacement 707 c.c. Max. b.h.p. 15 at 3,000 r.p.m. 4 speeds. Max. speed approx. 70 m.p.h. Front wheel drive. Never in series production.

TRIUMPH　　　　　　　　　　**GREAT BRITAIN 1946**

1800, 2/2 pass. sports tourer. 4-cyl. o.h.v. engine in line. Bore and stroke 73 x 106 mm. Displacement 1,776 c.c. Max. b.h.p. 65 at 4,500 r.p.m. 4 speeds. Max. speed 84 m.p.h. Standard Vanguard engine in 1949 model.

CISITALIA   **ITALY 1946**

D46, racing car. 4-cyl. o.h.v. engine in line. Bore and stroke 68 × 75 mm. Displacement 1,090 c.c. Max. b.h.p. 60 at 5,500 r.p.m. 3 speeds. Max. speed 110 m.p.h. Engine based on Fiat 508C.

BENTLEY   **GREAT BRITAIN 1947**

Mark VI, 4 pass. sedanca coupé. 6-cyl. F-head engine in line. Bore and stroke 89 x 114 m.m. Displacement 4,256 c.c. Max. b.h.p. 140 at 4,500 r.p.m. 4 speeds. Max. speed 100 m.p.h.

RAILTON   **GREAT BRITAIN 1947**

World speed record car. Two 12-cyl. engines with superchargers (Napier-Lion). Bore and stroke 140 x 130 mm. Displacement (total) 47,872 c.c. Max. b.h.p. 2,500 at 3,600 r.p.m. Max. speed approx. 404 m.p.h. Record 397 m.p.h. Record held from 1947 until 1965.

FIAT   **ITALY 1947**

1100/S, 2-seater sports coupé. 4-cyl. o.h.v. engine in line. Bore and stroke 68 × 75 mm. Displacement 1,089 c.c. Max. b.h.p. 51 at 5,200 r.p.m. 4 speeds. Max. speed 93 m.p.h. Body style created for 1940 Mille Miglia.

LINCOLN U.S.A. 1947

Continental, 4/5 pass. convertible coupé. V-12 s.v. engine. Bore and stroke 2.88 x 3.75 inches. Displacement 292 cu. in. Max. b.h.p. 125 at 3600 r.p.m. 3 speeds. Max. speed 95 m.p.h. Developed by Edsel Ford for his own use. 5,320 sold from 1940 - 1948.

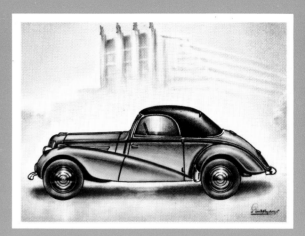

IMPERIA BELGIUM 1948

T.A.P., 4 pass. cabriolet. 4-cyl. o.h.v. engine in line. Bore and stroke 67 x 95 mm. Displacement 1,340 c.c. Max. b.h.p. 45 at 4,000 r.p.m. 3 speeds. Max. speed 70 m.p.h. Front-wheel drive. Built under Adler license.

TATRA CZECHOSLOVAKIA 1948

600 (Tatraplan), 5/6 pass. sedan. 4-cyl. horizontally opposed, air-cooled, rear-mounted, o.h.v. engine. Bore and stroke 85 x 86 mm. Displacement 1,950 c.c. Max. b.h.p. 56 at 4,000 r.p.m. 4 speeds. Max. speed 87 m.p.h.

HOTCHKISS FRANCE 1948

686, 4/5 pass. berline. 6-cyl. o.h.v. engine in line. Bore and stroke 86 x 100 mm. Displacement 3,485 c.c. Max. b.h.p. 100 at 4,000 r.p.m. 4 speeds. Max. speed 87 m.p.h. Consistently placed well in international rallies.

RENAULT FRANCE 1948

R1060 (4 CV) 750, 4 pass. berline. 4-cyl. o.h.v. engine in line at rear. Bore and stroke 55 × 80 mm. Displacement 748 c.c. Max. b.h.p. 18 at 4,200 r.p.m. 3 speeds. Max. speed 62 m.p.h. Competitor of VW.

TALBOT FRANCE 1948

Lago Record, 4 pass. berline. 6-cyl. o.h.v. engine in line. Bore and stroke 93 × 110 mm. Displacement 4,482 c.c. Max. b.h.p. 170 at 4,200 r.p.m. 4 speeds. Max. speed 105 m.p.h. Cotal pre-selector transmission.

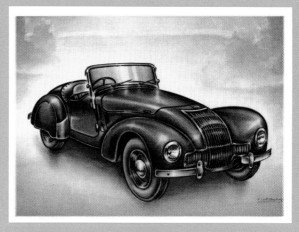

VOLKSWAGEN GERMANY 1948

11A, 4 pass. limousine. 4-cyl. horizontally opposed, air-cooled, rear-mounted o.h.v. engine. Bore and stroke 75 × 64 mm. Displacement 1,131 c.c. Max. b.h.p. 25 at 3,300 r.p.m. 4 speeds. Max. speed 62 m.p.h. Swing-axle rear suspension.

ALLARD GREAT BRITAIN 1948

V8, 2-seater sportscar. V-8 s.v. engine (Ford). Bore and stroke 78 × 95 mm. Displacement 3,622 c.c. Max. b.h.p. 90 at 3,800 r.p.m. 4 speeds. Max. speed 90 m.p.h. Front suspension with divided axle and leaf springs.

ARMSTRONG-SIDDELEY   GREAT BRITAIN 1948

Hurricane, coupé. 6-cyl. o.h.v. engine. Bore and stroke 65 x 100 m.m. Displacement 1991 c.c. Max. b.h.p. 70 at 4200 r.p.m. 4 speeds. Max. speed 92 m.p.h. Body design by Percy Riman.

AUSTIN   GREAT BRITAIN 1948

A40 Devon, 4/5 pass. saloon. 4-cyl. o.h.v. engine in line. Bore and stroke 65 x 89 mm. Displacement 1,200 c.c. Max. b.h.p. 40 at 4,300 r.p.m. 4 speeds. Max. speed 68 m.p.h. Coil spring front suspension.

DAIMLER   GREAT BRITAIN 1948

Straight Eight, 5/6 pass. drophead coupé. 8-cyl. o.h.v. engine in line. Bore and stroke 85 x 120 mm. Displacement 5,460 c.c. Max. b.h.p. 150 at 3,600 r.p.m. 4 speeds. Max. speed 95 m.p.h. Body by Hooper. One of Britain's last straight-eights.

HEALEY   GREAT BRITAIN 1948

Sportsmobile 2-seater sports-roadster. 4-cyl. o.h.v. engine in line (Riley). Bore and stroke 80.5 x 120 mm. Displacement 2,443 c.c. Max. b.h.p. 100 at 4,500 r.p.m. 4 speeds. Max. speed 105 m.p.h. All-coil chassis suspension.

H.R.G.   GREAT BRITAIN 1948

1500, 2-seater sports roadster. 4-cyl. s.o.h.c. engine in line (Singer Motors). Bore and stroke 68×103 mm. Displacement 1,496 c.c. Max. b.h.p. 61 at 4,800 r.p.m. 4 speeds. Max. speed approx. 85 m.p.h.

JOWETT   GREAT BRITAIN 1948

Javelin, 4/5 pass. saloon. 4-cyl. o.h.v. horizontally opposed engine. Bore and stroke 72.5 × 90 mm. Displacement 1,486 c.c. Max. b.h.p. 50 at 4,100 r.p.m. 4 speeds. Max. speed 77 m.p.h. Design inspired by Lancia Aprilia.

LAGONDA   GREAT BRITAIN 1948

$2^1/_2$ Liter, 4/5 pass. drophead coupé. 6-cyl. d.o.h.c. engine in line. Bore and stroke 78 × 90 mm. Displacement 2,580 c.c. Max. b.h.p. 106 at 5,000 r.p.m. 4 speeds. Max. speed 90 m.p.h. Body by Tickford.

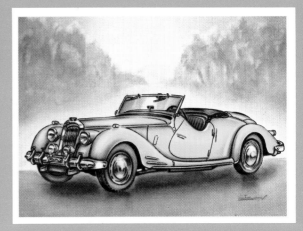

RILEY   GREAT BRITAIN 1948

$2^1/_2$ Liter, 3-seater sports tourer. 4-cyl. o.h.v. engine in line. Bore and stroke 80.5 × 120 mm. Displacement 2,443 c.c. Max. b.h.p. 100 at 4,500 r.p.m. 4 speeds. Max. speed 95 m.p.h. Made for North American market.

ROLLS-ROYCE　　　　　　　　**GREAT BRITAIN 1948**

Silver Wraith, touring limousine, 6-cyl. F-head engine. Bore and stroke 88.9 x 114.3 m.m. Displacement 4,566 c.c. Max. speed 87 m.p.h. Silver Dawn was a smaller model of the Wraith.

ALFA ROMEO　　　　　　　　**ITALY 1948**

6C 2500 Sport, 4/5 pass. touring coupé. 6-cyl. d.o.h.c. engine in line. Bore and stroke 72 x 100 mm. Displacement 2,442 c.c. Max. b.h.p. 95 at 4,600 r.p.m. 4 speeds. Max. speed 95 m.p.h. Swing-axle independent rear suspension.

CISITALIA　　　　　　　　**ITALY 1948**

Porsche Type 360, Formula One racing car. 12-cyl. horizontally opposed d.o.h.c. engine with supercharger. Bore and stroke 56 x 50.5 mm. Displacement 1,493 c.c. Max. b.h.p. 300 at 8,500 r.p.m. 5 speeds. Max. speed approx. 217 m.p.h. 4-wheel drive.

MASERATI　　　　　　　　**ITALY 1948**

A6G 1500, 2/3 seater sport Gran Turismo. 6-cyl. s.o.h.c. engine in line. Bore and stroke 66 x 72.5 mm. Displacement 1,500 c.c. Max. b.h.p. 65 at 4,700 r.p.m. 4 speeds. Max. speed 95 m.p.h. Tubular steel frame.

MASERATI ITALY 1948

4 CLT/1500, Formula One racing car. 4-cyl. d.o.h.c. engine in line with supercharger. Bore and stroke 78 × 78 mm. Displacement 1,492 c.c. Max. b.h.p. 260 at 7,000 r.p.m. 4 speeds. Max. speed 160 m.p.h. Called San Remo after winning its first race there in 1948.

VOLVO SWEDEN 1948

PV 444, 4/5 pass. sedan. 4-cyl. o.h.v. engine in line. Bore and stroke 75 × 80 mm. Displacement 1,410 c.c. Max. b.h.p. 44 at 3,800 r.p.m. 3 speeds. Max. speed 74 m.p.h. All-coil suspension.

CADILLAC U.S.A. 1948

62, 6 pass. convertible coupé. V-8 s.v. engine. Bore and stroke 3.5 x 4.5 inches. Displacement 346 cu. in. Max. b.h.p. 150 at 3400 r.p.m. 3 speeds. Max. speed 95 m.p.h. Body design under direction of Harley J. Earl.

STUDEBAKER U.S.A. 1948

Commander, 5/6 pass. Regal De Luxe coupé. 6-cyl. s.v. engine in line. Bore and stroke 3.31 x 4.37 inches. Displacement 226.2 cu. in. Max. b.h.p. 94 at 3600 r.p.m. 3 speeds. Max. speed 85 m.p.h. Body design by Raymond Loewy.

ZISS U.S.S.R. 1948

110, 6 pass. limousine. 8-cyl. s.v. engine in line. Bore and stroke 90 × 118 mm. Displacement 6,000 c.c. Max. b.h.p. 140 at 3,600 r.p.m. 3 speeds. Max. speed 68 m.p.h. 1940 Packard copy.

SKODA CZECHOSLOVAKIA 1949

1101, 4 pass. sedan. 4-cyl. o.h.v. engine in line. Bore and stroke 68 × 75 mm. Displacement 1,089 c.c. Max. b.h.p. 32 at 4,000 r.p.m. 4 speeds. Max. speed 62 m.p.h. Swing-axle independent rear suspension.

PANHARD FRANCE 1949

Dyna, 4 pass. berline. 2-cyl. o.h.v. horizontally opposed air-cooled engine. Bore and stroke 72 × 75 mm. Displacement 610 c.c. Max. b.h.p. 25 at 5,000 r.p.m. 4 speeds. Max. speed 62 m.p.h. Front-wheel drive. Aluminum chassis and body.

BRISTOL GREAT BRITAIN 1949

400, 4/5 pass. saloon. 6-cyl. o.h.v. engine in line. Bore and stroke 66 × 96 mm. Displacement 1,971 c.c. Max. b.h.p. 85 at 4,500 r.p.m. 4 speeds. Max. speed 95 m.p.h. Engine copy of BMW 328.

JAGUAR GREAT BRITAIN 1949

XK 120, 2-seater super sports-roadster. 6-cyl. d.o.h.c. engine in line. Bore and stroke 83 × 106 mm. Displacement 3,442 c.c. Max. b.h.p. 162 at 5,200 r.p.m. 4 speeds. Max. speed 125 m.p.h. Most responsible for popularity of sports cars.

LEA FRANCIS GREAT BRITAIN 1949

14 HP, 2/3 pass. roadster. 4-cyl. o.h.v. engine in line. Bore and stroke 75 × 100 mm. Displacement 1,767 c.c. Max. b.h.p. 77 at 5,100 r.p.m. 4 speeds. Max. speed 90 m.p.h. Out of business in 1963.

MORRIS GREAT BRITAIN 1949

Minor, 4 pass. saloon. 4-cyl. s.v. engine in line. Bore and stroke 57 × 90 mm. Displacement 919 c.c. Max. b.h.p. 27 at 4,400 r.p.m. 4 speeds. Max. speed 62 m.p.h. O.h.v. flat-four engine in prototype; Morris 8's s.v. engine in production model.

STANDARD GREAT BRITAIN 1949

Vanguard, 4/5 pass. saloon. 4-cyl. o.h.v. engine in line. Bore and stroke 85 × 92 mm. Displacement 2,088 c.c. Max. b.h.p. 68 at 4,200 r.p.m. 3 speeds. Max. speed 77 m.p.h. First standard with hydraulic brakes.

CISITALIA   **ITALY 1949**

1100, 2-seater Gran Sport cabriolet. 4-cyl. o.h.v. engine in line. Bore and stroke 68 × 75 mm. Displacement 1,089 c.c. Max. b.h.p. 60 at 5,500 r.p.m. 4 speeds. Max. speed 93 m p.h. Carrozzeria Pininfarina. Set international styling trends for a decade.

ISOTTA FRASCHINI   **ITALY 1949**

8C Monterosa, 5/6 pass. berlina. V-8 o.h.v. rear-mounted engine. Displacement 3,400 c.c. Max. b.h.p. 125 at 4,200 r.p.m. 4 speeds. Max. speed 105 m.p.h. Body design by Fabio Luigi Rapi.

GATSO   **THE NETHERLANDS 1949**

4000, 4 pass. Aero sports coupé. V-8 s.v. engine (Mercury). Bore and stroke 81 × 95 mm. Displacement 3,917 c.c. Max. b.h.p. 120 at 4,000 r.p.m. 3 speeds. Max. speed 93 m.p.h. Design by Maurice Gatsonides (race- and rally-driver).

BUICK   **U.S.A. 1949**

Series 50, 6 pass. Super sedan. 8-cyl. o.h.v. engine in line. Bore and stroke 3.09 × 4.11 inches. Displacement 248.1 cu.in. Max. b.h.p. 115 at 3600 r.p.m. 3 speeds. Max. speed 93 m.p.h. Dynaflow automatic transmission available.

CHEVROLET U.S.A. 1949

2103 Styleline, 6 pass. de luxe sedan. 6-cyl. o.h.v. engine in line. Bore and stroke 3.50 x 3.75 inches. Displacement 216.5 cu. in. Max. b.h.p. 90 at 3300 r.p.m. 3 speeds. Max. speed 87 m.p.h. Powerglide available in 1950.

FORD U.S.A. 1949

98 BA-101, 4/5 pass. coupé. V-8 s.v engine. Bore and stroke 3.18 x 3.75 inches. Displacement 239.4 cu. in. Max. b.h.p. 100 at 3600 r.p.m. 3 speeds. Max. speed 90 m.p.h. First Ford with independent front suspension.

HUDSON U.S.A. 1949

Commodore, 6 pass. convertible. 8-cyl. s.v. engine in line. Bore and stroke 3.0 x 4.5 inches. Displacement 254 cu. in. Max. b.h.p. 128 at 4200 r.p.m. 3 speeds. Max. speed 93 m.p.h. Body design by Frank S. Spring.

KAISER U.S.A. 1949

492 Virginian, 6 pass. convertible sedan. 6-cyl. s.v. engine in line. Bore and stroke 3.31 x 4.37 inches. Displacement 226.2 cu. in. Max. b.h.p. 100 at 3600 r.p.m. 3 speeds. Max. speed 87 m.p.h. Body designed by Howard Darrin.

PACKARD U.S.A. 1949

Eight Golden Anniversary. 6 pass. sedan. 8-cyl. s.v. engine in line. Bore and stroke 3.5 x 4.62 inches. Displacement 356 cu. in. Max. b.h.p. 160 at 3600 r.p.m. 3 speeds. Max. speed 93 m.p.h. Ultramatic transmission available.

WILLYS U.S.A. 1949

Jeep 6-63, 6 pass. station wagon. 6-cyl. s.v. engine in line. Bore and stroke 3.0 x 3.5 inches. Displacement 148.5 inches. Displacement 148.5 inches. Max. b.h.p. 72 at 4000 r.p.m. 3 speeds. Max. speed 70 m.p.h. Optional 4-cyl. engine.

GORDINI FRANCE 1950

18C, 2-seater super sports roadster. 4-cyl. o.h.v. engine in line. Bore and stroke 78 x 78 mm. Displacement 1,490 c.c. Max. b.h.p. 80 at 5,500 r.p.m. 4 speeds. Max. speed 125 m.p.h. Engine based on Simca.

TALBOT FRANCE 1950

Grand Prix, Formula One racing car. 6-cyl. o.h.v. engine in line. Bore and stroke 93 x 110 mm. Displacement 4,485 c.c. Max. b.h.p. 280 at 5,000 r.p.m. 4 speeds. Max. speed 160 m.p.h. Cotal pre-selector transmission.

MERCEDES-BENZ **GERMANY 1950**

170 S, 2/3 pass. A cabriolet. 4-cyl. s.v. engine in line. Bore and stroke 75 × 100 mm. Displacement 1,767 c.c. Max. b.h.p. 52 at 4,000 r.p.m. 4 speeds. Max. speed 75 m.p.h. Independent coil-spring suspension in wheels.

FIAT **ITALY 1950**

1400, 4/5 pass. convertible. 4-cyl. o.h.v. engine in line. Bore and stroke 82 × 66 mm. Displacement 1,395 c.c. Max. b.h.p. 44 at 4,400 r.p.m. 4 speeds. Max. speed 75 m.p.h. Rear suspension with both coil and leaf springs.

ZIM **U.S.S.R. 1950**

ZIM, 7 pass. limousine. 6-cyl. o.h.v. engine in line. Bore and stroke 82 × 101 mm. Displacement 3,480 c.c. Max. b.h.p. 94 to 3,600 r.p.m. 3 speeds. Max. speed 80 m.p.h. Body design by Boris Lebedev.

HOLDEN **AUSTRALIA 1951**

48/215, 5/6 pass. saloon. 6-cyl. o.h.v. engine in line. Bore and stroke 76 × 79 mm. Displacement 2,166 c.c. Max. b.h.p. 61 at 3,800 r.p.m. 3 speeds. Max. speed 74 m.p.h. Holden part of General Motors.

B.R.M.   **GREAT BRITAIN 1951**

G.P., racing car. V-16 d.o.h.c. engine with centrifugal super-chargers. Bore and stroke 49.5 × 48 mm. Displacement 1,488 c.c. Max. b.h.p. 450 at 12,000 r.p.m. 5 speeds. Max. speed approx. 200 m.p.h. All wheels with air/oil suspension.

JAGUAR   **GREAT BRITAIN 1951**

XK 120C, 2-seater super sports competition. 6-cyl. d.o.h.c. engine in line. Bore and stroke 83 × 106 mm. Displacement 3,442 c.c. Max. b.h.p. 203 at 5,800 r.p.m. 4 speeds. Max. speed 165 m.p.h. Disk brakes standardized on 1953 model.

FERRARI   **ITALY 1951**

Gran Premio, Formula One racing car. V-12 d.o.h.c. engine. Bore and stroke 80 × 74.5 mm. Displacement 4,490 c.c. Max. b.h.p. 380 at 7,500 r.p.m. 4 speeds. Max. speed 175 m.p.h. Ladder-type tubular steel frame.

EUCORT   **SPAIN 1951**

51,4 pass. sedan. 3-cyl. 2-stroke engine in line. Bore and stroke 76 × 76 mm. Displacement 1,034 c.c. Max. b.h.p. 31 at 3,900 r.p.m. 3 speeds. Max. speed 60 m.p.h.

CHRYSLER   **U.S.A. 1951**

New Yoker, 5/6 pass. Newport coupé. V-8, o.h.v. engine.
Bore and stroke 3.8 x 3.62 inches. Displacement 331 cu. in.
Max. b.h.p. 180 at 4000 r.p.m. Max. speed 106 m.p.h. Auto-
matic transmission. Hemispherical combustion chambers.

BUGATTI   **FRANCE 1952**

101C, 4/5 pass. sports coupé. 8-cyl. d.o.h.c. engine in line
with supercharger. Bore and stroke 72 x 100 mm. Displacement 3,257 c.c. Max. b.h.p. 190 at 5,400 r.p.m. 4 speeds. Max.
speed 112 m.p.h. Among the last with rigid front axles.

FORD   **FRANCE 1952**

Comète, 4 pass. coupé. V-8 s.v. engine. Bore and stroke
66 x 79 mm. Displacement 2,158 c.c. Max. b.h.p. 66 at 4,500
r.p.m. 3 speeds. Max. speed 80 m.p.h. Body by Facel-
Metallon.

HOTCHKISS GREGOIRE   **FRANCE 1952**

2.2 Liter, 5/6 pass. berline. 4-cyl. o.h.v. horizontally opposed
engine. Bore and stroke 86 x 90 mm. Displacement 2,200
c.c. Max. b.h.p. 70 at 4,000 r.p.m. 4 speeds. Max. speed 95
m.p.h. Front-wheel drive.

RENAULT   FRANCE 1952

Fregate R1100, 5/6 pass. berline. 4-cyl. o.h.v. engine in line. Bore and stroke 85 × 88 mm. Displacement 1,997 c.c. Max. b.h.p. 60 at 3,800 r.p.m. 4 speeds. Max. speed 80 m.p.h. Transfluide automatic transmission. All-independent suspension.

SIMCA   FRANCE 1952

9, 2/3 pass. sports coupé. 4-cyl. o.h.v. engine in line. Bore and stroke 72 × 75 mm. Displacement 1,221 c.c. Max. b.h.p. 50 at 4,800 r.p.m. 4 speeds. Max. speed 85 m.p.h. Body design by Jean Daninos.

MERCEDES-BENZ   GERMANY 1952

300 SL, 2-seater super sports coupé. 6-cyl. s.o.h.c. engine in line. Bore and stroke 85 × 88 mm. Displacement 2,996 c.c. Max. b.h.p. 175 at 5,200 r.p.m. 4 speeds. Max. speed 155 m.p.h. First and second in Le Mans 24-hour race.

PORSCHE   GERMANY 1952

356, 2/3 pass. sports coupé. 4-cyl. o.h.v. horizontally opposed, air-cooled, rear-mounted engine. Bore and stroke 80 × 64 mm. Displacement 1,286 c.c. Max. b.h.p. 46 at 4,000 r.p.m. 4 speeds. Max. speed 87 m.p.h. Body design by Erwin Komenda.

ARMSTRONG SIDDELEY   **GREAT BRITAIN** 1952

Sapphire, 4/5 pass. saloon. 6-cyl. o.h.v. engine in line. Bore and stroke 90 × 90 mm. Displacement 3,435 c.c. Max. b.h.p. 120 at 4,200 r.p.m. 4 speeds. Max. speed 85 m.p.h. Optional Wilson pre-selector transmission.

AUSTIN   **GREAT BRITAIN** 1952

A125 Sheerline, 5/6 pass. saloon. 6-cyl. o.h.v. engine in line. Bore and stroke 87 × 111 mm. Displacement 3,993 c.c. Max. b.h.p. 127 at 3,700 r.p.m. 4 speeds. Max. speed 85 m.p.h. Same engine for prestige model and trucks.

BENTLEY   **GREAT BRITAIN** 1952

Mark VI. 4 pass. Continental sports saloon (Mulliner body). 6-cyl. F-head engine in line. Bore and stroke 92 × 114.3 m.m. Displacement 4,566 c.c. Max. b.h.p 150 at 3750 r.p.m. 4 speed. Max. speed 120 m.p.h.

BENTLEY   **GREAT BRITAIN** 1952

Mark VI. 4 pass. Continental sports saloon (Mulliner body). 6-cyl. F-head engine in line. Bore and stroke 92 × 114,3 mm. Displacement 4,566 c.c. Max. b.h.p. not quoted. Weight lowered by 200 kg to ± 1700 kg. 4 speeds. Max. speed 118.5 m.p.h./192 km/h.

JAGUAR   GREAT BRITAIN 1952

Mark VII, 4/5 pass. saloon. 6-cyl. d.o.h.c. engine in line.
Bore and stroke 83 × 106 mm. Displacement 3,442 c.c. Max.
b.h.p. 162 at 5,200 r.p.m. 4 speeds. Max. speed 106 m.p.h.
Heavy steel frame with X-bracing.

JOWETT   GREAT BRITAIN 1952

Jupiter, 2-seater sports convertible. 4-cyl. horizontally
opposed o.h.v. engine. Bore and stroke 72.5 × 90 mm. Displacement 1,486 c.c. Max. b.h.p. 63 at 4,500 r.p.m. 4 speeds.
Max. speed 87 m.p.h. Over 1,000 built.

ROVER   GREAT BRITAIN 1952

Land-Rover 4 × 4, Series I, regular. 4-cyl. F-head engine in
line. Bore and stroke 78 × 105 mm. Displacement 1,997 c.c.
Max. b.h.p. 52 at 4,000 r.p.m. 4 speeds. Max. speed 56 m.p.h.
80 in. wheelbase. English imitation of Willys Jeep.

TRIUMPH   GREAT BRITAIN 1952

Mayflower, 4 pass. saloon. 4-cyl. s.v. engine in line. Bore
and stroke 63 × 100 mm. Displacement 1,247 c.c. Max. b.h.p.
38 at 4,200 r.p.m. 3 speeds. Max. speed 65 m.p.h. Miniature
version of Triumph 2000 "knife-edge" saloon.

ALFA ROMEO   ITALY 1952

1900 C, 4/5 pass. Gran Turismo. 4-cyl. d.o.h.c. engine in line.
Bore and stroke 82.5 x 88 mm. Displacement 1,884 c.c. Max.
b.h.p. 100 at 5,500 r.p.m. 4 speeds. Max. speed 105 m.p.h.
Aluminum body hooked, but not welded, to chassis framework.

ALFA ROMEO   ITALY 1952

Disco Volante, 2-seater super sports-roadster. 6-cyl. d.o.h.c.
engine in line. Bore and stroke 82.5 x 92 mm. Displacement
2,995 c.c. Max. b.h.p. 200 at 6,000 r.p.m. 4 speeds. Max.
speed 155 m.p.h. Prototype abandoned because of tenden-
cy to fly at high speeds.

FERRARI   ITALY 1952

342 America, 2-seater super sports-roadster. V-12 s.o.h.c.
engine. Bore and stroke 80 x 68 mm. Displacement 4,102 c.c.
Max. b.h.p. 200 at 5,000 r.p.m. 5 speeds. Max. speed 148
m.p.h. Carrozzeria Pininfarina.

LANCIA   ITALY 1952

B20 Aurelia, 4/5 pass. Gran turismo coupé. V-6 o.h.v. engine.
Bore and stroke 72 x 81.5 mm. Displacement 1,991 c.c. Max.
b.h.p. 75 at 4,500 r.p.m. 4 speeds. Max. speed 103 m.p.h.
Consistently won 2-liter class in 1951-52 races.

TOYOPET   **JAPAN 1952**

SF, 4 pass. sedan. 4-cyl. s.v. engine in line. Bore and stroke 65 × 75 mm. Displacement 995 c.c. Max. b.h.p. 28 at 4,000 r.p.m. 4 speeds. Max. speed 62 m.p.h.

CHRYSLER   **U.S.A. 1952**

Experimental, 4/5 pass. K-310 coupe. V-8 o.h.v. engine. Bore and stroke 3.81 x 3.63 inches. Displacement 331 cu.in. Max. b.h.p. 235 at 4000 r.p.m. Max. speed 125 m.p.h. Body by Carrozzeria Ghia. One of Chrysler's most useful experimental cars.

GENERAL MOTORS   **U.S.A. 1952**

Le Sabre, 2-seater roadster. V-8 d.o.h.c. engine. Bore and stroke inches. Displacement 214.3 cu. in. Max. b.h.p. 300 at 4500 r.p.m. Max. speed 125 m.p.h. Automatic transmission. Fuel injection body by General Motors Research.

NASH HEALEY   **U.S.A./GREAT BRITAIN 1952**

Le Mans, 2-seater roadster. 6-cyl. o.h.v. engine in line. Bore and stroke 89 × 111 mm. Displacement 4,138 c.c. Max. b.h.p. 135 at 4,000 r.p.m. 3 speeds. Max. speed 110 m.p.h. Body design in consultation with Pininfarina.

POBIEDA   U.S.S.R. 1952

GAZ M-20, 4/5 pass. saloon. 4-cyl. s.v. engine in line. Bore
and stroke 82 × 100 mm. Displacement 2,120 c.c. Max. b.h.p.
49 at 3,600 r.p.m. 3 speeds. Max. speed 68 m.p.h. One of first
Russian designed cars.

PANHARD   FRANCE 1953

Dyna, 4/5 pass. berline. 2-cyl. horizontally opposed, air-
cooled, o.h.v. engine. Bore and stroke 85 × 75 mm. Displacement 850 c.c. Max. b.h.p. 42 at 4,000 r.p.m. 4 speeds. Max.
speed 80 m.p.h. Front-wheel drive. Aluminum unit-construction body.

PEUGEOT   FRANCE 1953

203, 2-seater cabriolet. 4-cyl. o.h.v. engine in line. Bore and
stroke 75 × 73 mm. Displacement 1,290 c.c. Max. b.h.p. 46
at 4,500 r.p.m. 4 speeds. Max. speed 71 m.p.h. Hemispherical
combustion chambers in aluminum cylinder head.

TALBOT   FRANCE 1953

T-26, 2-seater grand sport. 6-cyl. o.h.v. engine in line. Bore
and stroke 93 × 110 mm. Displacement 4,483 c.c. Max. b.h.p.
250 at 4,800 r.p.m. 4 speeds. Max. speed 136 m.p.h. Cotal
pre-selector transmission.

IFA   EAST GERMANY 1953

F9, 4 pass. convertible. 3-cyl. 2-stroke engine in line. Bore
and stroke 70 x 78 mm. Displacement 900 c.c. Max. b.h.p.
30 at 3,800 r.p.m. 4 speeds. Max. speed 68 m.p.h. Front wheel
drive. Production version of 1940 experimental D.K.W., F-89.

BORGWARD HANSA   GERMANY 1953

2400 Sedan, 6-cyl. Displacement 2337 c.c. Max. b.h.p. 82
r.p.m. Max. speed 150 km/93 m.p.h.

MERCEDES-BENZ   GERMANY 1953

300 S, 2/3 pass. sports-roadster. 6-cyl. s.o.h.c. engine in
line. Bore and stroke 85 x 88 mm. Displacement 2,996 c.c.
Max. b.h.p. 150 at 4,850 r.p.m. 4 speeds. Max. speed 112
m.p.h. Several hundred built.

OPEL   GERMANY 1953

1.5 L Olympia Rekord, 4/5 pass. sedan. 4-cyl. o.h.v. engine
in line. Bore and stroke 80 x 74 mm. Displacement 1,488 c.c.
Max. b.h.p. 51 at 4,400 r.p.m. 3 speeds. Max. speed 77 m.p.h.
Unit-construction body.

ASTON MARTIN   **GREAT BRITAIN 1953**

DB2 Vantage, 4 pass. sports saloon. 6-cyl. d.o.h.c. engine in line. Bore and stroke 78 × 90 mm. Displacement 2,580 c.c. Max. b.h.p. 127 at 5,000 r.p.m. 4 speeds. Max. speed 125 m.p.h. All-coil suspension chassis.

AUSTIN   **GREAT BRITAIN 1953**

A30, 4 pass. saloon. 4-cyl. o.h.v. engine in line. Bore and stroke 58 × 76 mm. Displacement 803 c.c. Max. b.h.p. 30 at 4,800 r.p.m. 4 speeds. Max. speed 62 m.p.h. Austin's version of the Mini-Minor (Austin and Morris merged in 1952 as British Motor Corp.).

HILLMAN   **GREAT BRITAIN 1953**

Minx Mark VI, 4/5 pass. Californian hardtop coupé. 4-cyl. s.v. engine in line. Bore and stroke 65 × 95 mm. Displacement 1,265 c.c. Max. b.h.p. 38 at 4,200 r.p.m. 4 speeds. Max. speed 68 m.p.h. Unit-construction from 1937.

H.W.M.   **GREAT BRITAIN 1953**

2 Liter, Formula Two racing car. 4-cyl. d.o.h.c. engine in line (Alta). Bore and stroke 83.5 × 90 mm. Displacement 1,960 c.c. Max. b.h.p. 150 at 5,800 r.p.m. 4 speeds. Max. speed approx. 135 m.p.h.

SUNBEAM TALBOT GREAT BRITAIN 1953

Alpine, 2-seater sports convertible. 4-cyl. o.h.v. engine in line. Bore and stroke 81 x 110 mm. Displacement 2,267 c.c. Max. b.h.p. 81 at 4,200 r.p.m. 4 speeds. Max. speed 115 m.p.h. Rootes Group merged Sunbeam and Talbots, dropped Talbot name later.

MASERATI ITALY 1953

A6 GCS, 2-seater super sports-roadster. 6-cyl. d.o.h.c. engine in line. Bore and stroke 72 x 80 mm. Displacement 1,978 c.c. Max. b.h.p. 130 at 6,000 r.p.m. 4 speeds. Max. speed 140 m.p.h. Weight 1,411 lbs.

PEGASO SPAIN 1953

Z-102 B, 2-seater sports coupé. V-8 d.o.h.c. engine. Bore and stroke 75 x 70 mm. Displacement 2,472 c.c. Max. b.h.p. 170 at 6,000 r.p.m. 5 speeds. Max. speed 127 m.p.h. Body by Carrozzeria Touring.

CADILLAC U.S.A. 1953

Le Mans, 2-seater experimental car (plastic) 8-cyl. o.h.v. engine in vee. Bore and stroke 3.81 x 3.62 inches. Displacement 331 cu. in. Max. b.h.p. 250 at 4600 r.p.m. Max. speed 135 m.p.h. Automatic transmission.

CHEVROLET   U.S.A. 1953

2402 Bel Air, 6 pass. sedan 6-cyl. o.h.v. engine in line. Bore and stroke 3.56 x 4.06 inches. Displacement 235.5 cu. in. Max. b.h.p. 108 at 3600 r.p.m. 3 speeds. Max. speed 87 m.p.h.

CUNNINGHAM   U.S.A. 1953

C3 Continental, 4/5 pass. coupé. V-8 o.h.v. engine. (Chrysler). Bore and stroke 3.81 x 3.62 inches. Displacement 331 cu. in. Max. b.h.p. 220 at 4400 r.p.m. Max. speed 118 m.p.h. Automatic transmission. Body by Vignale. 26 built.

DODGE   U.S.A. 1953

D-48 Coronet, 6 pass. Sierra station wagon. V-8 o.h.v. engine. Bore and stroke 3.19 x 4.0 inches. Displacement 255.4 cu. in. Max. b.h.p. 125 at 3800 r.p.m. Max. speed 93 m.p.h. Engine: smaller version of Chryslers hemispherical-head V-8.

FORD   U.S.A. 1953

Crestline, 6 pass. Station wagon. V-8 s.v. engine. Bore and stroke 3.19 x 3.75 inches. Displacement 239 x 4 cu. in. Max. b.h.p. 110 at 3800 r.p.m. 3 speeds. Max. speed 90 m.p.h. Mercury engine extended to Ford in 1953.

HUDSON U.S.A. 1953

Super Jet, 6 pass. sedan. 6-cyl. s.v. engine in line. Bore and stroke 3.56 x 3.87 inches. Displacement 232 cu. in. Max. b.h.p. 112 at 4000 r.p.m. 3 speeds. Max. speed 90 m.p.h. Competition for Rambler.

KURTIS-KRAFT U.S.A. 1953

500, A Fuel Injection Special, Indianapolis racing car. V-8 o.h.v. engine. Bore and stroke 3.94 x 3.63 inches. Displacement 354 cu. in. Max. b.h.p. 325 at 5000 r.p.m. engine in line. Bore and stroke 3.50 x 4.37 inches. Displacement 252 cu. in. Max. b.h.p. 120 at 3700 r.p.m. 3 speeds. Max. speed 93 m.p.h. Body design in consultation with Pininfarina.

LINCOLN U.S.A. 1953

Capri, 6 pass. special custom sedan. V-8 o.h.v. engine. Bore and stroke 3.8 x 3.5 inches. Displacement 317.5 cu. in. Max. b.h.p. 205 at 4200 r.p.m. Max. speed 106 m.p.h. Ball-joint front suspension 1952.

NASH U.S.A. 1953

Ambassador, 6 pass. Country Club sedan. 6-cyl. o.h.v. engine in line. Bore and stroke 89 x 111 mm. Displacement 4,138 c.c. Max. b.h.p. 142 at 4,000 r.p.m. 3 speeds. Max. speed 93 m.p.h. Body design in consultation with Pininfarina.

STUDEBAKER U.S.A. 1953

Commander, 5 pass. Regal Starlight coupé. V-8 o.h.v. engine. Bore and stroke 3.37 x 3.25 inches. Displacement 232.6 cu. in. Max. b.h.p. 120 at 4000 r.p.m. 3 speeds. Max. speed 90 m.p.h. Body design by Robert Loewy.

CITROËN FRANCE 1954

15 Six, 5 pass. sedan. 6-cyl. o.h.v. engine in line. Bore and stroke 78 x 100 mm. Displacement 2,867 c.c. Max. b.h.p. 80 at 4,000 r.p.m. 3 speeds. Max. speed 85 m.p.h. Front wheel drive. Rear wheels with air-oil suspension.

GORDINI FRANCE 1954

GP 2500, Formula One racing car. 6-cyl. d.o.h.c. engine in line. Bore and stroke 82 x 80 mm. Displacement 2,473 c.c. Max. b.h.p. 220 at 6,000 r.p.m. 4 speeds. Max. speed 160 m.p.h. Sports version available.

SALMSON FRANCE 1954

2300, 4 pass. sports coupé. 4-cyl. d.o.h.c. engine in line. Bore and stroke 84 x 105 mm. Displacement 2,328 c.c. Max. b.h.p. 110 at 5,000 r.p.m. 4 speeds. Max. speed 112 m.p.h. Cotal transmission. Body design by Eugene Martin.

MERCEDES-BENZ   GERMANY 1954

180, 4/5 pass. sedan. 4-cyl. s.v. engine in line. Bore and stroke 75 × 100 mm. Displacement 1,767 c.c. Max. b.h.p. 52 at 4,000 r.p.m. 4 speeds. Max. speed 77 m.p.h. Mercedes Benz's first unit-construction body.

MERCEDES-BENZ   GERMANY 1954

190 SL, 2-seater sports-roadster. 4-cyl. s.o.h.c. engine in line. Bore and stroke 85 × 83.5 mm. Displacement 1,897 c.c. Max. b.h.p. 125 at 5,500 r.p.m. 4 speeds. Max. speed 118 m.p.h.

MERCEDES-BENZ   GERMANY 1954

300, 5 pass. B cabriolet. 6-cyl. s.o.h.c. engine in line. Bore and stroke 85 × 88 mm. Displacement 2,996 c.c. Max. b.h.p. 138 at 4,500 r.p.m. 4 speeds. Max. speed 100 m.p.h. Chassis built upon cruciform frame.

MERCEDES-BENZ   GERMANY 1954

W 196, Grand Prix, Formula One racing car. 8-cyl. d.o.h.c. engine in line. Bore and stroke 70 × 69 mm. Displacement 2,496 c.c. Max. b.h.p. 300 at 8,500 r.p.m. 5 speeds. Max. speed 186 m.p.h. Bosch fuel injection.

PORSCHE GERMANY 1954

550, 2-seater sports-roadster. 4-cyl. horizontally opposed d.o.h.c. engine. Bore and stroke 85 x 66 mm. Displacement 1,498 c.c. Max. b.h.p. 110 at 7,000 r.p.m. 4 speeds. Max. speed 136 m.p.h. Known as Carrera from its participation in the Mexican road race.

AUSTIN-HEALEY GREAT BRITAIN 1954

100, 2-seater sports-roadster. 4-cyl. o.h.v. engine in line. Bore and stroke 87 x 111 mm. Displacement 2,660 c.c. Max. b.h.p. 91 at 4,000 r.p.m. 4 speeds. Max. speed 105 m.p.h. Healey chassis and Austin 16 engine.

BRISTOL GREAT BRITAIN 1954

404/100C, 2/4 pass. sports coupé. 6-cyl. o.h.v. engine in line. Bore and stroke 66 x 96 mm. Displacement 1,971 c.c. Max. b.h.p. 125 at 5,500 r.p.m. 4 speeds. Max. speed 118 m.p.h. Chrysler V-8 engine in later model.

FRAZER NASH GREAT BRITAIN 1954

Targa Florio, 2-seater Grand sport coupé. 6-cyl. o.h.v. engine in line. Bore and stroke 66 x 96 mm. Displacement 1,971 c.c. Max. b.h.p. 150 at 5,750 r.p.m. 4 speeds. Max. speed approx. 125 m.p.h. Engine based on pre-war B.M.W.

M.G.   **GREAT BRITAIN 1954**

TF Midget, 2-seater sports roadster. 4-cyl. o.h.v. engine in line. Bore and stroke 66.5 x 90 mm. Displacement 1,250 c.c. Max. b.h.p. 57 at 5,500 r.p.m. 4 speeds. Max. speed 80 m.p.h. 1,500 c.c. displacement in 1955.

TRIUMPH   **GREAT BRITAIN 1954**

TR2, 2-seater sports roadster. 4-cyl. o.h.v. engine in line. Bore and stroke 83 x 99 mm. Displacement 1,991 c.c. Max. b.h.p. 91 at 4,800 r.p.m. 4 speeds. Max. speed 105 m.p.h. Body styling by W. J. Belgrove.

FIAT   **ITALY 1954**

1100 TV, 4 pass. berlina. 4-cyl. o.h.v. engine in line. Bore and stroke 68 x 75 mm. Displacement 1,089 c.c. Max. b.h.p. 48 at 5,200 r.p.m. 4 speeds. Max. speed 80 m.p.h. TV stands for Turismo Veloce – fast touring.

LANCIA   **ITALY 1954**

Formula One, racing car. V-8 o.h.v. engine. Bore and stroke 76 x 68.5 mm. Displacement 2,487 c.c. Max. b.h.p. 260 at 8,500 r.p.m. 5 speeds. Max. speed approx. 200 m.p.h. Fairings between wheels contain fuel tanks.

MASERATI   **ITALY 1954**

A6GCS 2000 sport, 2-seater spider (aluminum). 6-cyl. d.o.h.c. engine in line. Bore and stroke 76.5 x 72 mm. Displacement 1,988 c.c. Max. b.h.p. 165 at 6,750 r.p.m. 4 speeds. Max. speed 148 m.p.h.

OSCA   **ITALY 1954**

MT/4, 2-seater spider. 4-cyl. d.o.h.c. engine in line. Bore and stroke 78 x 78 mm. Displacement 1,490 c.c. Max. b.h.p. 110 at 6,200 r.p.m. 4 speeds. Max. speed approx. 125 m.p.h. OSCA stands for Officine Specializzate di Costruzione Automobili.

BUICK   **U.S.A. 1954**

Series 40 Special, 6 pass. convertible coupé. V-8 o.h.v. engine. Bore and stroke 3.62 x 3.21 inches. Displacement 264 cu. in. Max. b.h.p. 188 at 4200 r.p.m. 3 speeds. Max. speed 90 m.p.h. Dynaflow automatic transmission optional.

CHEVROLET   **U.S.A. 1954**

Corvette, 2-seater sports roadster. 6-cyl. o.h.v. engine in line. Bore and stroke 3.56 x 3.93 inches. Displacement 235.5 cu. in. Max. b.h.p. 150 at 4200 r.p.m. Max. speed over 100 m.p.h. 300 Corvettes built the first year.

DODGE U.S.A. 1954

Fire Arrow, 2 pass. Spider. V-8 o.h.v. engine. Bore and stroke 3.43 x 3.25 inches. Displacement 241 cu. in. Max. b.h.p. 150 at 4400 r.p.m. Max. speed 100 m.p.h. Body by Carrozzeria Ghia. Never produced for sale.

FORD U.S.A. 1954

Thunderbird, 2-seater sports car (hardtop) V-8 o.h.v. engine. Bore and stroke 3.75 x 3.29 inches. Displacement 292 cu. in. Max. b.h.p. 192 at 4400 r.p.m. Max. speed approx. 110 m.p.h. Fordomatic automatic transmission. Fords First American built o.h.v. V-8.

HUDSON U.S.A. 1954

Italia, 4 pass. show model coupé. 6-cyl. s.v. engine in line. Bore and stroke 3.0 x 4.75 inches. Displacement 202 cu. in. Max. b.h.p. 104 at 4000 r.p.m. 3 speeds. Max. speed 95 m.p.h. Aluminium body by Carrozzeria Touring.

MERCURY U.S.A. 1954

Monterey, 6 pass. Sun Valley hardtop coupé. V-8 o.h.v. engine. Bore and stroke 3.62 x 3.10 inches. Displacement 256 cu. in. Max. b.h.p. 161 at 4400 r.p.m. 3 speeds. Max. speed 100 m.p.h. Merc-O-Matic automatic transmission optional.

OLDSMOBILE   **U.S.A. 1954**

Ninety Eight, 6 pass. de luxe Holiday coupé (hardtop). V-8
o.h.v. engine. Bore and stroke 3.87 x 3.43 inches. Displacement 324 cu. in. Max. b.h.p. 185 at 4000 r.p.m. Max. speed
100 m.p.h. Hydramatic automatic transmission.

CITROËN   **FRANCE 1955**

2 CV AZ, 4 pass. cabrio-berline. 2-cyl. horizontally
opposed o.h.v. engine, air-cooled. Front-wheel drive. Bore
and stroke 66 x 62 mm. Displacement 425 c.c. Max. b.h.p.
12 at 3,500 r.p.m. 4 speeds. Max. speed 50 m.p.h.

FACEL-VEGA   **FRANCE 1955**

Vega, 4 pass. sports-coupé. V-8 o.h.v. engine (Chrysler-
built). Bore and stroke 92 x 85 mm. Displacement 4,528 c.c.
Max. b.h.p. 180 at 4,500 r.p.m. 4 speeds. Max. speed approx.
112 m.p.h. Body design by Jean Daninos, head of Facel-
Metallon.

GORDINI   **FRANCE 1955**

G.P. 2500, Formula One racing car. 8-cyl. d.o.h.c. engine in
line. Bore and stroke 75 x 70 mm. Displacement 2,498 c.c.
Max. b.h.p. 256 at 7,300 r.p.m. 5 speeds. Max. speed approx.
193 m.p.h. Gordini merged with Renault in 1959.

FORD   FRANCE 1955

Vedette Versailles, 5/6 pass. berline. V-8 s.v. engine. Bore
and stroke 66 x 86 mm. Displacement 2,353 c.c. Max. b.h.p.
80 at 4,600 r.p.m. 3 speeds. Max. speed 85 m.p.h. Later
became the Simca Vedette.

PEUGEOT   FRANCE 1955

403, 4/5 pass. berline. 4-cyl. o.h.v. engine in line. Bore
and stroke 80 x 73 mm. Displacement 1,468 c.c. Max.
b.h.p. 58 at 4,900 r.p.m. 4 speeds. Max. speed 85 m.p.h.
Body design by Boschetti and Pininfarina.

TALBOT   FRANCE 1955

Grand Sport, 2 pass. coupé. 6-cyl. o.h.v. engine in
line. Bore and stroke 93 x 110 mm. Displacement 4,482
c.c. Max. b.h.p. 210 at 4,300 r.p.m. 4 speeds. Max: speed
125 m.p.h. Later available with B.M.W. V-8.

B.M.W.   GERMANY 1955

502, 5/6 pass. limousine. V-8 o.h.v. engine. Bore and
stroke 74 x 75 mm. Displacement 2,850 c.c. Max. b.h.p.
105 at 4,800 r.p.m. 4 speeds. Max. speed 103 m.p.h. Oval-
tube steel frame.

B.M.W.   **GERMANY 1955**

503, 4 pass. cabriolet (convertible). **V-8 o.h.v. engine.**
Bore and stroke 82 x 75 mm. Displacement 3,168 **c.c.**
Max. b.h.p. 140 at 4,800 r.p.m. 4 speeds. Max. speed
120 m.p.h.

BORGWARD   **GERMANY 1955**

Isabella, 4/5 pass. limousine. 4-cyl. o.h.v. engine in line.
Bore and stroke 75 x 85 mm. Displacement 1,493 c.c.
Max. b.h.p. 60 at 4,700 r.p.m. 4 speeds. Max. speed 80
m.p.h. Borgward works closed in 1961.

D.K.W.   **GERMANY 1955**

Sonderklasse F91, 4 pass. Allsicht hardtop coupé. 3-cyl.
2-stroke engine in line. Bore and stroke 71 x 76 mm.
Displacement 896 c.c. Max. b.h.p. 38 at 4,500 r.p.m. 4
speeds. Max. speed 77 m.p.h. Front wheel drive. 1 cyl.
added to existing vertical-twin engine.

FORD   **GERMANY 1955**

15M Taunus, 4 pass. limousine. 4-cyl. o.h.v. engine in
line. Bore and stroke 82 x 71 mm. Displacement 1,498
c.c. Max. b.h.p. 55 at 4,250 r.p.m. 3 or 4 speeds. Max.
speed 75 m.p.h. Ford resumed manufacturing in Germany
in 1949.

MERCEDES-BENZ **GERMANY 1955**

300 SLR, 2-seater super sport 8-cyl. d.o.h.c. engine in line. Bore and stroke 78 x 78 mm. Displacement 2,982 c.c. Max. b.h.p. 300 at 7,500 r.p.m. 5 speeds. Max. speed. approx. 200 m.p.h. Multi-tube steel frame.

ALVIS **GREAT BRITAIN 1955**

TC21/100, 4 pass. drophead coupé. 6-cyl. o.h.v. engine in line. Bore and stroke 84 x 90 mm. Displacement 2,993 c.c. Max. b.h.p. 104 at 4,000 r.p.m. 4 speeds. Max. speed 100 m.p.h. Body designed and built by Tickford. Taken over by Rover in 1965.

AUSTIN **GREAT BRITAIN 1955**

A90 Six Westminster 5 pass. saloon. 6-cyl. o.h.v. engine in line. Bore and stroke 79 x 89 mm. Displacement 2,639 c.c. Max. b.h.p. 210 at 4,300 r.p.m. 4 speeds. Max. speed 90 m.p.h. First Austin with optional automatic transmission.

B.R.M. **GREAT BRITAIN 1955**

2.5 Liter G.P., Formula One racing car. 4-cyl. d.o.h.c. engine in line. Bore and stroke 100 x 80 mm. Displacement 2,500 c.c. Max. b.h.p. 260 at 6,000 r.p.m. 4 speeds. Max. speed approx. 175 m.p.h. Disk brake mounted on transmission for rear wheels.

JAGUAR GREAT BRITAIN 1955

D, Le Mans super sports. 6-cyl. d.o.h.c. engine in line. Bore and stroke 83 x 106 mm. Displacement 3,442 c.c. Max. b.h.p. 285 at 5,750 r.p.m. 4 speeds. Max. speed 195 m.p.h. Won 24-hour Le Mans race in 1955, 1956, 1957.

JAGUAR GREAT BRITAIN 1955

XK 140, 2/4 pass. coupé. 6-cyl. d.o.h.c. engine in line. Bore and stroke 83 x 106 mm. Displacement 3,442 c.c. Max. b.h.p. 192 at 5,500 r.p.m. 4 speeds. Max. speed 112 m.p.h.

JENSEN GREAT BRITAIN 1955

541, 5 pass. sports saloon (fiberglass). 6-cyl. o.h.v. engine in line (Austin). Bore and stroke 87 x 111 mm. Displacement 3,993 c.c. Max. b.h.p. 131 at 3,700 r.p.m. 4 speeds. Max. speed 105 m.p.h.

M.G. GREAT BRITAIN 1955

EX 182, Le Mans 2-seater. 4-cyl. o.h.v. engine in line. Bore and stroke 73 x 89 mm. Displacement 1,489 c.c. Max. b.h.p. 82 at 5,500 r.p.m. 4 speeds. Max. speed approx. 115 m.p.h. Prototype for 1957 M.G.A.

RILEY GREAT BRITAIN 1955

1 1/2 Liter, 4 pass. saloon. 4-cyl. o.h.v. engine in line. Bore and stroke 69 x 100 mm. Displacement 1,496 c.c. Max. b.h.p. 56 at 4,500 r.p.m. 4 speeds. Max. speed 77 m.p.h. Torsion bar independent front suspension.

RILEY GREAT BRITAIN 1955

Pathfinder, 4/5 pass. saloon. 4-cyl. o.h.v. engine in line. Bore and stroke 81 x 120 mm. Displacement 2,443 c.c. Max. b.h.p. 102 at 4,400 r.p.m. 4 speeds. Max. speed 100 m.p.h. Last of big Rileys. In production only 3 years.

ROVER GREAT BRITAIN 1955

75, 5 pass. saloon. 6-cyl. F-head engine in line. Bore and stroke 73 x 89 mm. Displacement 2,230 c.c. Max. b.h.p. 80 at 4,500 r.p.m. 4 speeds. Max. speed 85 m.p.h. Rovermatic transmission available in 1956.

VAUXHALL GREAT BRITAIN 1955

Cresta, 5 pass. saloon. 6-cyl. o.h.v. engine in line. Bore and stroke 79 x 76 mm. Displacement 2,262 c.c. Max. b.h.p. 67 at 4,000 r.p.m. 3 speeds. Max. speed 80 m.p.h. Unit-construction body since 1937.

ABARTH   **ITALY 1955**

207A, super sports 2-seater. 4-cyl. o.h.v. engine in
line. (supercharged Fiat 1100). Bore and stroke 68 x 75
mm. Displacement 1,089 c.c. Max. b.h.p. 66 at 6,000
r.p.m. 4 speeds. Max. speed approx. 112 m.p.h.

FERRARI   **ITALY 1955**

118 Le Mans, 2-seater spider. 6-cyl. d.o.h.c. engine in
line. Bore and stroke 94 x 90 mm. Displacement 3,750 c.c.
Max. b.h.p. 330 at 6,300 r.p.m. 5 speeds. Max. speed
approx. 200 m.p.h. Body by Carrozzeria Pininfarina.

FERRARI   **ITALY 1955**

555 Super Squalo, Formula One racing car. 4-cyl. d.o.h.c.
engine in line. Bore and stroke 100 x 79.5 mm. Displacement 2,488 c.c. Max. b.h.p. 265 at 7,000 r.p.m. 5 speeds.
Max. speed 200 m.p.h. Fuel tanks removed from tail,
placed in body sides.

FIAT   **ITALY 1955**

1100 TV, 2-seater spider. 4-cyl. o.h.v. engine in line.
Bore and stroke 68 x 75 mm. Displacement 1,089 c.c.
Max. b.h.p. 50 at 5,400 r.p.m. 4 speeds. Max. speed
84 m.p.h. Body by Carrozzeria Pininfarina.

FIAT   **ITALY 1955**

600 COACH, 4-cyl. o.h.v. engine in line, at rear. Bore and stroke 60 x 56 mm. Displacement 633 c.c. Max. b.h.p. 2.15 at 4,600 r.p.m. 4 speeds. Max. speed 55 m.p.h. With special body by Pininfarina.

GHIA   **ITALY 1955**

Gilda, 2-seater experimental coupé. Suitable for fitting gas turbine. External brake drums. Overall height 48 in. Purchased by the Henri Ford Museum, Dearborn, U.S.A.

LANCIA   **ITALY 1955**

Aurelia GT2500, 2-seater spider. V-6 o.h.v. engine. Bore and stroke 78 x 86 mm. Displacement 2,451 c.c. Max. b.h.p. 118 at 5,000 r.p.m. 4 speeds. Max. speed 115 m.p.h. Body by Carrozzeria Pininfarina. GT coupé available with same engine.

LANCIA   **ITALY 1955**

Florida, 4 pass. berlina. V-6 o.h.v. engine. Bore and stroke 78 x 86 mm. Displacement 2,451 c.c. Max. b.h.p. 118 at 5,000 r.p.m. 4 speeds. Max. speed 95 m.p.h. Body by Carrozzerina Pininfarina. Styling prototype for Flaminia.

MASERATI   **ITALY 1955**

GP 2500, racing car. 6-cyl. d.o.h.c. engine in line. Bore
and stroke 84 x 75 mm. Displacement 2,493 c.c. Max.
b.h.p. 260 at 7,700 r.p.m. 4 speeds. Max. speed 175
m.p.h. Fuel injection experimented with.

NARDI-LANCIA   **ITALY 1955**

Rayon d'Azur, 2-seater coupé, 6-cyl. o.h.v. engine in vee.
Bore and stroke 78 x 85.5 mm. Displacement 2,451 c.c.
Max. b.h.p. 190 at 5,500 r.p.m. 4 speeds. Max. speed
130 m.p.h. Body by Vignale.

VOLVO   **SWEDEN 1955**

1500, 2-seater sports roadster (fiberglass). 4-cyl. o.h.v.
engine in line. Bore and stroke 75 x 80 mm. Displacement
1,414 c.c. Max. b.h.p. 70 at 6,000 r.p.m. 5 speeds. Max.
speed 95 m.p.h. Delivery van frame.

CHEVROLET   **U.S.A. 1955**

Biscayne, 4 pass. experimental sedan. V-8 o.h.v. engine.
Bore and stroke 3.75 x 3.0 inches. Displacement 265. cu. in.
Max. b.h.p. 215 at 4500 r.p.m. Max. speed 105 m.p.h. Auto-
matic transmission.

CHRYSLER U.S.A. 1955

Imperial Newport, 6 pass. hardtop coupé. V-8 o.h.v. engine. Bore and stroke 3.71 x 3.62 inches. Displacement 331 cu. in. Max. b.h.p. 250 at 4600 r.p.m. Max. speed 105 m.p.h. Body design under direction of Virgil Exner.

DE SOTO U.S.A. 1955

Fireflite S-21, 6 pass. Sportsman hardtop coupé. V-8 o.h.v. engine. Bore and stroke 3.71 x 3.34 inches. Displacement 291 cu. in. Max. b.h.p. 185 at 4400 r.p.m. 3 speeds. Max. speed 105 m.p.h. Powerflite automatic transmission optional.

FORD U.S.A. 1955

Fairlane, 5/6 pass. sedan. V-8 o.h.v. engine. Bore and stroke 3.62 x 3.60 inches. Displacement 272 cu. in. Max. b.h.p. 162 at 4400 r.p.m. 3 speeds. Max. speed 100 m.p.h. Fordomatic automatic transmission optional.

HUDSON U.S.A. 1955

Hornet, 5/6 pass. Hollywood coupé. 6-cyl. s.v. engine in line. Bore and stroke 3.81 x 4.50 inches. Displacement 308 cu. in. Max. b.h.p. 160 at 3800 r.p.m. 3 speeds. Max. speed 95 m.p.h. Nash Rambler with Hudson grille.

NASH   U.S.A. 1955

Rambler Cross Country, 5/6 pass. station wagon. 6-cyl. s.v. engine in line. Bore and stroke 3.12 x 3.25 inches. Displacement 195.6 cu. in. Max. b.h.p. 100 at 3800 r.p.m. 3 speeds. Max. speed 85 m.p.h. Nash name dropped in 1957, changed to Rambler.

OLDSMOBILE   U.S.A. 1955

88 Delta, 4 pass. experimental hardtop coupé. V-8 o.h.v. engine. Bore and stroke 3.87 x 3.43 inches. Displacement 324 cu. in. Max. b.h.p. 250 at 4000 r.p.m. Max. speed approx. 125 m.p.h. Automatic transmission.

PACKARD   U.S.A. 1955

Patrician, 5/6 pass. sedan. V-8 o.h.v. engine. Bore and stroke 4.0 x 3.5 inches. Displacement 352 cu. in. Max. b.h.p. 260 at 4600 r.p.m. Max. speed 112 m.p.h.

PONTIAC   U.S.A. 1955

Star Chief, 5/6 pass. convertible coupé. V-8 o.h.v. engine. Bore and stroke 3.75 x 3.25 inches. Displacement 287.2 cu. in. Max. b.h.p. 180 at 4600 r.p.m. Max. speed 100 m.p.h. Hydra-Matic automatic transmission.

STUDEBAKER   U.S.A. 1955

Commander, 5 pass. hardtop coupé. V-8 o.h.v. engine.
Bore and stroke 3.56 x 3.25 inches. Displacement 259.2
cu. in. Max. b.h.p. 162 at 4500 r.p.m. 3 speeds. Max. speed
93 m.p.h.

VOLGA   U.S.S.R. 1955

Type GAZ M-21, 5 pass. sedan. 4-cyl. o.h.v. engine
in line. Bore and stroke 82 x 100 mm. Displacement
2,200 c.c. Max. b.h.p. 75 at 3,600 r.p.m. Max. speed
80 m.p.h. 3-speed manual transmission standard; automatic optional.

DENZEL   AUSTRIA 1956

1500 Sport International, 3 pass. roadster. 4-cyl. air-
cooled horizontally opposed, rear-mounted, o.h.v. engine.
Bore and stroke 80 x 74 mm. Displacement 1,488 c.c. Max.
b.h.p. 80 at 5,800 r.p.m. 4 speeds. Max. speed 112 m.p.h.
When Denzel stopped making cars, he became the Austrian distributor for B.M.W.

TATRA   CZECHOSLOVAKIA 1956

603, 5/6 pass. limousine. V-8 air-cooled, rear-mounted,
o.h.v. engine. Bore and stroke 75 x 72 mm. Displacement 2,545 c.c. Max. b.h.p. 100 at 4,800 r.p.m. 4 speeds,
Max. speed 105 m.p.h. Swing-axle independent rear suspension.

CITROEN   **FRANCE** 1956

DS 19, 5/6 pass. sedan. 4-cyl. o.h.v. engine in line. Bore and stroke 78 x 100 mm. Displacement 1,911 c.c. Max. b.h.p. 75 at 4,500 r.p.m. 4 speeds. Max. speed 87 m.p.h. Front wheel drive. All wheels with air-oil suspension. Disk brakes on front wheels standard.

RENAULT   **FRANCE** 1956

A 106, 2 pass. „Alpine Mille Milles" coach. 4-cyl. o.h.v. engine in line. Bore and stroke 54.5 x 80 mm. Displacement 747 c.c. Max. b.h.p. 43 at 6,200 r.p.m. 5 speeds. Max. speed 95 m.p.h.

WARTBURG   **EAST GERMANY** 1956

P-311 Wartburg, 4 pass. sedan. 3-cyl. 2-stroke engine. Bore and stroke 70 x 78 mm. Displacement 900 c.c. Max. b.h.p. 38 at 4,000 r.p.m. 4 speeds. Max. speed 78 m.p.h. Weight 970 kg. Based on pre-WWII D.K.W.

A.W.Z.-ZWICKAU   **EAST GERMANY** 1956

P 70, 4 pass. coach (plastic). 2-cyl. 2-stroke engine in line. Bore and stroke 76 x 76 mm. Displacement 690 c.c. Max. b.h.p. 22 at 3,500 r.p.m. 3 speeds. Max. speed 55 m.p.h. Front wheel drive. Based on pre-WWII D.K.W.

B.M.W.   Germany 1956

507, 2 pass. touring sports. V-8 o.h.v. engine. Bore and stroke 82 x 75 mm. Displacement 3,168 c.c. Max. b.h.p. 140 at 4,800 r.p.m. 5 speeds. Max. speed 135 m.p.h. Body design by Albrecht Goertz.

VOLKSWAGEN   GERMANY 1956

143 Karmann Ghia, 2/4 pass. coupé. 4-cyl. air-cooled, horizontally opposed, rear-mounted, o.h.v. engine. Bore and stroke 77 x 64 mm. Displacement 1,192 c.c. Max. b.h.p. 30 at 3,400 r.p.m. 4 speeds. Max. speed 72 m.p.h. Body designed by Carrozzeria Ghia, built by Karmann.

ASTON-MARTIN   GREAT BRITAIN 1956

DB 3 S, 2-seater road-racing car 6-cyl. d.o.h.c. engine in line. Bore and stroke 83 x 90 mm. Displacement 2,922 c.c. Max. b.h.p. 213 at 6,000 r.p.m. 4 speeds. Max. speed 145 m.p.h. Body styling by Frank Feeley.

BENTLEY   GREAT BRITAIN 1956

Series S, 5 pass. saloon. 6-cyl. F-head engine. Bore and stroke 95 x 114 mm. Displacement 4,875 c.c. Max. b.h.p. 170 at 4,200 r.p.m. Max. speed 106 m.p.h. Automatic transmission. Bentley and Rolls-Royce made their own Hydra-Matic transmissions.

COOPER-CLIMAX　　　　**GREAT BRITAIN 1956**

Formula II, racing car. 4-cyl. d.o.h.c. engine in line. Bore and stroke 76 x 80 mm. Displacement 1,460 c.c. Max. b.h.p. 100 at 6,100 r.p.m. 4 speeds. Max. speed approx. 145 m.p.h. Enlarged in 1958 for Formula One racing.

DAIMLER　　　　**GREAT BRITAIN 1956**

One-O-Four, 5 pass. lady's model saloon. 6-cyl. o.h.v. engine in line. Bore and stroke 83 x 108 mm. Displacement 3,468 c.c. Max. b.h.p. 139 at 4,400 r.p.m. Max. speed 100 m.p.h. Replaced the Regency.

FRAZER NASH　　　　**GREAT BRITAIN 1956**

Sebring Grand Sport, 2-seater roadster. 6-cyl. o.h.v. engine in line. Bore and stroke 66 x 96 mm. Displacement 1,971 c.c. Max. b.h.p. 142 at 5,750 r.p.m. 4 speeds. Max. speed 130 m.p.h.

HILLMAN　　　　**GREAT BRITAIN 1956**

Minx Series I, 4 pass. drophead coupé. 4-cyl. o.h.v. engine in line. Bore and stroke 76 x 76 mm. Displacement 1,390 c.c. Max. b.h.p. 51 at 4,600 r.p.m. 4 speeds. Max. speed 72 m.p.h. Styling consultant: Raymond Loewy.

JAGUAR **GREAT BRITAIN 1956**

2.4 Liter, 5 pass. saloon. 6-cyl. d.o.h.c. engine in line. Bore and stroke 83 x 76.5 mm. Displacement 2,483 c.c. Max. b.h.p. 114 at 5,750 r.p.m. 4 speeds. Max. speed 100 m.p.h. Jaguar's first unit-construction body.

LANCHESTER **GREAT BRITAIN 1956**

Sprite, 5 pass. sedan. 4-cyl. o.h.v. engine. Bore and stroke 76 x 89 mm. Displacement 1,622 c.c. Max. b.h.p. 61 at 4,200 r.p.m. Max. speed 78 m.p.h. Pre-selector transmission. Last of the Lanchesters similar to small Daimlers.

M.G. **GREAT BRITAIN 1956**

Magnette, 4 pass. saloon. 4-cyl. o.h.v. engine in line. Bore and stroke 73 x 89 mm. Displacement 1,489 c.c. Max. b.h.p. 60 at 4,600 r.p.m. 4 speeds. Max. speed 85 m.p.h. B.M.C. built the same car with another name plate: Wolseley 4/44.

MORGAN **GREAT BRITAIN 1956**

4/4 Series II, 2-seater roadster. 4-cyl. s.v. engine in line (Ford 100E). Bore and stroke 63.5 x 92.5 mm. Displacement 1,172 c.c. Max. b.h.p. 37 at 4,500 r.p.m. 3 speeds. Max. speed 77 m.p.h. Design basically unchanged from 1936.

ROLLS-ROYCE   **GREAT BRITAIN** 1956

Silver Cloud, 5 pass. saloon. 6-cyl. F-head engine in
line. Bore and stroke 95 x 114 mm. Displacement 4,887
c.c. Max. b.h.p. not disclosed. Max. speed 103 m.p.h.
Hydra-Matic transmission standard.

TRIUMPH   **GREAT BRITAIN** 1956

TR 3 Francorchamps, 2 pass. coupé 4-cyl. o.h.v. engine.
Bore and stroke 83 x 92 mm. Displacement 1,991 c.c.
Max. b.h.p. 96 at 4,800 r.p.m. 4 speeds. Max. speed 106
m.p.h. Weight 947 kg.

MASERATI   **ITALY 1956**

250 F, racing car. 6-cyl. d.o.h.c. engine in line. Bore and
stroke 84 x 75 m.m. Displacement 2493 c.c. Max. 270 at
7,600 r.p.m.s. speeds. Max. speed 185 m.p.h. V-12 added in
1957; however; 6-cyl. won the Monte Carlo championship
in 1956.

PEGASO   **SPAIN** 1956

Z-103, 2-seater sports-coupé. V-8 o.h.v. engine. Bore
and stroke 93 x 82.5 mm. Displacement 4,459 c.c. Max.
b.h.p. 300 at 5,500 r.p.m. 5 speeds. Max. speed 125
m.p.h. Body by Carrozzeria Touring.

CHECKER U.S.A. 1956

A8 Standard, 6 pass. sedan (taxicab). 6-cyl. s.v. engine in line (Continental Motors). Bore and stroke 84 x 111 mm. Displacement 3,703 c.c. Max. b.h.p. 91 at 3,000 r.p.m. 3 speeds. Max. speed 75 m.p.h.

LINCOLN U.S.A. 1956

Continental Mark II, 5 pass. coupé. V-8 o.h.v. engine. Bore and stroke 4 x 3 21/32 inches. Displacement 368 cu. in. Max. b.h.p. 300 at 4800 r.p.m. Max. speed 112 m.p.h. Body design by John M. Reinhardt.

HOLDEN AUSTRALIA 1957

Special sedan. 6-cyl. o.h.v. engine in line. Bore and stroke 76 x 80 mm. Displacement 2,171 c.c. Max. b.h.p. 70 at 4,000 r.p.m. 3 speeds. Max. speed $\pm$ 80 m.p.h. First built in 1948. Cross between Vauxhall and Chevrolet.

FACEL-VEGA FRANCE 1957

Excellence, 5 pass. sedan. V-8 o.h.v. engine (Chrysler) Bore and stroke 94.5 x 96.5 mm. Displacement 5,413 c.c. Max. b.h.p. 250 at 4,400 r.p.m. 4 speeds. Max. speed 118 m.p.h. Pont-a-Mousson 4-speed manual or Chrysler automatic transmission.

SIMCA   **FRANCE** 1957

Pichon Parat, coupé. 4-cyl. water-cooled engine in line. Bore and stroke 74 x 75 mm. Displacement 1,290 c.c. Max. b.h.p. 65 at 5,500 r.p.m. 4 speeds. Max. speed 95 m.p.h.

RENAULT   **FRANCE** 1957

4 CV Sport, 4 pass. berline. 4-cyl. rear-mounted o.h.v. engine in line. Bore and stroke 54.5 x 80 mm. Displacement 747 c.c. Max. b.h.p. 21 at 4,500 r.p.m. 3 speeds. Max. speed 62 m.p.h. Phased out in favor of Dauphine.

SIMCA   **FRANCE** 1957

Plein Ciel, 2-seater coupé. 4-cyl. o.h.v. engine in line (Aronde 1300). Bore and stroke 74 x 75 mm. Displacement 1,290 c.c. Max. b.h.p. 55 at 5,200 r.p.m. 4 speeds. Max. speed 135 m.p.h. Body built by Facel-Metallon.

BORGWARD   **GERMANY** 1957

Isabella T.S., 2/4 pass. Coupé. 4-cyl. o.h.v. engine in line. Bore and stroke 75 x 84.5 mm. Displacement 1,493 c.c. Max. b.h.p. 75 at 5,200 r.p.m. 4 speeds. Max. speed 95 m.p.h. Swing-axle rear suspension.

D.K.W. GERMANY 1957

Monza, coupe (fiberglass). 3-cyl. 2-stroke engine in line. Bore and stroke 71 x 76 mm. Displacement 896 c.c. Max. b.h.p. 44 at 4,500 r.p.m. 4 speeds. Max. speed 80 m.p.h. Freewheel or Saxomat automatic clutch. Front wheel drive.

MERCEDES-BENZ GERMANY 1957

220S, 4 pass. A cabriolet. 6-cyl. s.o.h.c. engine in line. Bore and stroke 80 x 73 mm. Displacement 2,195 c.c. Max. b.h.p. 112 at 4,800 r.p.m. 4 speeds. Max. speed 100 m.p.h. Hydrak automatic clutch available.

OPEL GERMANY 1957

1.5 Liter Olympia Rekord, 4 pass. limousine. 4 cyl. o.h.v. engine in line. Bore and stroke 80 x 74 mm. Displacement 1,488 c.c. Max. b.h.p. 52 at 3,900 r.p.m. 3 speeds. Max. speed 72 m.p.h. Grew larger with frequent styling changes.

ALLARD GREAT BRITAIN 1957

J2R, 2-seater super-sports roadster. V-8 o.h.v. engine (Cadillac). Bore and stroke 97 x 92 mm. Displacement 5,422 c.c. Max. b.h.p. 272 at 4,600 r.p.m. 3 speeds. Max. speed 125 m.p.h. Led for one lap, then blew up at Le Mans in 1957.

BERKELEY   **GREAT BRITAIN 1957**

Roadster, 2-seater (plastic). 2-cyl. 2-stroke air-cooled engine in line (British Anzani). Bore and stroke 60 x 57 mm. Displacement 322 c.c. Max. b.h.p. 15 at 5,000 r.p.m. 3 speeds. Max. speed approx. 65 m.p.h. Albion transmission. Front wheel drive.

JAGUAR   **GREAT BRITAIN 1957**

SS, 2-seater sports. 6-cyl. d.o.h.c. engine in line. Bore and stroke 83 x 106 mm. Displacement 3,442 c.c. Max. b.h.p. 250 at 5,200 r.p.m. 4 speeds. Max. speed 125 m.p.h.

MORRIS   **GREAT BRITAIN 1957**

Oxford series III, saloon. 4-cyl. o.h.v. engine in line. Bore and stroke 73 x 89 mm. Displacement 1,489 c.c. Max. b.h.p. 56 at 4,400 r.p.m. 4 speeds. Max. speed 75 m.p.h.

ROVER   **GREAT BRITAIN 1957**

T3, experimental 2-seater coupé. Max. b.h.p. 110 at 5,200 r.p.m. Max. speed 103 m.p.h. Gas turbine at rear. With plastic body.

STANDARD   **GREAT BRITAIN 1957**

Sportsman, sedan. 4-cyl. o.h.v. engine in line. Bore and stroke 85 x 92 mm. Displacement 2,088 c.c. Max. b.h.p. 91 at 4,500 r.p.m. Max. speed 90 m.p.h. 3-speed with overdrive. Styling variation of the Vanguard.

VAUXHALL   **GREAT BRITAIN 1957**

Cresta EIPC, 5/6 pass. saloon. 6-cyl. o.h.v. engine in line. Bore and stroke 79 x 76 mm. Displacement 2,262 c.c. Max. b.h.p. 68.4 at 4,000 r.p.m. 3 speeds. Max. speed 80 m.p.h. Body design by David B. Jones.

ABARTH   **ITALY 1957**

Convertible. 4-cyl. o.h.v. engine in line (Fiat 600-based). Bore and stroke 61 x 64 mm. Displacement 747 c.c. Max. b.h.p. 41.5 at 5,500 r.p.m. 4 speeds. Max. speed 80 m.p.h. Body by Carrozzeria Viotti.

FIAT   **ITALY 1957**

600 Multipla, 6 pass. tourer or barchetta. 4-cyl. rear-mounted o.h.v. engine. Bore and stroke 60 x 56 mm. Displacement 633 c.c. Max. b.h.p. 22 at 4,600 r.p.m. 4 speeds. Max. speed 56 m.p.h. Weight 750 kg. Fuel consumption 1 : 14. 1956 600 Fiat's first rear-engine.

FIAT ITALY 1957

1400 B, saloon. 4-cyl. engine in line. Bore and stroke 82 x 66 m.m. Displacement 1395 c.c. Max. b.h.p. 58 at 4600 r.p.m. 4 speeds. Max. speed 84 m.p.h. replaced by 1300/1500 series in 1962.

DATSUN JAPAN 1957

1000, saloon. 4-cyl. o.h.v. engine in line. Bore and stroke 73 x 59 mm. Displacement 988 c.c. Max. b.h.p. 34 at 4,400 r.p.m. 4 speeds. Max. speed 65 m.p.h. Based on Austin A-40.

TOYOPET JAPAN 1957

Corona ST, saloon. 4-cyl. s.v. engine in line. Bore and stroke 65 x 75 mm. Displacement 995 c.c. Max. b.h.p. 33 at 4,500 r.p.m. 3 speeds. Max. speed 55 m.p.h. 1,000 manufactured per day.

SAAB SWEDEN 1957

Sonett, 2-seater sports roadster (fiberglass). 3-cyl. 2-stroke engine in line. Bore and stroke 66 x 73 mm. Displacement 743 c.c. Max. b.h.p. 58 at 5,000 r.p.m. 3 speeds. Max. speed 125 m.p.h. Front wheel drive. Body design by Sixten Sason.

VOLVO　　　　　　　　　　　　　　**SWEDEN 1957**

122S (formerly Amazon), 5 pass. sedan. 4-cyl. o.h.v. engine in line. Bore and stroke 79.4 x 80 mm. Displacement 1,582 c.c. Max. b.h.p. 85 at 5,500 r.p.m. 4 speeds. Max. speed 93 m.p.h. 90 h.p. engine in 1962; 96 h.p. in 1965.

BUICK　　　　　　　　　　　　　　**U.S.A. 1957**

Roadmaster Riviera 73, 4-door hardtop. V-8 o.h.v. engine. Bore and stroke 4.13 x 3.40 inches. Displacement 365 cu. in. Max. b.h.p. 300 at 4600 r.p.m. Max. speed 120 m.p.h. Dynaflow transmission.

CADILLAC　　　　　　　　　　　　**U.S.A. 1957**

Eldorado Brougham. V-8 o.h.v. engine. Bore and stroke 4.0 x 3.6 inches. Displacement 365 cu. in. Max. b.h.p. 330 at 4800 r.p.m. Hydra-Matic transmission. First American car with air suspension.

CHEVROLET　　　　　　　　　　　　**U.S.A. 1957**

2934 Corvette, 2-seater sports roadster. V-8 o.h.v. engine. Bore and stroke 3.88 x 3.0 inches. Displacement 283 cu. in. Max. b.h.p. 220 at 4800 r.p.m. 3 speeds. Max. speed 120 m.p.h. 265 cu. in. engine in 1956.

CHRYSLER U.S.A. 1957

300 C, pass. coupé. V-8 o.h.v. engine. Bore and stroke 4.0 x 3.9 inches. Displacement 392 cu. in. Max. b.h.p. 375 at 5200 r.p.m. Max. speed 145 m.p.h. Imperial engine and grille added to New Yorker.

FORD U.S.A. 1957

Fairlane, town sedan. V-8 o.h.v. engine. Bore and stroke 3.75 x 3.30 inches. Displacement 292 cu. in. Max. b.h.p. 206 at 4500 r.p.m. Max. speed 95-100 m.p.h. 3-speed or Fordomatic transmission. Body design under direction of George W. Walker.

MERCURY U.S.A. 1957

Montclair, phaeton sedan. V-8 o.h.v. engine. Bore and stroke 3.8 x 3.4 inches. Displacement 312 cu. in. Max. b.h.p. 255 at 4600 r.p.m. 3-speed or Merc-O-Matic transmission. Max. speed 100-110 m.p.h.

PLYMOUTH U.S.A. 1957

Savoy, sedan. 6-cyl. water-cooled s.v. engine in line. Bore and stroke 3.25 x 4.63 inches. Displacement 230 cu. in. Max. b.h.p. 132 at 3600 r.p.m. 3 speeds with or without over-drive or automatic transmission. Max. speed 90 m.p.h.

STUDEBAKER   U.S.A. 1957

Silver Hawk. V-8 water-cooled o.h.v. engine. Bore and stroke 3.56 x 3.25 inches. Displacement 259 cu. in. Max. b.h.p. 180 at 4500 r.p.m. 3 speeds with or without overdrive or automatic transmission. Max. speed 103 m.p.h.

MOSKVITCH   U.S.S.R. 1957

402. 4-cyl. s.v. engine in line. Bore and stroke 72 x 75 mm. Displacement 1,220 c.c. Max. b.h.p. 35 at 4,200 r.p.m. 3 speeds. Max. speed 65 m.p.h. Direct copy of 1938 Opel Kadett.

CHRYSLER   AUSTRALIA 1958

Royal. 6-cyl. s.v. engine in line. Bore and stroke 83 x 114 mm. Displacement 3,772 c.c. Max. b.h.p. 115 at 3,600 r.p.m. Max. speed 90 m.p.h. 3-speed or PowerFlite automatic transmission. Chrysler has large plants in Australia.

MORRIS   AUSTRALIA 1958

Major Mk I, saloon. 4-cyl. o.h.v. engine in line. Bore and stroke 73 x 89 mm. Displacement 1,489 c.c. 4 speeds. B.M.C. has large plants in Australia.

ALPINE   FRANCE 1958

Convertible. 4-cyl. o.h.v. engine in line (Renault 4 CV). Bore and stroke 55 x 80 mm. Displacement 747 c.c. Max. b.h.p. 26 at 4,100 r.p.m. 5 speeds. Max. speed 90 m.p.h. Body design by Giovanni Michelotti.

BRISSONNEAU et LOTZ   FRANCE 1958

Convertible (fiberglass). 4-cyl. o.h.v. engine in line (Renault 4 CV). Bore and stroke 55 x 80 mm. Displacement 747 c.c. Max. b.h.p. 26 at 4,100 r.p.m. 3 speeds. Max. speed 65 m.p.h.

U.M.A.P.   FRANCE 1958

2 CV, coupé. 2-cyl. air-cooled, horizontally opposed, o.h.v. engine (tuned Citroën AZ). Bore and stroke 66 x 62 mm. Displacement 425 c.c. Max. b.h.p. 17 at 5,000 r.p.m. 4 speeds. Max. speed 65 m.p.h. Body by Charbonneau.

SIMCA   FRANCE 1958

Beaulieu. V-8. o.h.v. engine (Aronde). Bore and stroke 66 x 86 mm. Displacement 2,351 c.c. Max. b.h.p. 84 at 4,800 r.p.m. 3 speeds. Max. speed 85 m.p.h. Simcamatic automatic clutch optional. Became successful as the Ariane.

D.K.W. GERMANY 1958

1000, coupé de luxe. 3-cyl. 2-stroke engine in line. Bore and stroke 74 x 76 mm. Displacement 980 c.c. Max. b.h.p. 50 at 4,500 r.p.m. 4 speeds. Max. speed 80 m.p.h. Saxomat automatic clutch optional. Front wheel drive.

FORD GERMANY 1958

Taunus 17 M, convertible. 4-cyl. o.h.v. engine in line. Bore and stroke 84 x 77 mm. Displacement 1,698 c.c. Max. b.h.p. 67 at 4,250 r.p.m. 3/4 speeds. Max. speed 75 m.p.h.

GOGGOMOBILE GERMANY 1958

TS/TC 400, sport coupé, 2-cyl. air-cooled, rear-mounted, 2-stroke engine. Bore and stroke 67 x 56 mm. Displacement 392 c.c. Max. b.h.p. 20 at 5,000 r.p.m. Max. speed 62 m.p.h. 4-speed Selectomat electrically actuated pre-selective gear shift.

MAICO GERMANY 1958

500, sports convertible. 2-cyl. 2-stroke engine in line. Bore and stroke 66 x 66 mm. Displacement 425 c.c. Max. b.h.p. 20 at 4,500 r.p.m. 4 speeds. Max. speed 65 m.p.h.

MERCEDES-BENZ GERMANY 1958

300 SL, roadster. 6-cyl. s.o.h.c. engine in line. Fuel injection. Bore and stroke 85 x 88 mm. Displacement 2,996 c.c. Max. b.h.p. 250 at 6,200 r.p.m. 4 speeds. Max. speed 150 m.p.h. Gullwing coupé discontinued with this roadster's introduction.

OPEL GERMANY 1958

Rekord, coach. 4-cyl. o.h.v. engine in line. Bore and stroke 80 x 74 mm. Displacement 1,488 c.c. Max. b.h.p. 52 at 4,200 r.p.m. 3 speeds. Max. speed 72 m.p.h.

ALLARD GREAT BRITAIN 1958

Mark II Gran Turismo, coupé. 6-cyl. d.o.h.c. engine in line (Jaguar type C). Bore and stroke 83 x 106 mm. Displacement 3,442 c.c. Max. b.h.p. 210 at 5,500 r.p.m. Max. speed 115 m.p.h. 4-speed with or without Overdrive. Never in production.

BRISTOL GREAT BRITAIN 1958

406. 6-cyl. o.h.v. engine in line. Bore and stroke 68.69 x 99.64 mm. Displacement 2,216 c.c. Max. b.h.p. 107 at 4,700 r.p.m. Max. speed 100 m.p.h. 4-speed with Overdrive. Body by Beutler (Switzerland). Last 6-cyl. Bristol.

FRAZER NASH   **GREAT BRITAIN 1958**

Continental, coupé. V-8 o.h.v. engine (BMW). Bore and stroke 74 x 75 mm. Displacement 2,580 c.c. Max. b.h.p. 140 at 5,000 r.p.m. 4 speeds. Max. speed 135 m.p.h. Body by Pininfarina.

HUMBER   **GREAT BRITAIN 1958**

Hawk, saloon. 4-cyl. o.h.v. engine in line. Bore and stroke 81 x 110 mm. Displacement 2,267 c.c. Max. b.h.p. 78 at 4,400 r.p.m. Max. speed 80 m.p.h. 4-speed or Borg-Warner automatic transmission. Power unit inherited from Sunbeam-Talbot.

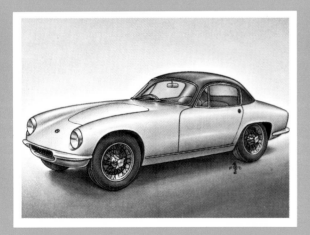

LOTUS   **GREAT BRITAIN 1958**

Elite, sports coupé (fiberglass). 4-cyl. s.o.h.c. engine in line (Coventry Climax). Bore and stroke 76 x 67 mm. Displacement 1,220 c.c. Max. b.h.p. 76 at 6,100 c.c. 4 speeds. Max. speed 115 m.p.h. Body design by John Frayling.

PEERLESS   **GREAT BRITAIN 1958**

Gran Turismo, coupé (fiberglass). 4-cyl. o.h.v. engine in line (Triumph TR 3). Bore and stroke 83 x 92 mm. Displacement 1,991 c.c. Max. b.h.p. 101 at 5,000 r.p.m. 4 speeds. Max. speed 115. Body design by John Gordon.

PRINCESS   GREAT BRITAIN 1958

IV, 8-pass. limousine. 6-cyl. o.h.v. engine in line. Bore and stroke 87 x 111 mm. Displacement 3,995 c.c. Max. b.h.p. 132 at 3,700 r.p.m. Max. speed 70 m.p.h. Engine based on Austin truck.

VAUXHALL   GREAT BRITAIN 1958

Victor, super saloon. 4-cyl. o.h.v. engine. Bore and stroke 79 x 76 mm. Displacement 1,507 c.c. Max. b.h.p. 55 at 4,200 r.p.m. 3 speeds. Max. speed 75 m.p.h. Replaced the Wyvern.

ALFA ROMEO   ITALY 1958

2000, berlina. 4-cyl. d.o.h.c. engine in line. Bore and stroke 84.5 x 88 mm. Displacement 1,975 c.c. Max. b.h.p. 105 at 5,300 r.p.m. 5 speeds. Max. speed 100 m.p.h. Derived from the 1900 series.

FERRARI   ITALY 1958

250 GT, coupé. V-12 s.o.h.c. engine. Bore and stroke 73 x 59 mm. Displacement 2,953 c.c. Max. b.h.p. 240 at 7,000 r.p.m. 4 speeds. Max. speed 150 m.p.h. Body by Pininfarina. Engine changed in detail only after 19 years.

LANCIA   ITALY 1958

Appia, coupé. V-4 s.o.h.c. engine. Bore and stroke 68 x 75
mm. Displacement 1,090 c.c. Max. b.h.p. 53 at 5,200 r.p.m.
4 speeds. Max. speed 85 m.p.h. Body by Pininfarina.
Replaced by the Fulvia in 1963.

MORETTI   ITALY 1958

750 Superpanoramica. 4-cyl. s.o.h.c. engine in line. Bore
and stroke 60 x 66 mm. Displacement 748 c.c. Max. b.h.p.
35 at 4,800 r.p.m. 4 speeds. Max. speed 70 m.p.h.

NARDI-LANCIA   ITALY 1958

GT 2500. V-6 o.h.v. engine (Lancia Flaminia). Bore and
stroke 78 x 85.5 mm. Displacement 2,451 c.c. Max. b.h.p.
138. 4 speeds. Max. speed 120 m.p.h. Body by Michelotti-
Vignale.

SIATA   ITALY 1958

500, spider sports convertible. 2-cyl. air-cooled o.h.v.
engine in line (Fiat 500). Bore and stroke 66 x 70 mm.
Displacement 479 c.c. Max. b.h.p. 18 at 4,700 r.p.m.
4 speeds. Max. speed 60 m.p.h.

FUJI JAPAN 1958

Subaru 360, cabrio-coach. 2-cyl. air-cooled, horizontally opposed, 2-stroke, rear-mounted engine. Bore and stroke 61.5 x 60 mm. Displacement 356 c.c. Max. b.h.p. 16 at 4,500 r.p.m. 3 speeds. Max. speed 50 m.p.h. 450 c.c. engine optional in 1961.

PRINCE JAPAN 1958

Skyline de luxe. 4-cyl. o.h.v. engine in line. Bore and stroke 75 x 84 mm. Displacement 1,484 c.c. Max. b.h.p. 60 at 4,400 r.p.m. 4 speeds. Max. speed 75 m.p.h. Began car manufacture in 1951.

SYRENA POLAND 1958

101, saloon. 2-cyl. 2-stroke engine in line. Bore and stroke 76 x 82 mm. Displacement 746 c.c. Max. b.h.p. 27 at 4,200 r.p.m. 4 speeds. Max. speed ± 65 m.p.h.

BUICK U.S.A./ITALY 1958

Lido, coupé. V-8 water-cooled o.h.v. engine. Bore and stroke 104.8 x 86.4 mm. Displacement 5,957 c.c. Max. b.h.p. 247 at 4,400 r.p.m. Automatic transmission. Max. speed 106 m.p.h.

CHEVROLET　　　　　　　　　　　　　　**U.S.A. 1958**

Bel Air, sport sedan. V-8 o.h.v. engine. Bore and stroke 3.87 x 3.00 inches. Displacement 283 cu. in. Max. b.h.p. 185 at 4600 r.p.m. 4 speeds. Max. speed ± 105 m.p.h. 3-speed or Powerglide automatic transmission. Available with air springs.

DE SOTO　　　　　　　　　　　　　　**U.S.A. 1958**

FireFlite, convertible, V-8 o.h.v. engine. Bore and stroke 4.12 x 3.38 inches. Displacement 361 cu. in. Max. b.h.p. 305 at 4600 r.p.m. Max. speed 110 m.p.h. Torque Flite automatic transmission. Body design under direction of Virgil Exner.

DODGE　　　　　　　　　　　　　　**U.S.A. 1958**

Coronet, 2-door sedan. V-8 water-cooled o.h.v. engine. Bore and stroke 3.69 x 3.80 inches. Displacement 325 cu. in. Max. b.h.p. 252 at 4400 r.p.m. 3 speeds or automatic transmission. Max. speed 110 m.p.h.

EDSEL　　　　　　　　　　　　　　**U.S.A. 1958**

Pacer, 2-door hardtop. V-8 o.h.v. engine. Bore and stroke 4.05 x 3.50 inches. Displacement 361 cu. in. Max. b.h.p. 303 at 4600 r.p.m. 3-speeds or Mile-O-Matic transmission. Max. speed 105 m.p.h. Body design under direction of George W. Walker.

CHRYSLER U.S.A. 1958

Imperial Crown, 2-door hardtop. V-8 o.h.v. engine. Bore and stroke 4.18 x 3.75 inches. Displacement 413 cu. in. Max. b.h.p. 350 at 4600 r.p.m. Max. speed 110-115 m.p.h. Torqueflite transmission mechanically unchanged between 1957 and 1966.

PACKARD U.S.A. 1958

Town sedan V-8 o.h.v. engine. Bore and stroke 3 9/16 x 3 5/8 inches. Displacement 289 cu. in. Max. b.h.p. 275 at 4800 r.p.m. Max. speed 95-105 m.p.h. Automatic transmission. Studebaker with a Packard Nameplate.

RAMBLER U.S.A. 1958

American, coach, 6-cyl. water-cooled s.v. engine in line. Bore and stroke 3.12 x 4.25 inches. Displacement 195 cu. in. Max. b.h.p. 127 at 4200 r.p.m. 3-speeds with or without overdrive or automatic transmission. Max. speed approx. 84 m.p.h.

ASCORT AUSTRALIA 1959

TSV 1300 GT, sports coupé. 4-cyl. air-cooled, horizontally opposed, rear-mounted, o.h.v. engine (VW). Bore and stroke 77 x 70 mm. Displacement 1,296 c.c. Max. b.h.p. 55 at 4,300 r.p.m. 4 speeds. Max. speed 95 m.p.h.

ARISTA   FRANCE 1959

RENAULT   FRANCE 1959

Passy, coupé (fiberglass). 2-cyl. air-cooled, horizontally opposed o.h.v. engine (Panhard). Bore and stroke 85 x 75 mm. Displacement 851 c.c. Max. b.h.p. 42 at 5,000 r.p.m. 4 speeds. Max. speed 80 m.p.h. Automatic clutch optional. Front wheel drive.

Floride, convertible. 4-cyl. rear-mounted o.h.v. engine in line. Bore and stroke 58 x 80 mm. Displacement 845 c.c. Max. b.h.p. 40 at 5,200 r.p.m. 3/4 speeds. Max. speed 80 m.p.h. Sports model based on Dauphine.

SIMCA   FRANCE 1959

VESPA   FRANCE 1959

Aronde Monaco, 2-door hardtop. 4-cyl. o.h.v. engine in line. Bore and stroke 74 x 75 mm. Displacement 1,290 c.c. Max. b.h.p. 60 at 5,200 r.p.m. 4 speeds. Max. speed 80 m.p.h. First non-Fiat based Simca design.

400, cabrio-coupé. 2-cyl. 2-stroke air-cooled, rear-mounted, engine. Bore and stroke 63 x 63 mm. Displacement 394 c.c. Max. b.h.p. 14 at 4,350 r.p.m. 3 speeds. Max. speed 50 m.p.h. Discontinued in 1962.

TRABANT   **EAST GERMANY 1959**

P-50, coach (fiberglass). 2-cyl. air-cooled, two-stroke, engine. Bore and stroke 66 x 73 mm. Displacement 500 c.c. Max. b.h.p. 18 at 3,750 r.p.h. 4 speeds. Max. speed 55 m.p.h. Front wheel drive.

GOGGOMOBILE   **GERMANY 1959**

Isar T 700. 2-cyl. air-cooled, horizontally opposed, o.h.v. engine. Bore and stroke 78 x 72 mm. Displacement 688 c.c. Max. b.h.p. 30 at 4,900 r.p.m. 4 speeds. Max. speed 65 m.p.h. Marque became Glas.

LLOYD   **GERMANY 1959**

Alexander, coupé. 2-cyl. horizontally opposed o.h.v. engine. Bore and stroke 77 x 64 mm. Displacement 596 c.c. Max. b.h.p. 30 at 5,000 r.p.m. 4 speeds. Max. speed 72 m.p.h. Front wheel drive. Body by Carrozzeria Frua. Part of the Borgward Group.

MERCEDES-BENZ   **GERMANY 1959**

300 Automatic, hardtop limousine. 6-cyl. s.o.h.c. engine in line. Fuel injection. Bore and stroke 85 x 88 mm. Displacement 2,996 c.c. Max. b.h.p. 160 at 5,300 r.p.m. Max. speed 100 m.p.h. Borg-Warner automatic transmission. Hand-controlled auxiliary rear springs to keep car level regardless of load.

N.S.U.   **GERMANY 1959**

Sport Prinz. 2-cyl. air-cooled, rear-mounted s.o.h.c. engine in line. Bore and stroke 75 x 66 mm. Displacement 583 c.c. Max. b.h.p. 34 at 5,800 r.p.m. 4 speeds. Max. speed 80 m.p.h. Sports model based on Prinz 3.

OPEL   **GERMANY 1959**

Kapitän, standard sedan. 6-cyl. o.h.v. engine in line. Bore and stroke 80 x 82 mm. Displacement 2,473 c.c. Max. b.h.p. 96 at 4,300 r.p.m. 3 speeds. Max. speed 85 m.p.h. German version of Chevrolet.

PORSCHE   **GERMANY 1959**

356A/1600. 4-cyl. air-cooled, horizontally opposed, o.h.v. engine (2 carburetors). Bore and stroke 82.5 x 74 mm. Displacement 1,582 c.c. Max. b.h.p. 60 at 4,500 r.p.m. 4 speeds. Max. speed 95 m.p.h. Body by Butler (Switzerland).

ARMSTRONG-SIDDELEY   **GREAT BRITAIN 1959**

Star Sapphire. 6-cyl. o.h.v. engine in line. Bore and stroke 97 x 90 mm. Displacement 3,990 c.c. Max. b.h.p. 165 at 4,250 r.p.m. Max. speed 95 m.p.h. Borg-Warner automatic transmission. Last of the Armstrong-Siddeleys; merged with Bristol.

ASTON MARTIN GREAT BRITAIN 1959

DB 4, coupé. 6-cyl. d.o.h.c. engine in line. Bore and stroke 92 x 92 mm. Displacement 3,670 c.c. Max. b.h.p. 267 at 5,700 r.p.m. 4 speeds. Max. speed 135 m.p.h. Body built by Tickford to designs by Carrozzeria Touring and Frank Feeley.

AUSTIN GREAT BRITAIN 1959

A 40 Futura. 4-cyl. o.h.v. engine in line. Bore and stroke 63 x 76 mm. Displacement 948 c.c. Max. b.h.p. 39 at 5,000 r.p.m. 4 speeds. Max. speed 70 m.p.h. Body design by Pininfarina.

BRISTOL GREAT BRITAIN 1959

405, 2-door coupé. 6-cyl. o.h.v. engine in line. Bore and stroke 69 x 100 mm. Displacement 2,216 c.c. Max. b.h.p. 105 at 4,700 r.p.m. 4 speeds (Overdrive on top gear). Max. speed 100 m.p.h. Chrysler engine in later models.

ROVER GREAT BRITAIN 1959

3 Liter, saloon. 6-cyl. F-head engine in line. Bore and stroke 78 x 105 mm. Displacement 2,995 c.c. Max. b.h.p. 115 at 4,250 r.p.m. Max. speed 95 m.p.h. 4-speed or Borg-Warner automatic transmission. Unit-construction body in all Rovers except Land-Rover.

TRIUMPH　　　　　　　**GREAT BRITAIN 1959**

Herald, saloon. 4-cyl. o.h.v. engine in line. Bore and stroke 63 x 76 mm. Displacement 948 c.c. Max. b.h.p. 39 at 4,500 r.p.m. 4 speeds. Max. speed 70 m.p.h. Body design by Giovanni Michelotti.

WOLSELEY　　　　　　　**GREAT BRITAIN 1959**

15/60, saloon. 4-cyl. o.h.v. engine in line. Bore and stroke 73 x 89 mm. Displacement 1,489 c.c. Max. b.h.p. 55 at 4,400 r.p.m. 4 speeds. Max. speed 80 m.p.h. Body design by Pininfarina.

ALFA ROMEO　　　　　　　**ITALY 1959**

Giulietta Sprint speciale. 4-cyl. d.o.h.c. engine in line. Bore and stroke 74 x 75 mm. Displacement 1,290 c.c. Max. b.h.p. 100 at 6,000 r.p.m. 5 speeds. Max. speed 120 m.p.h. Body by Carrozzeria Bertone. Supplemented in 1963 by the Giulia.

AUTOBIANCHI　　　　　　　**ITALY 1959**

Bianchina. 2-cyl. air-cooled, rear-mounted, o.h.v. engine in line (Fiat 500 Sport). Bore and stroke 68 x 70 mm. Displacement 500 c.c. Max. b.h.p. 25 at 4,500 r.p.m. 4 speeds. Max. speed 65 m.p.h. De luxe version of Fiat 500.

FIAT   **ITALY 1959**

1200, saloon. 4-cyl. o.h.v. engine in line. Bore and stroke 72 x 75 mm. Displacement 1,221 c.c. Max. b.h.p. 63 at 5,300 r.p.m. 4 speeds. Max. speed 85 m.p.h. Variant of the Fiat 1100.

LANCIA   **ITALY 1959**

Flaminia, coupé. V-6 o.h.v. engine. Bore and stroke 80 x 82 mm. Displacement 2,458 c.c. Max. b.h.p. 118 at 5,100 r.p.m. 4 speeds. Body built by Pininfarina.

DATSUN   **JAPAN 1959**

1000 Fair Lady, sports convertible. 4-cyl. o.h.v. engine in line. Bore and stroke 73 x 59 mm. Displacement 988 c.c. Max. b.h.p. 37 at 4,600 r.p.m. 4 speeds. Max. speed 75 m.p.h. Based on the Austin A-40.

MIKASA   **JAPAN 1959**

Touring, sports roadster. 2-cyl. air-cooled, horizontally opposed, o.h.v. engine. Bore and stroke 73 x 70 mm. Displacement 585 c.c. Max. b.h.p. 17 at 3,800 r.p.m. Max. speed 55 m.p.h.

ENZMANN   **SWITZERLAND 1959**
506, Super 1300, sports convertible. 4-cyl. air-cooled, horizontally opposed o.h.v. engine (Volkswagen) with enlarged stroke, special cylinder heads, 2 carburetors. Bore and stroke 77 x 70 mm. Displacement 1,295 c.c. Max. b.h.p. 45 at 4,600 r.p.m. 4 speeds. Max. speed 95 m.p.h. Fiberglass body without doors.

CADILLAC   **U.S.A. 1959**

Series 75. V-8 o.h.v. engine. Bore and stroke 4.0 x 3.87 inches. Displacement 390 cu. in. Max. b.h.p. 325 at 4800 r.p.m. Max. speed 115 m.p.h. Hydra-Matic transmission. Body design under direction of Harley J. Earl.

DODGE   **U.S.A. 1959**

Custom Royal, 4-door hardtop. V-8 water-cooled o.h.v. engine. Bore and stroke 4.12 x 3.37 inches. Displacement 361 cu. in. Max. b.h.p. 305 at 4600 r.p.m. Automatic transmission. Max. speed 120 m.p.h.

FORD   **U.S.A. 1959**

Thunderbird, convertible. V-8 o.h.v. engine. Bore and stroke 4.00 x 3.50 inches. Displacement 352 cu. in. Max. b.h.p. 300 at 4600 r.p.m. Max. speed 105 m.p.h. 3-speed or Cruise-O-Matic transmission.

LINCOLN   U.S.A. 1959

Continental Mark IV. V-8 o.h.v. engine. Bore and stroke
4.30 x 3.70 inches. Displacement 430 cu. in. Max. b.h.p.
375 at 4800 r.p.m. Max. speed 110 m.p.h. Twin Range Turbo
Drive Transmission. Built to attract Cadillac market.

OLDSMOBILE   U.S.A. 1959

Super 88, Holiday Sceni, coupé. V-8 o.h.v. engine. Bore and
stroke 4.12 x 3.68 inches. Displacement 394 cu. in. Max.
b.h.p. 315 at 4600 r.p.m. Max. speed 110 m.p.h. Hydra-Matic
transmission or 3-speed manual.

PONTIAC   U.S.A. 1959

Bonneville, 4-door hardtop. V-8 o.h.v. engine. Bore and
stroke 3.06 x 3.75 inches. Displacement 389 cu. in. Max.
b.h.p. 245 at 4200 r.p.m. Max. speed 110 m.p.h. Hydra-Matic
transmission. First Wide-track Pontiac.

RAMBLER   U.S.A. 1959

Ambassador, 4-door hardtop. V-8 water cooled o.h.v. engine. Bore and stroke 4.00 x 3.25 inches. Displacement 327
cu. in. Max. b.h.p. 270 at 4700 r.p.m. 3 speeds with overdrive
or automatic transmission. Max. speed 106 m.p.h.

STUDEBAKER   **U.S.A. 1959**

Lark, 2-door hardtop. 6-cyl. s.v. engine in line. Bore and stroke 3.00 x 4.00 inches. Displacement 170 cu. in. Max. b.h.p. 90 at 4000 r.p.m. Max. speed 80 m.p.h. 3-speed or Borg-Warner automatic transmission. Engine converted to overhead valves in 1960.

TCHAIKA   **U.S.S.R. 1959**

M-13, sedan. V-8 o.h.v. engine. Bore and stroke 100 x 88 mm. Displacement 5,500 c.c. Max. b.h.p. 195 at 4,400 r.p.m. Max. speed 95 m.p.h. Automatic transmission. Body design by Boris Lebedev.

ZIL   **U.S.S.R. 1959**

111, limousine. V-8 o.h.v. engine. Bore and stroke 100 x 95 mm. Displacement 5,980 c.c. Max. b.h.p. 220 at 4,200 r.p.m. Max. speed 95 m.p.h. Automatic transmission. Body design by Boris Lebedev.

GRACIELA   **ARGENTINA 1960**

Coach. 3-cyl. 2-stroke engine in line (Wartburg). Bore and stroke 70 x 78 mm. Displacement 900 c.c. Max. b.h.p. 37 at 4,000 r.p.m. 4 speeds. Max. speed 70 m.p.h. Front wheel drive.

VAUXHALL   **CANADA** 1960

Envoy Special, saloon. 4-cyl. o.h.v. engine. Bore and stroke 79 x 76 mm. Displacement 1,508 c.c. Max. b.h.p. 56 at 4,200 r.p.m. 3 speeds. Max. speed 75 m.p.h. Canadian version of the Victor.

HONGCHI   **CHINA** 1960

Red Flag, limousine. V-8 o.h.v. engine. Bore and stroke 100 x 90 mm. Displacement 5,650 c.c. Max. b.h.p. 220 at 4,900 r.p.m. Max. speed 95 m.p.h. Automatic transmission.

ALPINE   **FRANCE** 1960

A 108-850, coupé. 4-cyl., rear-mounted o.h.v. engine in line (Renault Dauphine). Bore and stroke 58 x 80 mm. Displacement 845 c.c. Max. b.h.p. 40 at 5,000 r.p.m. 3 speeds. Max. speed 85 m.p.h.

PANHARD   **FRANCE** 1960

PL 17, convertible. 2-cyl. air-cooled, horizontally opposed, o.h.v. engine. Bore and stroke 85 x 75 mm. Displacement 851 c.c. Max. b.h.p. 42 at 5,300 r.p.m. 4 speeds. Max. speed 80 m.p.h. Jaeger automatic clutch optional. Front wheel drive.

SERA-PANHARD   **FRANCE 1960**

Hardtop, 2 pass. 2-cyl. air-cooled, horizontally opposed o.h.v. engine (Panhard Tigre). Bore and stroke 85 x 75 mm. Displacement 851 c.c. Max. b.h.p. 50 at 6,300 r.p.m. 4 speeds. Max. speed 95 m.p.h. Front wheel drive.

B.M.W.   **GERMANY 1960**

700, coupé. 2-cyl. air-cooled, rear-mounted, horizontally opposed o.h.v. engine. Bore and stroke 78 x 73 mm. Displacement 697 c.c. Max. b.h.p. 35 at 5,200 r.p.m. 4 speeds. Max. speed 75 m.p.h.

BORGWARD   **GERMANY 1960**

2.3 Liter, sedan. 6-cyl. o.h.v. engine in line. Bore and stroke 75 x 84.5 mm. Displacement 2,238. Max. b.h.p. 100 at 5,100 r.p.m. Max. speed 95 m.p.h. 4-speed or Hansa-matic automatic transmission. Air springs standard.

D.K.W.   **GERMANY 1960**

Junior. 3-cyl. 2-stroke engine in line. Bore and stroke 68 x 68 mm. Displacement 741 c.c. Max. b.h.p. 39 at 4,300 r.p.m. 4 speeds. Max. speed 70 m.p.h. Front wheel drive.

FORD GERMANY 1960

Taunus 12 M Super, coach. 4-cyl. o.h.v. engine in line. Bore and stroke 82 x 71 mm. Displacement 1,498 c.c. Max. b.h.p. 60 at 5,500 r.p.m. 3/4 speeds. Max. speed 75 m.p.h.

LLOYD GERMANY 1960

Arabella. 4-cyl. o.h.v. engine. Bore and stroke 69 x 60 mm. Displacement 897 c.c. Max. b.h.p. 42 at 4,800 r.p.m. 4 speeds. Max. speed 70 m.p.h. Front wheel drive. German built Fiat 500. Last of the Lloyds.

MERCEDES-BENZ GERMANY 1960

220. 6-cyl. s.o.h.c. engine in line. Bore and stroke 80 x 73 mm. Displacement 2,195 c.c. Max. b.h.p. 105 at 5,000 r.p.m. 4 speeds. Max. speed 95 m.p.h. Body design by Karl Wilfert.

PORSCHE GERMANY 1960

1600 G.S. Carrera GTL (Abarth), coupé. 4-cyl. air-cooled, horizontally opposed o.h.v. engine. Bore and stroke 88 x 66 mm. Displacement 1,588 c.c. Max. b.h.p. 115 at 6,500 r.p.m. 4 speeds. Max. speed 130 m.p.h.

AUSTIN   **GREAT BRITAIN 1960**

A 99, sedan. 6-cyl. o.h.v. engine in line. Bore and stroke 83 x 89 mm. Displacement 2,912 c.c. Max. b.h.p. 113.5 at 4,750 r.p.m. Max. speed ± 95 m.p.h. 3-speed with Overdrive or automatic transmission (Borg-Warner).

DAIMLER   **GREAT BRITAIN 1960**

SP 250 Sport (fiberglass). V-8 o.h.v. engine. Bore and stroke 76 x 70 mm. Displacement 2,548 c.c. Max. b.h.p. 142 at 5,800 r.p.m. Max. speed 120 m.p.h. 4-speed or Borg-Warner automatic transmission.

ELVA   **GREAT BRITAIN 1960**

Courier, roadster. 4-cyl. o.h.v. engine in line. Bore and stroke 75 x 89 mm. Displacement 1,588 c.c. Max. b.h.p. 79.5 at 5,500 r.p.m. 4 speeds. Max. speed 95 m.p.h. M.G.A. engine, gearbox and rear axle.

FORD   **GREAT BRITAIN 1960**

Anglia 105E. 4-cyl. o.h.v. engine in line. Bore and stroke 81 x 48 mm. Displacement 997 c.c. Max. b.h.p. 41 at 5,000 r.p.m. 4 speeds. Max. speed 72 m.p.h.

GORDON GREAT BRITAIN 1960

G.T. V-8 o.h.v. engine (Chevrolet Corvette). Bore and stroke 98 x 76 mm. Displacement 4,639 c.c. Max. b.h.p. 294 at 6,250 r.p.m. 4 speeds. Max. speed 135 m.p.h. Body by Carrozzeria Bertone. Based on Peerless.

MORRIS GREAT BRITAIN 1960

Mini Minor (850). 4-cyl. transverse mounted o.h.v. engine. Bore and stroke 63 x 68 mm. Displacement 848 c.c. Max. b.h.p. 38 at 5,500 r.p.m. 4 speeds. Max. speed 70 m.p.h. Front wheel drive. Gearbox in unit with differential.

ROLLS-ROYCE GREAT BRITAIN 1960

Phantom V. V-8 o.h.v. engine. Bore and stroke 104 x 91 mm. Displacement 6,230 c.c. Max. b.h.p. approx. 300. Body by Park Ward. Straight-eight engine in Phantom IV.

SUNBEAM GREAT BRITAIN 1960

Alpine, coupé. 4-cyl. o.h.v. engine in line. Bore and stroke 79 x 76 mm. Displacement 1,495 c.c. Max. b.h.p. 79 at 5,300 r.p.m. 4 speeds. Max. speed 95 m.p.h. Sports version of Hillman Minx.

ABARTH   ITALY 1960

850 Coupe Scorpione. 4-cyl. o.h.v. engine in line (Fiat-based). Bore and stroke 62 x 69 mm. Displacement 833 c.c. Max. b.h.p. 52 at 6,000 r.p.m. 4 speeds. Max. speed 95 m.p.h. Body by Carrozzeria Allemano.

CISITALIA   ITALY 1960

750, coupé. 4-cyl. o.h.v. engine in line (Fiat 600-based). Bore and stroke 60 x 65 mm. Max. b.h.p. 35 at 5,500. 4 speeds. Max. speed 70 m.p.h.

FIAT   ITALY 1960

2100, sedan. 6-cyl. o.h.v. engine in line. Bore and stroke 77 x 73.5 mm. Displacement 2,054 c.c. Max. b.h.p. 95 at 5,000 r.p.m. 4 speeds. Max. speed 90 m.p.h. Developed into the 2300.

MASERATI   ITALY 1960

3500 GT, coupé. 6-cyl. d.o.h.c. engine in line. Bore and stroke 86 x 100 mm. Displacement 3,485 c.c. Max. b.h.p. 235 at 5,800 r.p.m. (fuel injection) or 220 at 5,800 (engine with carburetor). 4/5 speeds. Max. speed 140 m.p.h. Body by Carrozzeria Touring.

DATSUN   **JAPAN 1960**

Bluebird de luxe. 4-cyl. o.h.v. engine in line. Bore and stroke 73 x 71 mm. Displacement 1,189 c.c. Max. b.h.p. 48 at 4,800 r.p.m. 3 speeds. Max. speed 75 m.p.h. Based on Austin A-50.

SUZULIGHT   **JAPAN 1960**

360 TL, coach with tailgate. 2-cyl. air-cooled, 2-stroke engine in line. Bore and stroke 59 x 66 mm. Displacement 360 c.c. Max. b.h.p. 21 at 5,300 r.p.m. 3 speeds. Max. speed 50 m.p.h.

G.S.M.   **SOUTH AFRICA 1960**

Dart 65, hardtop. 4-cyl. o.h.v. engine in line (tuned Ford 105E Anglia). Bore and stroke 81 x 48 mm. Displacement 997 c.c. Max. b.h.p. 56 at 6,000 r.p.m. 4 speeds. Max. speed 95 m.p.h.

VOLKSWAGEN   **SWITZERLAND 1960**

Italsuisse Sun-Valley, coach. 4-cyl. air-cooled, horizontally opposed, rear-mounted, o.h.v. engine. Bore and stroke 77 x 64 mm. Displacement 1,192 c.c. Max. b.h.p. 36 at 3,700 r.p.m. 4 speeds. Max. speed 70 m.p.h. Built by Carrozzeria Frua on VW chassis. Never in series production.

CHEVROLET   U.S.A. 1960

Corvair 700 de luxe. 6-cyl. air-cooled rear mounted hori-zontally opposed o.h.v. engine. Bore and stroke 86 x 66 mm. Displacement 2,287 c.c. Max. speed 80 m.p.h. 3-speed or Powerglide transmission. Swing axle indepen-dent rear suspension.

CHRYSLER   U.S.A. 1960

New Yorker, 2-door hardtop. V-8 o.h.v. engine. Bore and stroke 106 x 95 mm. Displacement 6,769 c.c. Max. b.h.p. 355 at 4600 r.p.m. TorqueFlite transmission. Unit-construc-tion body.

CHRYSLER   U.S.A. 1960

Valiant V-200. 6-cyl. o.h.v. engine in line. Bore and stroke 86 x 79 mm. Displacement 2,789 c.c. Max. b.h.p. 355 at 4600 r.p.m. TorqueFlite transmission. Unit-construction body.

DODGE   U.S.A. 1960

Dart, club sedan. 6-cyl. water-cooled o.h.v. engine in line. Bore and stroke 86.36 x 104.77· mm. Displacement 3,682 c.c. Max. b.h.p. 147 at 4,000 r.p.m. 3 speeds. Max. speed approx. 88 m.p.h.

FORD   U.S.A. 1960

Falcon, Tudor sedan. 6-cyl. o.h.v. engine in line. Bore and stroke 3.50 x 2.50 inches. Displacement 144.3 cu. in. Max. b.h.p. 90 at 4200 r.p.m. Max. speed 80 m.p.h. 3-speed or Ford-O-Matic automatic transmission. First Ford compact.

IMPERIAL   U.S.A. 1960

Le Baron, 4-door hardtop. V-8 water-cooled o.h.v. engine. Bore and stroke 4.18 x 3.75 inches. Displacement 413 cu. in. Max. b.h.p. 350 at 4600 r.p.m. Automatic transmission. Max. speed approx. 118 m.p.h.

MERCURY   U.S.A. 1960

Monterey, 4-door hardtop V-8 o.h.v. engine. Bore and stroke 3.80 x 3.44 inches. Displacement 312 cu. in. Max. b.h.p. 205 at 4000 r.p.m. Max. speed 95 m.p.h. 3-speed or Merc-O-Matic transmission.

PONTIAC   U.S.A. 1960

Catalina, sports sedan. V-8 water-cooled o.h.v. engine Bore and stroke 4.06 x 3.75 inches. Displacement 389 cu. in. Max. b.h.p. 215 at 3600 r.p.m. 3-speeds or automatic transmission. Max. speed approx. 110 m.p.h.

SKODA CZECHOSLOVAKIA 1961

Felicia, convertible. 4-cyl. o.h.v. engine in line. Bore and stroke 68 x 75 mm. Displacement 1,089 c.c. Max. b.h.p. 53 at 5,500 r.p.m. 4 speeds. Max. speed 85 m.p.h. Convertible body based on Octavia chassis.

D.B. (Deutsch et Bonnet). FRANCE 1961

Le Mans, convertible. 2-cyl. air-cooled, horizontally opposed, o.h.v. engine (Panhard). Bore and stroke 85 x 75 mm. Displacement 850 c.c. Max. b.h.p. 58 at 6,200 r.p.m. 4 speeds. Max. speed 100 m.p.h. D.B. partnership terminated in 1962.

FACEL FRANCE 1961

Facellia. 4-cyl. d.o.h.c. engine in line. Bore and stroke 82 x 78 mm. Displacement 1,647 c.c. Max. b.h.p. 115 at 6,400 r.p.m. 4 speeds. Max. speed 105 m.p.h. Volvo or Austin-Healey engines in later models.

PEUGEOT FRANCE 1961

404, saloon. 4-cyl. o.h.v. engine in line. Bore and stroke 84 x 73 m.m. Displacement 1,618 c.c. Max. b.h.p. 72 at 5,400 r.p.m. 4 speeds. Max. speed 85 m.p.h. Body design by Pininfarina, modified by Boschetti.

RENAULT FRANCE 1961

R4 L. 4-cyl. o.h.v. engine in line. Bore and stroke 54 x 80 mm. Displacement 747 c.c. Max. b.h.p. 28 at 4,500 r.p.m. 3 speeds. Max. speed 65 m.p.h. Front wheel drive. Renault's first front-drive car.

BORGWARD GERMANY 1961

Isabella TS, convertible. 4-cyl. engine. Bore and stroke 65 x 72 mm. Displacement 956 c.c. Max. b.h.p. 41 at 4,500 r.p.m. 4 speeds. Max. speed 80 m.p.h.

FORD GERMANY 1961

Taunus 17M, tourenlimousine. 4-cyl. o.h.v. engine in line. Bore and stroke 84 x 77 mm. Displacement 1,698 c.c. Max. b.h.p. 60 at 4,250 r.p.m. 3/4 speeds. Max. speed 80 m.p.h. Saxomat automatic clutch optional. Body design by Wesley P. Dahlberg.

GOLIATH GERMANY 1961

1100, coupé. 4-cyl. o.h.v. engine. Bore and stroke 74 x 64 mm. Displacement 1,093 c.c. Max. b.h.p. 55 at 5,000 r.p.m. 4 speeds. Max. speed 80 m.p.h. Last of the Goliaths.

N.S.U.-FIAT   GERMANY 1961

Weinsberg, coupé. 2-cyl. air-cooled, rear-mounted, o.h.v. engine in line. Bore and stroke 67 x 70 mm. Displacement 499 c.c. Max. b.h.p. 21 at 4,000 r.p.m. 4 speeds. Max. speed 55 m.p.h.

OPEL   GERMANY 1961

Kapitän L, sedan. 6-cyl. o.h.v. engine in line. Bore and stroke 85 x 77 mm. Displacement 2,605 c.c. Max. b.h.p. 100 at 4,300 r.p.m. Max. speed 95 m.p.h. 3-speed or automatic transmission. Restyled in 1964.

A.C.   GREAT BRITAIN 1961

Greyhound, 4 pass. sports coupé. 6-cyl. o.h.v. engine in line (Bristol). Bore and stroke 66 x 96 mm. Displacement 1,971 c.c. Max. b.h.p. 126 at 6,000 r.p.m. Max. speed 110 m.p.h. 4 speeds with or without Overdrive.

ALEXANDER-TURNER   GREAT BRITAIN 1961

Sports roadster. 4-cyl. o.h.v. engine in line (tuned Austin). Bore and stroke 63 x 76 mm. Displacement 948 c.c. Max. b.h.p. 61 at 6,000 r.p.m. 4 speeds. Max. speed 90 m.p.h.

BENTLEY GREAT BRITAIN 1961

S 2 Continental, hardtop. V-8 o.h.v. engine (aluminum).
Bore and stroke 104 x 91 mm. Displacement 6,230 c.c.
Max. b.h.p. approx. 300. Rolls-Royce Hydra-Matic trans-
mission.

FAIRTHORPE GREAT BRITAIN 1961

Zeta, roadster. 6-cyl. o.h.v. engine in line (6 carburetors;
Ford Zephyr tuned by Raymond Mays). Bore and stroke
82 x 80 mm. Displacement 2,553 c.c. Max. b.h.p. 143 at
5,800 r.p.m. 4 speeds. Max. speed 115 m.p.h.

FORD GREAT BRITAIN 1961

Consul Classic 315, sedan. 4-cyl. o.h.v. engine in line.
Bore and stroke 81 x 65 mm. Displacement 1,340 c.c.
Max. b.h.p. 54 at 4,900 r.p.m. 4 speeds. Max. speed 75
m.p.h. Replaced in 1963 by the Cortina.

JAGUAR GREAT BRITAIN 1961

E, convertible. 6-cyl. d.o.h.c. engine in line. Bore and
stroke 87 x 106 mm. Displacement 3,781 c.c. Max. b.h.p.
265 at 5,500 r.p.m. 4 speeds. Max. speed 145 m.p.h.
All-independent suspension.

FERRARI   ITALY 1961

Superamerica, 400/SA. V-12 s.o.h.c. engine. Bore and
stroke 77 x 71 mm. Displacement 3,967 c.c. Max. b.h.p.
400 at 6,750 r.p.m. Max. speed 180 m.p.h. 4-speed with
Overdrive. Body by Pininfarina. Made to order.

INNOCENTI   ITALY 1961

950, convertible. 4-cyl. o.h.v. engine in line. Bore and
stroke 63 x 76 mm. Displacement 948 c.c. Max. b.h.p. 48
at 5,200 r.p.m. 4 speeds. Max. speed 85 m.p.h. Body by
Carrozzeria Ghia. Italian-built Austin-Healey Sprite.

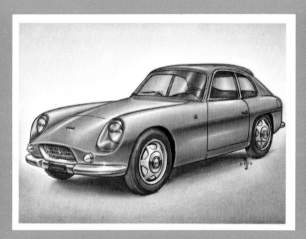

OSCA   ITALY 1961

1600 GT (aluminum). 4-cyl. d.o.h.c. engine in line. Bore
and stroke 80 x 78 mm. Displacement 1,568 c.c. Max.
b.h.p. 95 at 6,600 r.p.m. 4 speeds. Max. speed 105 m.p.h.
Body by Carrozzeria Zagato.

SIATA   ITALY 1961

750, coupé. 4-cyl. o.h.v. engine in line. Bore and stroke
62 x 64 mm. Displacement 767 c.c. Max. b.h.p. 36 at
5,000 r.p.m. 4 speeds. Max. speed 70 m.p.h. Based on
the Fiat 600.

MAZDA JAPAN 1961

R 360, coupé de luxe. V-2 air-cooled o.h.v. engine. Bore and stroke 60 x 63 mm. Displacement 356 c.c. Max. b.h.p. 16 at 5,300 r.p.m. Max. speed 55 m.p.h. (50 m.p.h. with automatic transmission). 4-speed or 2-speed automatic transmission. Built in Hiroshima by Toyo Kogyo.

MITSUBISHI JAPAN 1961

500, coach. 2-cyl. air-cooled, o.h.v. engine. Bore and stroke 70 x 64 mm. Displacement 493 c.c. Max. b.h.p. 21 at 5,000 r.p.m. 3 speeds. Max. speed 55 m.p.h.

NISSAN JAPAN 1961

Cedric. 4-cyl. o.h.v. engine in line. Bore and stroke 85 x 83 mm. Displacement 1,883 c.c. Max. b.h.p. 88 at 4,800 r.p.m. Max. speed 85 m.p.h. 4-speed or automatic transmission.

TOYOPET JAPAN 1961

Publica, coach. 2-cyl. air-cooled, horizontally opposed, o.h.v. engine. Bore and stroke 78 x 78 mm. Displacement 697 c.c. Max. b.h.p. 28 at 4,300 r.p.m. 4 speeds. Max. speed 65 m.p.h. 2-speed automatic transmission optional.

TOYOPET   JAPAN 1961

Tiara, sedan. 4-cyl. o.h.v. engine in line. Bore and stroke 77 x 78 mm. Displacement 1,453 c.c. Max. b.h.p. 63 at 4,500 r.p.m. Max. speed 80 m.p.h. Export version of Corona.

SAAB   SWEDEN 1961

GT 750, coach. 3-cyl. 2-stroke engine in line. Bore and stroke 66 x 73 mm. Displacement 748 c.c. Max. b.h.p. 58 at 5,000 r.p.m. 4 speeds. Max. speed 95 m.p.h. Front wheel drive.

VOLVO   SWEDEN 1961

P 1800. 4-cyl. o.h.v. engine in line. Bore and stroke 84 x 80 mm. Displacement 1,780 c.c. Max. b.h.p. 100 at 5,500 r.p.m. 4 speeds. Max. speed 105 m.p.h. Overdrive optional. Body design by Pelle Pettersson.

BUICK   U.S.A. 1961

Special V-8 o.h.v. engine (Aluminum). Bore and Stroke 3.50 x 2.80 inches. Displacement 215 cu. in. Max. b.h.p. 155 at 4400 r.p.m. Max. speed 95 m.p.h. 3-speed or automatic transmission. (Dual Path Turbine Drive).

DODGE   U.S.A. 1961

Lancer 770, 2-door hardtop. 6-cyl. o.h.v. engine in line.
Bore and stroke 3.40 x 3.12 inches. Displacement 170 cu. in.
Max. b.h.p. 101 at 4400 r.p.m. Max. speed 85 m.p.h. 3-speed
or Torqueflite transmission. Replaced by the Dart in 1962.

FORD   U.S.A. 1961

Galaxie, sedan. V-8 o.h.v. engine. Bore and stroke 4.04 x
3.78 inches. Displacement 390 cu. in. Max. b.h.p. 300 at
4600 r.p.m. Max. speed 120 m.p.h. 3-speed or automatic
transmission.

LINCOLN   U.S.A. 1961

Convertible. V-8 water-cooled o.h.v. engine. Bore and
stroke 4.30 x 3.70 inches. Displacement 430 cu. in. Max.
b.h.p. 315 at 4100 r.p.m. Automatic transmission. Max.
speed approx. 113 m.p.h.

MERCURY   U.S.A. 1961

Comet 144, 6-cyl. o.h.v. engine in line. Bore and stroke
3.50 x 2.50 inches. Displacement 144 cu. in. Max. b.h.p. 90
at 4200 r.p.m. Max. speed 78 m.p.h. 3-speed automatic
transmission. De luxe Falcon.

OLDSMOBILE U.S.A. 1961

Dynamic 88 Holiday, sedan. V-8 o.h.v. engine. Bore and stroke 4.12 x 3.68 inches. Displacement 394 cu. in. Max. b.h.p. 250 at 4200 r.p.m. Max. speed 100 m.p.h. 3-speed manual or hydra-matic transmission.

PONTIAC U.S.A. 1961

Tempest, sedan. 4-cyl. water-cooled o.h.v. engine in line. Bore and stroke 4.06 x 3.75 inches. Displacement 194.5 cu. in. Max. b.h.p. 110 at 3800 r.p.m. Max. speed approx. 84 m.p.h. 3-speeds. V-8 engine available.

RAMBLER U.S.A. 1961

American, custom saloon. 6-cyl. s.v. engine in line. Bore and stroke 3.12 x 4.25 inches. Displacement 196 cu. in. Max. b.h.p. 125 at 4200 r.p.m. Max. speed 85 m.p.h. 3-speed or automatic transmission. Body design by Edmund Anderson.

ZAPOROZHETS U.S.S.R. 1961

ZAZ, coupé. V-4 air-cooled, rear-mounted, o.h.v. engine. Bore and stroke 66 x 55 mm. Displacement 746 c.c. Max. b.h.p. 20 at 4,000 r.p.m. 4 speeds. Max. speed 55 m.p.h.

AUSTIN   **AUSTRALIA 1962**

Freeway 6 saloon. 6-cyl. o.h.v. engine in line. Bore and stroke 76 x 89 mm. Displacement 2,433 c.c. Max. b.h.p. 82 at 4,300 r.p.m. Max. speed 85 m.p.h. 3-speed or Borg-Warner automatic transmission. BMC has large plants in Australia.

RAMSES   **EGYPT 1962**

Gamila. 2-cyl. air-cooled engine in line (N.S.U. Prinz III). Bore and stroke 75 x 66 mm. Displacement 583 c.c. Max. b.h.p. 35 at 5,500 r.p.m. 4 speeds. Max. speed 70 m.p.h.

CITROËN   **FRANCE 1962**

Ami-6, saloon. 2-cyl. air-cooled, horizontally opposed o.h.v. engine. Bore and stroke 74 x 70 mm. Displacement 602 c.c. Max. b.h.p. 22 at 5,000 r.p.m. 4 speeds. Max. speed 65 m.p.h. Front wheel drive. Front and rear springs interconnected on each side.

RENAULT   **FRANCE 1962**

Caravelle, coupé. 4-cyl. rear-mounted, o.h.v. engine in line. Bore and stroke 65 x 72 mm. Displacement 956 c.c. Max. b.h.p. 44 at 5,500 r.p.m. 4 speeds. Max. speed 80 m.p.h. Known as Floride in Europe.

SIMCA FRANCE 1962

1000 saloon, 4-cyl. rear-mounted o.h.v. engine in line. Bore and stroke 86 x 65 m.m. Displacement 944 c.c. Max. b.h.p. 52 at 4400 r.p.m. 4-speeds. Max. speed 42 m.p.h. First rear-engine Simca.

B.M.W. GERMANY 1962

1500. 4-cyl. s.o.h.c. engine. Bore and stroke 82 x 71 mm. Displacement 1,499 c.c. Max. b.h.p. 80 at 5,700 r.p.m. 4 speeds. Max. speed 90 m.p.h. Developed into the 1600, 1800 and 2000.

B.M.W. GERMANY 1962

3200 CS, coupé. V-8 o.h.v. engine. Bore and stroke 82 x 75 mm. Displacement 3,168 c.c. Max. b.h.p. 160 at 5,600 r.p.m. 5 speeds. Max. speed 120 m.p.h. Body by Carrozzeria Bertone. Limited production.

GLAS GERMANY 1962

1004 S, convertible. 4-cyl. s.o.h.c. engine in line. Bore and stroke 72 x 61 mm. Displacement 992 c.c. Max. b.h.p. 42 at 4,800 r.p.m. 4 speeds. Max. speed 80 m.p.h. First Glas (formerly Goggomobil) sports car.

MERCEDES-BENZ GERMANY 1962

220 SE, cabriolet. 6-cyl. s.o.h.c. engine. Fuel injection. Bore and stroke 80 x 73 mm. Displacement 2,195 c.c. Max. b.h.p. 134 at 5,000 r.p.m. Max. speed 110 m.p.h. 4-speed or Daimler-Benz automatic transmission. Single-joint swing axle independent rear suspension with low pivot point.

N.S.U.-FIAT GERMANY 1962

Jagst 770 Riviera, spider. 4-cyl. rear-mounted, o.h.v. engine in line. Bore and stroke 62 x 64 mm. Displacement 767 c.c. Max. b.h.p. 32 at 4,800 r.p.m. 4 speeds. Max. speed 72 m.p.h. Body by Vignale. German sports model of Fiat 600.

N.S.U. GERMANY 1962

Prinz, coach. 2-cyl. air-cooled, rear-mounted, o.h.v. engine in line. Bore and stroke 76 x 66 mm. Displacement 598 c.c. Max. b.h.p. 36 at 5,500 r.p.m. 4 speeds. Max. speed 72 m.p.h. Engine derived from motorcycle engineering.

OPEL GERMANY 1962

Rekord, coupé. 4-cyl. o.h.v. engine in line. Bore and stroke 85 x 74 mm. Displacement 1,680 c.c. Max. b.h.p. 67 at 4,300 r.p.m. 3 speeds. Max. speed 85 m.p.h. Olymat automatic clutch optional. Series restyled in 1963.

VOLKSWAGEN GERMANY 1962

VW 1500, saloon. 4-cyl. air-cooled, rear-mounted, horizontally opposed o.h.v. engine. Bore and stroke 83 x 69 mm. Displacement 1,493 c.c. Max. b.h.p. 53 at 4,000 r.p.m. 4 speeds. Max. speed ± 80 m.p.h. Swing-axle independent rear suspension.

ALVIS GREAT BRITAIN 1962

TD 21, super coupé. 6-cyl. o.h.v. engine in line. Bore and stroke 84 x 90 mm. Displacement 2,993 c.c. Max. b.h.p. 119 at 4,500 r.p.m. Max. speed ± 110 m.p.h. 4-speed with Overdrive. Body by Graber (Switzerland).

DAIMLER GREAT BRITAIN 1962

Majestic Major. V-8 o.h.v. engine. Bore and stroke 95 x 80 mm. Displacement 4,560 c.c. Max. b.h.p. 223 at 5,500 r.p.m. Max. speed 110 m.p.h. Borg-Warner automatic transmission. Built as Rolls-Royce rival.

FORD GREAT BRITAIN 1962

Zodiac Mk III, sedan. 6-cyl. o.h.v. engine in line. Bore and stroke 83 x 80 mm. Displacement 2,553 c.c. Max. b.h.p. 109 at 4,800 r.p.m. Max. speed 95 m.p.h. 4-speed or Borg-Warner automatic transmission. De luxe version of the Zephyr.

JAGUAR GREAT BRITAIN 1962

Mk X. 6-cyl. d.o.h.c. engine in line. Bore and stroke 87 x 106 mm. Displacement 3,781 c.c. Max. b.h.p. 265 at 5,500 r.p.m. Max. speed 115 m.p.h. 4-speed or Borg-Warner automatic transmission. All-independent suspension.

LAGONDA GREAT BRITAIN 1962

Rapide. 6-cyl. d.o.h.c. engine in line (Aston Martin). Bore and stroke 96 x 92 mm. Displacement 3,995 c.c. Max. b.h.p. 236 at 5,000 r.p.m. Max. speed $\pm$ 120 m.p.h. Borg-Warner automatic transmission or 4-speed David Brown gearbox.

RILEY GREAT BRITAIN 1962

1.5, saloon. 4-cyl. o.h.v. engine in line (2 carburetors). Bore and stroke 73 x 89 mm. Displacement 1,489 c.c. Max. b.h.p. 69 at 5,400 r.p.m. 4 speeds. Max. speed 85 m.p.h. Introduced in 1957.

SINGER GREAT BRITAIN 1962

Vogue, saloon. 4-cyl. o.h.v. engine in line. Bore and stroke 82 x 76 mm. Displacement 1,592 c.c. Max. b.h.p. 67 at 4,800 r.p.m. Max. speed 80 m.p.h. 4-speed or Easidrive automatic transmission. De luxe version of Hillman Super Minx.

TRIUMPH　　　　　　　　　　**GREAT BRITAIN** 1962

TR 4, roadster. 4-cyl. o.h.v. engine in line. Bore and stroke 86 x 92 mm. Displacement 2,138 c.c. Max. b.h.p. 105 at 4,750 r.p.m. Max. speed 105 m.p.h. 4-speed with or without Overdrive. Body design by Giovanni Michelotti.

VANDEN PLAS　　　　　　　**GREAT BRITAIN** 1962

Princess Mk II, 3 Liter saloon. 6-cyl. o.h.v. engine in line. Bore and stroke 83 x 89 mm. Displacement 2,913 c.c. Max. b.h.p. 120 at 4,750 r.p.m. Max. speed 110 m.p.h. 3-speed or automatic transmission. Replaced in 1965 by Rolls-Royce engined Princess R.

SABRA　　　　　　　　　　　**ISRAEL** 1962

Sports convertible. 4-cyl. o.h.v. engine in line. Bore and stroke 83 x 80 mm. Displacement 1,703 c.c. Max. b.h.p. 61 at 4,400 r.p.m. 4 speeds. Max. speed 90 m.p.h. Built in Israel under Reliant license.

FIAT　　　　　　　　　　　　　**ITALY** 1962

1300, saloon. 4-cyl. o.h.v. engine in line. Bore and stroke 72 x 80 mm. Displacement 1,295 c.c. Max. b.h.p. 72 at 5,200 r.p.m. 4 speeds. Max. speed 80 m.p.h. Available with 1500 engine.

LANCIA   ITALY 1962

Flavia, convertible. 4-cyl. horizontally opposed, o.h.v.
engine. Bore and stroke 82 x 71 mm. Displacement 1,500
c.c. Max. b.h.p. 78 at 5,200 r.p.m. 4 speeds. Max. speed
90 m.p.h. Body by Carrozzeria Vignale. First front wheel
drive Lancia.

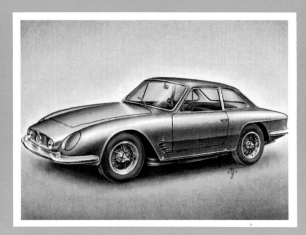

MASERATI   ITALY 1962

5000 GT. V-8 d.o.h.c. engine. Fuel injection. Bore and
stroke 94 x 89 mm. Displacement 4,950 c.c. Max. b.h.p.
325 at 5,500 r.p.m. Max. speed 162 m.p.h. Body by
Carrozzeria Frua to design by Michelotti. Made to order.

HINO   JAPAN 1962

Contessa, saloon. 4-cyl. rear-mounted o.h.v. engine in
line. Bore and stroke 60 x 79 mm. Displacement 893 c.c.
3 speeds. Max. speed 65 m.p.h. Based on Renault 4 CV.

MAZDA   JAPAN 1962

Carol de luxe, coach. 4-cyl. rear transversely mounted
o.h.v. engine in line. Bore and stroke 46 x 54 mm. Displacement 358 c.c. Max. b.h.p. 22 at 6,800 r.p.m. 4 speeds.
Max. speed 60 m.p.h.

DAF   THE NETHERLANDS 1962

Daffodil. 2-cyl. air-cooled, horizontally opposed, o.h.v. engine. Bore and stroke 86 x 65 mm. Displacement 746 c.c. Max. b.h.p. 30 at 4,000 r.p.m. Max. speed 65 m.p.h. Variomatic all-mechanical automatic transmission. Front engine, rear wheel drive.

CADILLAC   U.S.A. 1962

Fleetwood 60 Special, sedan V-8 water-cooled o.h.v. engine. Bore and stroke 4.00 x 3.87 inches. Displacement 390 cu. in. Max. b.h.p. 325 at 4800 r.p.m. Automatic transmission. Max. speed approx. 125 m.p.h.

CHECKER   U.S.A. 1962

Marathon, sedan. 6-cyl. o.h.v. engine in line (continental). Bore and stroke 3.31 x 4.37 inches. Displacement 225.7 cu. in. Max. b.h.p. 142 at 4,400 r.p.m. Max. speed 85-90 m.p.h. 3-speed or automatic transmission.

CHEVROLET   U.S.A. 1962

Chevy II, 300, 2-door saloon. 4-cyl. o.h.v. engine in line. Bore and stroke 3.87 x 3.25 inches. Displacement 153 cu. in. Max. b.h.p. 90 at 4000 r.p.m. Max. speed 85 m.p.h. 3-speed or powerglide transmission. Available with 6-cyl. engine.

CHRYSLER U.S.A. 1962

Newport, sedan. V-8 water-cooled o.h.v. engine. Bore and stroke 4.12 x 3.37 inches. Displacement 361 cu. in. Max. b.h.p. 265 at 4400 r.p.m. 3-speed or automatic transmission. Max. speed approx. 103 m.p.h.

DODGE U.S.A. 1962

Dart, 4-door hardtop. V-8 o.h.v. engine. Bore and stroke 3.91 x 3.31 inches. Displacement 318 cu. in. Max. b.h.p. 230 at 4400 r.p.m Max. speed 100-110 m.p.h. 3-speed or automatic transmission. Replaced the Lancer.

FORD U.S.A. 1962

Thunderbird, convertible. V-8 water-cooled o.h.v. engine. Bore and stroke 4.05 x 3.78 inches. Displacement 390 cu. in. Max. b.h.p. 300 at 4600 r.p.m. Automatic transmission. Max. speed approx. 125 m.p.h.

OLDSMOBILE U.S.A. 1962

F-85 Cutlass, coupe. V-8 o.h.v. engine. Bore and stroke 3.50 x 2.80 inches. Displacement 215 cu. in. Max. b.h.p. 155 at 4800 r.p.m. Max. speed 95 m.p.h 3-speed or Hydra-matic transmission. Turbocharged engine available.

RAMBLER   U.S.A. 1962

Classic, de luxe sedan. 6-cyl. o.h.v. engine in line. Bore and stroke 3.12 x 4.25 inches. Displacement 195.6 cu. in. Max. b.h.p. 127 at 4200 r.p.m. Max. speed ± 90 m.p.h. 3-speed or automatic transmission.

HOLDEN   AUSTRALIA 1963

Sedan. 6-cyl. o.h.v. engine in line. Bore and stroke 79 x 76 mm. Displacement 2,262 c.c. Max. b.h.p. 75 at 4,200 r.p.m. Max. speed 85 m.p.h. Australian division of General Motors.

WILLYS   BRAZIL 1963

Aero 2600, sedan. 6-cyl. o.h.v. engine in line. Bore and stroke 79 x 89 mm. Displacement 2,638 c.c. Max. b.h.p. 110 at 4,400 r.p.m. 3 speeds. Max. speed 90 m.p.h. Built by Willys-Overland do Brazil.

ACADIAN   CANADA 1963

Hardtop. 6-cyl. o.h.v. engine in line. Bore and stroke 91 x 83 mm. Displacement 3,186 c.c. Max. b.h.p. 120 at 4,400 r.p.m. Max. speed 90 m.p.h. 3-speed or automatic transmission.

ALPINE   **FRANCE 1963**

2 + 2, coupé (fiberglass), 4-cyl. rear-mounted o.h.v. engine in line (Renault). Bore and stroke 58 x 80 mm. Displacement 845 c.c. Max. b.h.p. 40 at 5,000 r.p.m. 3/4 speeds. Max. 85 m.p.h.

RENAULT   **FRANCE 1963**

R 8. 4-cyl. o.h.v. engine in line. Bore and stroke 65 x 72 mm. Displacement 956 c.c. Max. b.h.p. 48 at 5,200 r.p.m. 4 speeds. Max. speed 75 m.p.h. 1,108 c.c. engine available later.

D.K.W.   **GERMANY 1963**

F 12, coach. 3-cyl. 2-stroke engine in line. Bore and stroke 75 x 68 mm. Displacement 889 c.c. Max. b.h.p. 45 at 4,300 r.p.m. 4 speeds. Max. speed 75 m.p.h. Saxomat automatic clutch optional. Front wheel drive.

FORD   **GERMANY 1963**

Taunus 12M, coach. V-4 o.h.v. engine. Bore and stroke 80 x 59 mm. Displacement 1,183 c.c. Max. b.h.p. 50 at 5,000 r.p.m. 4 speeds. Max. speed 75 m.p.h. Front wheel drive. Based on Cardinal prototype.

MERCEDES-BENZ   GERMANY 1963

230 SL, sports coupé. 6-cyl. s.o.h.c. engine in line. Fuel injection. Bore and stroke 82 x 73 mm. Displacement 2,306 c.c. Max. b.h.p. 170 at 5,600. 4 speeds. Max. speed 120 m.p.h. Automatic transmission optional. Replaced the 190 SL and 300 SL.

N.S.U.-FIAT   GERMANY 1963

Neckar Mistral 1500, coupé. 4-cyl. o.h.v. engine in line. Bore and stroke 77 x 80 mm. Displacement 1,481 c.c. Max. b.h.p. 94 at 6,200 r.p.m. 4 speeds. Max. speed 100 m.p.h. German version of the Fiat 1500.

OPEL   GERMANY 1963

Kadett, coach. 4-cyl. o.h.v. engine in line. Bore and stroke 72 x 61 mm. Displacement 993 c.c. Max. b.h.p. 47 at 5,200 r.p.m. 4 speeds. Max. speed 70 m.p.h. Body design by Clare McKichan.

FORD   GREAT BRITAIN 1963

Cortina de luxe. 4-cyl. o.h.v. engine in line. Bore and stroke 81 x 58 mm. Displacement 1,198 c.c. Max. b.h.p. 53 at 4,800 r.p.m. 4 speeds. Max. speed 75 m.p.h. Anglia engine in base-model.

DAIMLER   GREAT BRITAIN 1963

V-8 2½ Liter, saloon. V-8 o.h.v. engine. Bore and stroke 76 x 70 mm. Displacement 2,548 c.c. Max. b.h.p. 142 at 5,800 r.p.m. Max. speed 102 m.p.h. Borg-Warner automatic transmission. Jaguar with Daimler engine and grille.

HILLMAN   GREAT BRITAIN 1963

Super Minx MK II, convertible. 4-cyl. o.h.v. engine in line. Bore and stroke 82 x 76 mm. Displacement 1,592 c.c. Max. b.h.p. 67 at 4,400 r.p.m. Max. speed 80 m.p.h. 4-speed or Easi-drive automatic transmission.

LOTUS   GREAT BRITAIN 1963

Elan, sports convertible (fiberglass). 4-cyl. d.o.h.c. engine in line (Ford-based). Bore and stroke 81 x 73 mm. Displacement 1,499 c.c. Max. b.h.p. 105 at 5,700 r.p.m. 4 speeds. Max. speed 108 m.p.h. Body design by Ronald P. Hickman.

M.G.   GREAT BRITAIN 1963

M.G.B. convertible. 4-cyl. o.h.v. engine in line. Bore and stroke 80 x 89 mm. Displacement 1,798 c.c. Max. b.h.p. 94 at 5,500 r.p.m. 4 speeds. Max. speed 102 m.p.h. Replaced M.G.A.

MORRIS   GREAT BRITAIN 1963

1100, saloon. 4-cyl. transversely mounted o.h.v. engine in line. Bore and stroke 65 x 84 mm. Displacement 1,098 c.c. Max. b.h.p. 48 at 5,100 r.p.m. 4 speeds. Max. speed 75 m.p.h. Front wheel drive. Hydrolastic water suspension system.

OGLE   GREAT BRITAIN 1963

SX 1000, coupé. 4-cyl. o.h.v. engine in line (B.M.C.-Cooper Alexander). Bore and stroke 62 x 81 mm. Displacement 997 c.c. Max. b.h.p. 69 at 6,000 r.p.m. 4 speeds. Max. speed 95 m.p.h. Front wheel drive. Body design by David Ogle.

TRIUMPH   GREAT BRITAIN 1963

Spitfire 4, convertible. 4-cyl. o.h.v. engine in line. Bore and stroke 69 x 76 mm. Displacement 1,147 c.c. Max. b.h.p. 63 at 5,700 r.p.m. 4 speeds. Max. speed 85 m.p.h. Sports version of Herald.

VAUXHALL   GREAT BRITAIN 1963

Cresta, sedan. 6-cyl. o.h.v. engine in line. Bore and stroke 83 x 83 mm. Displacement 2,651 c.c. Max. b.h.p. 113 at 4,800 r.p.m. Max. speed 93 m.p.h. 3-speed or Hydra-Matic transmission. De luxe version of Velox.

SABRA   **ISRAEL 1963**

Carmel, coach. 4-cyl. o.h.v. engine in line (Ford Anglia Super). Bore and stroke 81 x 58 mm. Displacement 1,198 c.c. Max. b.h.p. 53 at 4,800 r.p.m. 4 speeds. Max. speed 80 m.p.h.

ALFA ROMEO   **ITALY 1963**

Giulia TI. 4-cyl. d.o.h.c. engine in line. Bore and stroke 78 x 82 mm. Displacement 1,570 c.c. Max. b.h.p. 106 at 6,200 r.p.m. 5 speeds. Max. speed 100 m.p.h. Unit-construction body.

ALFA ROMEO   **ITALY 1963**

2600 Sprint, coupé. 6-cyl. d.o.h.c. engine in line. Bore and stroke 83 x 80 mm. Displacement 2,584 c.c. Max. b.h.p. 165 at 5,900 r.p.m. 5 speeds. Max. speed 130. All-coil suspension system. Body by Carrozzeria Bertone.

ASA   **ITALY 1963**

1000, coupé. 4-cyl. s.o.h.c. engine in line. Bore and stroke 69 x 69 mm. Displacement 1,032 c.c. Max. b.h.p. 97 at 7,000 r.p.m. 4 speeds Max. speed 115 m.p.h. Engine design by Ferrari.

LANCIA   ITALY 1963

Fulvia 1100, saloon. V-4 s.o h.c. engine. Bore and stroke
72 x 67 mm. Displacement 1,091 c.c. Max. b.h.p. 60 at
5,800 r.p.m. 4 speeds. Max. speed 85 m.p.h. Front wheel
drive.

ISUZU   JAPAN 1963

Belle 2000 de luxe, sedan. 4-cyl. o.h.v. engine in line.
Bore and stroke 83 x 92 mm. Displacement 1,991 c.c.
Max. b.h.p. 85 at 4,600 r.p.m. 4 speeds. Max. speed
85 m.p.h. Began by building Hillmans in 1953.

PRINCE   JAPAN 1963

Gloria de luxe, saloon. 4-cyl. o.h.v. engine in line. Bore
and stroke 84 x 84 mm. Displacement 1,862 c.c. Max.
b.h.p. 100 at 5,000 r.p.m. 4 speeds. Max. speed 85
m.p.h. Body design by Giovanni Michelotti.

TOYOPET   JAPAN 1963

Crown de luxe, saloon. 4-cyl. o.h.v. engine in line. Bore
and stroke 88 x 78 mm. Displacement 1,897 c.c. Max.
b.h.p. 95 at 5,000 r.p.m. Max. speed 85 m.p.h. 3-speed
with Overdrive or Toyoglide automatic transmission.

BUICK   U.S.A. 1963

Riviera, 2-door coupé. V-8 o.h.v. engine. Bore and stroke
4.18 x 3.64 inches. Displacement 401 cu. in. Max. b.h.p. 325
at 4400 r.p.m. Max. speed 120 m.p.h. Turbine Drive transmission. Body design by David R. Holls.

CHEVROLET   U.S.A. 1963

Corvette Sting Ray, coupé (Fiberglass). V-8 o.h.v. engine.
Bore and stroke 4.00 x 3.25 inches. Displacement 327 cu. in.
Max. b.h.p. 250 at 4400 r.p.m. Max. speed 120 m.p.h. ¾
speed or Powerglide transmission. All-independent suspension.

FORD   U.S.A. 1963

Fairlane 500, sedan, 6-cyl. water-cooled o.h.v. engine in
line. Bore and stroke 3.50 x 2.94 inches. Displacement 170
cu. in. Max. b.h.p. 101 at 4400 r.p.m. 3 speeds or automatic
transmission. Max. speed approx. 90 m.p.h.

PLYMOUTH   U.S.A. 1963

Fury, 2-door hardtop. V-8 o.h.v. engine. Bore and stroke
3.91 x 3.31 inches. Displacement 318 cu. in. Max. b.h.p 230
at 4400 r.p.m. Max. speed 108 m.p.h. Torqueflite automatic
transmission. Torsion bar independent front suspension.

PONTIAC U.S.A. 1963

Tempest Le Mans, convertible. 4-cyl. o.h.v. engine in line. Bore and stroke 4.06 x 3.75 inches. Displacement 194.5 cu. in. Max. b.h.p. 115 at 4000 r.p.m. 3 speeds. Max. speed 85 m.p.h. Swing axle, independent rear suspension.

RAMBLER U.S.A. 1963

Ambassador 990. V-8 o.h.v. engine. Bore and stroke 4.0 x 3.25 inches. Displacement 327 cu. in. Max. b.h.p. 250 at 4700 r.p.m. Max. speed 105 m.p.h. 3-speed or automatic transmission. Body design by Richard A. Teague.

STUDEBAKER U.S.A. 1963

Avanti, sports coupé (Fiberglass). V-8 supercharged o.h.v. engine. Bore and stroke 3.56 x 3.62 inches. Displacement 289 cu. in. Max. b.h.p. 280 at 4800 r.p.m. Max. speed 145 m.p.h. 4-speed or automatic transmission. Body design by Raymond Loewy.

WILLYS JEEP U.S.A. 1963

Wagoneer, station wagon 6-cyl. s.o.h.c. engine in line. Bore and stroke 3.34 x 4.37 inches. Displacement 230 cu. in. Max. b.h.p. 140 at 4000 r.p.m. 3 speeds. 4-wheel drive, 2-speed transfer case, automatic transmission available. Willys Jeep now part of Kaiser Industries.

STEYR-PUCH AUSTRIA 1964

Adria TS, coupé. 2-cyl. air-cooled, horizontally opposed, o.h.v. engine. Bore and stroke 80 x 64 mm. Displacement 643 c.c. Max. b.h.p. 30 at ± 5,400 r.p.m. 4 speeds. Max. speed 75 m.p.h. Fiat 500 with a Puch engine.

STUDEBAKER CANADA 1964

Cruiser, sedan. V-8 o.h.v. engine (Chevrolet). Bore and stroke 91 x 92 mm. Displacement 4,736 c.c. Max. b.h.p. 210 at 4,500 r.p.m. Max. speed 100 m.p.h. 3-speed or automatic transmission. Studebaker moved to Canada; South Bend engine plant taken over by Chrysler.

ARISTA FRANCE 1964

2 + 2, sport coupé (fiberglass). 2-cyl. air-cooled, horizontally opposed, o.h.v. engine (Panhard Tigre). Bore and stroke 85 x 75 mm. Displacement 848 c.c. Max. b.h.p. 60 at 5,750 r.p.m. 4 speeds. Max. speed 85 m.p.h. Front wheel drive.

PANHARD FRANCE 1964

24 CT, coupé. 2-cyl. air-cooled, horizontally opposed, o.h.v. engine. Bore and stroke 85 x 75 mm. Displacement 848 c.c. Max. b.h.p. 60 at 5,800 r.p.m. 4 speeds. Max. speed 90 m.p.h. Front wheel drive.

SIMCA   FRANCE 1964

1500, saloon. 4-cyl. o.h.v. engine in line. Bore and stroke
75 x 83 mm. Displacement 1,482 c.c. 4 speeds. Replaced
the 1951-62 Aronde.

D.K.W.   GERMANY 1964

F102, saloon. 3-cyl. 2-stroke engine in line. Bore and
stroke 81 x 76 mm. Displacement 1,175 c.c. Max. b.h.p.
68 at 4,500 r.p.m. Max. speed 80 m.p.h. 4-speed with
freewheel. With or without Saxomat automatic clutch.
Front wheel drive.

GLAS   GERMANY 1964

1300 GT. 4-cyl. s.o.h.c. engine in line. Bore and stroke
75 x 73 mm. Displacement 1,289 c.c. Max. b.h.p. 75 at
5,800 r.p.m. 4 speeds. Max. speed 100 m.p.h. Body
by Carrozzeria Frua. Belt-driven overhead camshaft.

MERCEDES-BENZ   GERMANY 1964

600, limousine. V-8 s.o.h.c. engine. Fuel injection. Bore
and stroke 103 x 95 mm. Displacement 6,329 c.c. Max.
b.h.p. 300 at 4,000 r.p.m. Max. speed 125 m.p.h. Daimler-
Benz automatic transmission. Air springs.

N.S.U.   **GERMANY 1964**

Prinz 1000, coach. 4-cyl. air-cooled, rear-mounted, s.o.h.c. engine in line. Bore and stroke 69 x 67 mm. Displacement 996 c.c. Max. b.h.p. 43 at 5,000 r.p.m. 4 speeds. Max. speed 80 m.p.h. Developed from 1958 Prinz 3.

OPEL   **GERMANY 1964**

Kadett, 2 + 2, coupé. 4-cyl. o.h.v. engine in line. Bore and stroke 72 x 61 mm. Displacement 993 c.c. Max. b.h.p. 48 at 5,400 r.p.m. 4 speeds. Max. speed. 80 m.p.h. Smallest Opel built since 1940.

PORSCHE   **GERMANY 1964**

901, sports coupé. 6-cyl. air-cooled, horizontally opposed, rear-mounted, s.o.h.c. engine. Bore and stroke 80 x 66 mm. Displacement 1,991 c.c. Max. b.h.p. 130 at 6,200 r.p.m. 5 speeds. Max. speed 120 m.p.h. Developed into the 6-cyl. 911 and 4-cyl. 912.

BOND   **GREAT BRITAIN 1964**

Equipe GT, 2 + 2, coupé. 4-cyl. o.h.v. engine in line. Bore and stroke 69 x 76 mm. Displacement 1,147 c.c. Max. b.h.p. 63 at 5,750 r.p.m. 4 speeds. Triumph Herald with Spitfire engine and fiberglass body parts.

FORD   GREAT BRITAIN 1964

Consul Corsair, coach. 4-cyl. o.h.v. engine in line. Bore
and stroke 81 x 73 mm. Displacement 1,498 c.c. Max.
b.h.p. 78 x 5,200 r.p.m. Max. speed 90 m.p.h. 4-speed
or Borg-Warner automatic transmission. Body design
by Roy Brown.

JAGUAR   GREAT BRITAIN 1964

S, saloon. 6-cyl. d.o.h.c. engine. Bore and stroke 87 x 106
mm. Displacement 3,781 c.c. Max. b.h.p. 220 at 5,500
r.p.m. 4-speed or Borg-Warner automatic transmission.
Max. speed 120 m.p.h. Independent rear suspension
with dual coil springs.

MORGAN   GREAT BRITAIN 1964

Plus 4 Plus, sports coupé (fiberglass). 4-cyl. o.h.v. engine
in line (Triumph TR-4). Bore and stroke 86 x 92 mm.
Displacement 2,138 c.c. Max. b.h.p. 105 at 4,750 r.p.m.
4 speeds. Max. speed ± 110 m.p.h.

ROVER   GREAT BRITAIN 1964

2000, saloon. 4-cyl. s.o.h.c. engine in line. Bore and
stroke 86 x 86 mm. Displacement 1,978 c.c. Max. b.h.p.
90 at 5,000 r.p.m. 4 speeds. Max. speed 100 m.p.h. Body
design by David Bache.

TRIUMPH　　　　　　　　　**GREAT BRITAIN 1964**

2000, saloon. 6-cyl. o.h.v. engine. Bore and stroke 75 x 76 mm. Displacement 1,998 c.c. Max. b.h.p. 90 at 5,000 r.p.m. Max. speed 95 m.p.h. 4-speed or Borg-Warner automatic transmission. Body design by Giovanni Michelotti.

AUTOBIANCHI　　　　　　　　　**ITALY 1964**

Stellina, cabriolet. 4-cyl. o.h.v. engine. Bore and stroke 62 x 64 mm. Displacement 767 c.c. Max. b.h.p. 32 at 4,800 r.p.m. 4 speeds. Max. speed 75 m.p.h. Based on Fiat 600.

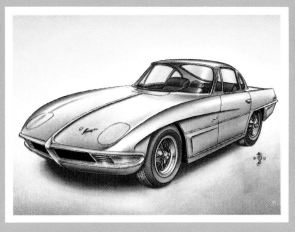

FERRARI　　　　　　　　　**ITALY 1964**

330 GT, 2 + 2, coupé. V-12 s.o.h.c. engine. Bore and stroke 77 x 71 mm. Displacement 3,967 c.c. Max. b.h.p. 300 at 7,000 r.p.m. Max. speed 150 m.p.h. 4-speed with Overdrive. Body by Pininfarina.

LAMBORGHINI　　　　　　　　　**ITALY 1964**

3500 GT Velox, coupé. V-12 d.o.h.c. engine. Bore and stroke 77 x 62 mm. Displacement 3,464 c.c. Max. b.h.p. 360 at 8,000 r.p.m. 5 speeds. Max. speed 170 m.p.h. Body by Carrozzeria Touring.

MASERATI   **ITALY 1964**

Quattroporte. V-8 d.o.h.c. engine. Bore and stroke 88 x 85 mm. Displacement 4,136 c.c. Max. b.h.p. 290 at 5,200 r.p.m. 5 speeds. Max. speed 140 m.p.h. Unit-construction body by Carrozzeria Frua.

MORETTI   **ITALY 1964**

2500 SS, spider. 6-cyl. o.h.v. engine in line (based on Fiat 2300 with 2 carburetors). Bore and stroke 81 x 80 mm. Displacement 2,454 c.c. Max. b.h.p. 150 at 5,800 r.p.m. 4 speeds. Max. speed 120 m.p.h.

SUNBEAM   **ITALY 1964**

Venezia, coupé. 4-cyl. o.h.v. engine in line. Bore and stroke 82 x 76 mm. Displacement 1,592 c.c. Max. b.h.p. 94 at 5,800 r.p.m. 4 speeds with Overdrive. Max. speed 100 m.p.h. Rapier with Touring body, assembled in Italy.

DATSUN   **JAPAN 1964**

410, sedan. 4-cyl. o.h.v. engine. Bore and stroke 73 x 71 mm. Displacement 1,189 c.c. Max. b.h.p. 60 at 5,000 r.p.m. 3/4 speeds. Max. speed 84 m.p.h. Body design in consultation with Pininfarina.

HONDA   JAPAN 1964

500, sports convertible. 4-cyl. d.o.h.c. engine. Bore and
stroke 54 x 58 mm. Displacement 531 c.c. Max. b.h.p.
42 at 8,000 r.p.m. 4/5 speeds. Max. speed 80 m.p.h.
Chain drive.

MITSUBISHI   JAPAN 1964

Colt 1000, sedan. 4-cyl. o.h.v. engine in line. Bore and
stroke 72 x 60 mm. Displacement 977 c.c. Max. b.h.p.
51 at 6,000 r.p.m. 4 speeds. Max. speed 75 m.p.h. Japan's
largest industrial combine.

APOLLO   U.S.A. 1964

3500 GT, sports coupé. V-8 o.h.v. engine (Buick aluminum
V-8). Bore and stroke 89 x 71 mm. Displacement 3,532
c.c. Max. b.h.p. 203 at 5,000 r.p.m. 4 speeds. Max. speed
130 m.p.h.

CHEVROLET   U.S.A. 1964

Chevelle, Malibu SS, coupé. V-8 o.h.v. engine. Bore and
stroke 3.87 x 3.0 inches. Displacement 283 cu. in. Max.
b.h.p. 195 at 4800 r.p.m. 3/4 speeds or powerglide transmission.

CHRYSLER   U.S.A. 1964

Turbo Dart, hardtop. Chrysler gas turbine engine with
rotating heat exchangers. Max. b.h.p. 130 at 44,600 r.p.m.
Max. speed 95 m.p.h. TorqueFlite transmission. Turbine
car for regular use. 50 built — none for sale.

DODGE   U.S.A. 1964

Polara 500, 2-door hardtop. V-8 o.h.v. engine. Bore and
stroke 4.25 x 3.38 inches. Displacement 383 cu. in. Max.
b.h.p. 330 at 4600 r.p.m. Max. speed 110 m.p.h. 3/4 speeds
or automatic transmission. Body design under direction of
Elwood P. Engel.

FORD   U.S.A. 1964

Thunderbird. V-8 o.h.v. engine. Bore and stroke 4.05 x 3.78
inches. Displacement 390 cu. in. Max. b.h.p. 300 at 4600
r.p.m. Max. speed 110-115 m.p.h. Cruise-O-Matic transmission.

IMPERIAL   U.S.A. 1964

Imperial Crown, 4-door hardtop. V-8 o.h.v. engine. Bore
and stroke 4.19 x 3.75 inches. Displacement 413 cu. in.
Max. b.h.p. 340 at 4600 r.p.m. Max. speed 115 m.p.h.
TorqueFlite automatic transmission. Seperate Frame and
body.

PONTIAC   U.S.A. 1964

Grand Prix sports coupé. 2-door hardtop. V-8 o.h.v. engine.
Bore and stroke 4.09 x 4.0 inches. Displacement 421 cu. in.
Max. b.h.p. 350 at 4600 r.p.m. Max. speed 120 m.p.h. Hydra-
Matic automatic transmission. Body design under direction
of Jack Humbert.

RAMBLER   U.S.A. 1964

American 440 H. hardtop. 6-cyl. o.h.v. engine in line. Bore
and stroke 3.12 x 4.25 inches. Displacement 195.6 cu. in.
Max. b.h.p. 138 at 4500 r.p.m. Max. speed ± 90 m.p.h.
3-speed or Borg-Warner automatic transmission. Body
design by Richard A. Teague.

SKODA   CZECHOSLOVAKIA 1965

1000 MB, sedan. 4-cyl. o.h.v. engine. Bore and stroke
68 x 68 mm. Displacement 988 c.c. Max. b.h.p. 45 at
4,650 r.p.m. 4 speeds. Max. speed 75 m.p.h. First rear-
engine Skoda.

MATRA   FRANCE 1965

Djet V S, coupé. 4-cyl. midships-mounted o.h.v. engine
(Renault). Bore and stroke 70 x 72 mm. Displacement
1,108 c.c. Max. b.h.p. 70 at 6,000 r.p.m. 4 speeds.
Max. speed 107 m.p.h. Based on Rene Bonnet's prototype.

RENAULT   FRANCE 1965

R 16, sedan/station wagon. 4-cyl. o.h.v. engine. Bore and stroke 76 x 81 mm. Displacement 1,470 c.c. Max. b.h.p. 59 at 5,000 r.p.m. 4 speeds. Max. speed 93 m.p.h. Front wheel drive.

TRABANT   EAST GERMANY 1965

601, coach. 2-cyl. 2-stroke engine in line. Bore and stroke 72 x 73 mm. Displacement 595 c.c. Max. b.h.p. 26 at 3,900 r.p.m. 4 speeds. Max. speed 62 m.p.h. Front wheel drive.

FORD   GERMANY 1965

Taunus 20M TS, coach. V-6 o.h.v. engine. Bore and stroke 84 x 60 mm. Displacement 1,998 c.c. Max. b.h.p. 90 at 5,000 r.p.m. 4 speeds. Max. speed 103 m.p.h. Body design by Wesley P. Dahlberg.

GLAS   GERMANY 1965

1700, sedan. 4-cyl. s.o.h.c. engine. Bore and stroke 78 x 88 mm. Displacement 1,682 c.c. Max. b.h.p. 80 at 4,800 r.p.m. 4 speeds. Max. speed 93 m.p.h. V-8 sports model available.

223

OPEL   GERMANY 1965

Diplomat, sedan. V-8 engine (Chevrolet). Bore and stroke
98 x 76 mm. Displacement 4,554 c.c. Max. b.h.p. 220 at
4,600 r.p.m. Max. speed 124 m.p.h. 4-speed or Powerglide
transmission. Body design by Clare McKichan.

VOLKSWAGEN   GERMANY 1965

Coach de luxe. 4-cyl. air-cooled, horizontally opposed,
rear-mounted, o.h.v. engine. Bore and stroke 77 x 64
mm. Displacement 1,192 c.c. Max. b.h.p. 40 at 3,900
r.p.m. 4 speeds. Max. speed 71 m.p.h. Body unchanged
since 1939 Berlin Auto Show.

AUSTIN   GREAT BRITAIN 1965

1800, sedan. 4-cyl. transversely mounted o.h.v. engine.
Bore and stroke 80 x 89 mm. Displacement 1,798 c.c.
Max. b.h.p. 84 at 5,300 r.p.m. 4 speeds. Max. speed 90
m.p.h. Front wheel drive.

HUMBER   GREAT BRITAIN 1965

Imperial, sedan. 6-cyl. o.h.v. engine (2 carburetors). Bore
and stroke 87 x 83 mm. Displacement 2,965 c.c. Max.
b.h.p. 128.5 at 5,000 r.p.m. Max. speed 100 m.p.h.
Borg-Warner automatic transmission. Rootes Group's
prestige car.

RELIANT   GREAT BRITAIN 1965

Rebel, coach. 4-cyl. o.h.v. engine. Bore and stroke
56 x 61 mm. Displacement 598 c.c. Max. b.h.p. 27 at
5,250 r.p.m. 4 speeds. Max. speed 62 m.p.h. Ford-
powered Scimitar also from Reliant.

SINGER   GREAT BRITAIN 1965

Chamois, coach. 4-cyl. s.o.h.c. rear-mounted engine. Bore
and stroke 68 x 60 mm. Displacement 875 c.c. Max. b.h.p.
42 at 5,000 r.p.m. 4 speeds. Max. speed 78 m.p.h. De
luxe version of Hillman Imp.

VAUXHALL   GREAT BRITAIN 1965

VX 4/90, saloon. 4-cyl. o.h.v. engine (2 carburetors).
Bore and stroke 82 x 76 mm. Displacement 1,594 c.c.
Max. b.h.p. 86 at 5,200 r.p.m. 4 speeds. Max. speed
91 m.p.h. Sports version of the Victor.

AUTOBIANCHI   ITALY 1965

Primula, station wagon. 4-cyl. transversely mounted o.h.v.
engine. Bore and stroke 72 x 75 mm. Displacement 1,221
c.c. Max. b.h.p. 57 at 5,200 r.p.m. 4 speeds. Max. speed
84 m.p.h. Front wheel drive. Design by Fiat's engineering
department.

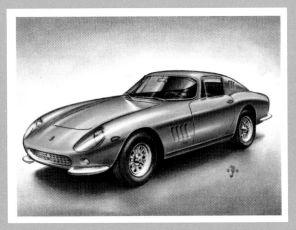

FERRARI   **ITALY 1965**

275 GTB, coupé. V-12 s.o.h.c. engine. Bore and stroke 77 x 59 mm. Displacement 3,285 c.c. Max. b.h.p. 280 at 7,500 r.p.m. 5 speeds. Max. speed 168 m.p.h. Body by Pininfarina.

FIAT   **ITALY 1965**

850 Super, coach. 4-cyl. rear-mounted o.h.v. engine. Bore and stroke 65 x 64 mm. Displacement 843 c.c. Max. b.h.p. 42 at 5,100 r.p.m. 4 speeds. Max. speed 78 m.p.h. Between Fiat 600 and 1100.

LANCIA   **ITALY 1965**

Flaminia C 3 2800, supersports. V-6 water-cooled o.h.v. engine (3 carburetors). Bore and stroke 85 x 81.5 mm. Displacement 2,775 c.c. Max. b.h.p. 150 at 5,400 r.p.m. 4 speeds. Max. speed 130 m.p.h. Body by Zagato.

SIATA   **ITALY 1965**

850 TS, coupé 2 + 2. 4-cyl. o.h.v. engine (tuned-up version of Fiat 850). Bore and stroke 65 x 64 mm. Displacement 843 c.c. Max. b.h.p. 44.5 at 6,000 r.p.m. 4 speeds. Max. speed 89 m.p.h.

HINO   **JAPAN** 1965

Contessa 1300, sedan. 4-cyl. o.h.v. engine. Bore and stroke 71 x 79 mm. Displacement 1,251 c.c. Max. b.h.p. 55 at 5,000 r.p.m. 3/4 speeds. Max. speed 81 m.p.h. Began by building Renaults in 1953.

MAZDA   **JAPAN** 1965

800, sedan de luxe. 4-cyl. o.h.v. engine. Bore and stroke 58 x 75 mm. Displacement 782 c.c. Max. b.h.p. 42 at 6,000 r.p.m. 4 speeds. Max. speed 72 m.p.h. Wankel-powered Cosmos also from Mazda.

BUICK   **U.S.A.** 1965

Skylark, sedan. V-8 water-cooled o.h.v. engine. Bore and stroke 3.75 x 3.40 inches. Displacement 300 cu. in. Max. b.h.p. 210 at 4600 r.p.m. 3/4 speed or automatic transmission. Max. speed approx. 110 m.p.h.

CHEVROLET   **U.S.A.** 1965

Corvair, 4-door hardtop. 6-cyl. air-cooled, horizontally opposed, rear-mounted, o.h.v. engine. Bore and stroke 3.43 x 2.94 inches. Displacement 164 cu. in. Max. b.h.p. 95 at 3600 r.p.m. Max. speed 91 m.p.h. 3/4 speed or Powerglide transmission.

CHRYSLER   U.S.A. 1965

300, 4-door hardtop. V-8 water-cooled o.h.v. engine. Bore
and stroke 4.25 x 3.38 inches. Displacement 383 cu. in.
Max. b.h.p. 315 at 4400 r.p.m. TorqueFlite transmission.
Max. speed approx. 125 m.p.h.

FORD   U.S.A. 1965

Mustang, coupe 2 + z. V-8 o.h.v. engine. Bore and
stroke 4.0 x 2.87 inches. Displacement 289 cu. in. Max.
b.h.p. 271 at 6000 r.p.m. Max. speed 117 m.p.h. 3/4 speed
or Cruise-O-Matic transmission. One million sold in less
than 2 years.

MERCURY   U.S.A. 1965

Comet Caliente, sedan. 6-cylinder water-cooled o.h.v.
engine in line. Bore and stroke 3.68 x 3.13 inches. Displacement 200 cu. in. Max. b.h.p. 120 at 4400 r.p.m. 3 speeds
or automatic transmission. Max. speed approx. 90 m.p.h.

OLDSMOBILE   U.S.A. 1965

98, sedan. V-8 o.h.v. engine (Super Rocket). Bore and
stroke 4.12 x 3.97 inches. Displacement 425 cu. in. Max.
b.h.p. 360 at 4800 r.p.m. Max. speed 124 m.p.h. Turbo.
Hydramatic transmission. Torque box perimeter Frame.

PLYMOUTH   U.S.A. 1965

Barracuda, sport coupe. V-8 o.h.v. engine. Bore and stroke 3.63 x 3.31 inches. Displacement 273.0 cu. in. Max. b.h.p. 235 at 5,200 r.p.m. Max. speed 125 m.p h. 3/4 speed or TorqueFlite transmission.

RAMBLER   U.S.A. 1965

Classic 550, coach. 6-cyl. o.h.v. engine. Bore and stroke 3.75 x 3.0. Displacement 199 cu. in. Max. b.h.p. 128 at 4400 r.p.m. Max. speed 100 m.p.h. 3-speed or Flash-O-Matic transmission. Unit-construction body.

MOSKVITCH   U.S.S.R. 1965

408, sedan. 4-cyl. o.h.v. engine. Bore and stroke 76 x 75 mm. Displacement 1,360 c.c. Max. b.h.p. 61 at 4,750 r.p.m. 4 speeds. Max. speed 78 m.p.h. Replaced the M-402.

STUDEBAKER   CANADA 1966

Cruiser, sedan. V-8 o.h.v. engine (Chevrolet). Bore and stroke 98 x 76 mm. Displacement 4,638 c.c. Max. b.h.p. 198 at 4,800 r.p.m. Max. speed 115 m.p.h. 3-speed or Flight-O-Matic automatic transmission. 425-h.p. hemi-head V-8 available. Last Studebaker built March 4, 1966.

CITROËN   FRANCE 1966

DS 21 Pallas, sedan. 4-cyl. hemi-head o.h.v. engine.
Bore and stroke 90 x 86 mm. Displacement 2,175 c.c.
Max. b.h.p. 109 at 5,500 r.p.m. 4 speeds. Max. speed
111 m.p.h. Front wheel drive. Inboard disk brakes on
front wheels.

PEUGEOT   FRANCE 1966

204, sedan. 4-cyl. hemi-head, transversely mounted s.o.h.c.
engine. Bore and stroke 75 x 64 mm. Displacement 1,130
c.c. Max. b.h.p. 58 x 5,800 r.p.m. 4 speeds. Max. speed
86 m.p.h. Front wheel drive. All-coil suspension.

RENAULT   FRANCE 1966

10 Major, sedan. 4-cyl. rear-mounted o.h.v. engine. Bore
and stroke 70 x 72 m.m. Displacement 1,108 c.c. Max.
b.h.p. 50 at 4,600 r.p.m. 4 speeds. Max. speed 82 m.p.h.
A lengthened R-8.

AUDI   GERMANY 1966

1700. 4-cyl. s.o.h.c. engine. Bore and stroke 80 x 84 mm.
Displacement 1,696 c.c. Max. b.h.p. 72 at 5,000 r.p.m.
4 speeds. Max. speed 92 m.p.h. Front wheel drive.
Engine developed by Daimler-Benz. Audi (Auto Union)
owned by Volkswagen.

B.M.W.   GERMANY 1966

2000 CS, coupé. 4-cyl. s.o.h.c. engine. Bore and stroke
89 x 80 mm. Displacement 1,990 c.c. Max. b.h.p. 120 at
5,600 r.p.m. Max. speed 115 m.p.h. 4-speed or 2F automatic transmission. Body design by Giovanni Michelotti.

MERCEDES-BENZ   GERMANY 1966

250 SE, sedan. 6-cyl. s.o.h.c. engine. Fuel injection. Bore
and stroke 82 x 79 mm. Displacement 2,496 c.c. Max.
b.h.p. 150 at 5,500 r.p.m. Max. speed 118 m.p.h. 4-speed
or automatic transmission. All-independent suspension
with coil springs.

OPEL   GERMANY 1966

Rekord, sedan. 4-cyl. s.o.h.c. engine. Bore and stroke
93 x 70 mm. Displacement 1,897 c.c. Max. b.h.p. 102 at
5,100 r.p.m. 3 speeds. Max. speed 100 m.p.h. Body design
by Clare McKichan.

VOLKSWAGEN   GERMANY 1966

1600 TL, coach. 4-cyl. air-cooled, horizontally opposed,
rear-mounted, o.h.v. engine. Bore and stroke 86 x 69 mm.
Displacement 1,584 c.c. Max. b.h.p. 65 at 4,600 r.p.m.
4 speeds. Max. speed 84 m.p.h. Available as a station
wagon and convertible.

JENSEN GREAT BRITAIN 1966

Interceptor, cabriolet (fiberglass). V-8 o.h.v. engine (Chrysler). Bore and stroke 93 x 84 mm. Displacement 4,475 c.c. Max. b.h.p. 238 at 5,000 r.p.m. Max. speed 112 m.p.h. 4-speed or TorqueFlight automatic transmission.

ROLLS-ROYCE GREAT BRITAIN 1966

Silver Shadow. V-8 o.h.v. engine (2 carburetors). Bore and stroke 104 x 91 mm. Displacement 6,230 c.c. Max. b.h.p. approx. 330. Max. speed 118 m.p.h. RR Hydra-Matic transmission. First Rolls-Royce unit-construction body.

TRIUMPH GREAT BRITAIN 1966

1300, sedan. 4-cyl. o.h.v. engine in line. Bore and stroke 74 x 76 mm. Displacement 1,296 c.c. Max. b.h.p. 61 at 5,000 r.p.m. 4 speeds. Max. speed 85 m.p.h. Front wheel drive. Body design by Giovanni Michelotti.

VAUXHALL GREAT BRITAIN 1966

Cresta, sedan. 6-cyl. o.h.v. engine. Bore and stroke 92 x 83 mm. Displacement 3,294 c.c. Max. b.h.p. 140 at 4,800 r.p.m. Max. speed 103 m.p.h. 3/4-speed or automatic transmission. Body design by David Jones.

WOLSELEY   **GREAT BRITAIN** 1966

1100, saloon. 4-cyl. transversely mounted o.h.v. engine
Bore and stroke 65 x 84 mm. Displacement 1,098 c.c
Max. b.h.p. 55 at 5,500 r.p.m. 4 speeds. Max. speed
87 m.p.h. Body design by Pininfarina.

ABARTH   **ITALY** 1966

OTR 1000, coupé. 4-cyl. o.h.v. engine. Bore and stroke
65 x 75 m.m. Displacement 982 c.c. Max. b.h.p. 73 at
6,500 r.p.m. 4 speeds. Max. speed 107 m.p.h. Based on
Fiat 850.

ALFA ROMEO   **ITALY** 1966

Giulia GTA, coupé (aluminum). 4-cyl. d.o.h.c. engine.
Bore and stroke 78 x 82 mm. Displacement 1,570 c.c.
Max. b.h.p. 133 at 6,000 r.p.m. 5 speeds. Max. speed
115 m.p.h.

ALFA ROMEO   **ITALY** 1966

2600, sedan. 6-cyl. d.o.h.c. engine. Bore and stroke
83 x 80 mm. Displacement 2,584 c.c. Max. b.h.p. 148 at
5,900 r.p.m. 5 speeds. Max. speed 109 m.p.h. Body by
Carrozzeria O.S.I. Body not in series production.

FIAT   **ITALY 1966**

124, sedan. 4-cyl. water-cooled o.h.v. engine in line. Bore and stroke 73 x 71.5 mm. Displacement 1,197 c.c. Max. b.h.p. 60 at 5,600 r.p.m. 4 speeds. Max. speed 86 m.p.h.

DAIHATSU   **JAPAN 1966**

Compagno, coach. 4-cyl. o.h.v. engine. Bore and stroke 62 x 66 mm. Displacement 797 c.c. Max. b.h.p. 41 at 5,000 r.p.m. 4 speeds. Max. speed 68 m.p.h.

NISSAN   **JAPAN 1966**

President C, limousine. V-8 o.h.v. engine. Bore and stroke 92 x 75 mm. Displacement 3,988 c.c. Max. b.h.p. 180. Max. speed 109 m.p.h. Borg-Warner automatic transmission. Body design in consultation with Pininfarina.

DAF   **THE NETHERLANDS 1966**

Daffodil de luxe, coach. 2-cyl. air-cooled o.h.v. engine. Bore and stroke 86 x 65 mm. Displacement 746 c.c. Max. b.h.p. 26 at 4,000 r.p.m. Max. speed 65 m.p.h. Automatic Variomatic transmission. (uses rubber belts running on cones).

CHEVROLET   U.S.A. 1966

Caprice, sedan. V-8 o.h.v. engine (Staggered valves).
Bore and stroke 3.87 x 3.0 inches. Displacement 283.0
cu. in. Max. b.h.p. 210 at 4,800 r.p.m. 3/4 speeds or automatic transmission. Max. speed 130 m.p.h. ,,Porcupine-
head" engine.

DODGE   U.S.A. 1966

Cornet 500, 2-door hardtop. 8-cyl. o.h.v. engine. Bore and
stroke 3.63 x 3.31 inches. Displacement 273 cu. in. Max.
b.h.p. 180 at 4,200 r.p.m. Max. speed 103 m.p.h.

FORD   U.S.A. 1966

Falcon Futura, sports coupé. 6-cyl. o.h.v. engine in line.
Bore and stroke 3.68 x 3.13 inches. Displacement 200.0
cu. in. Max. b.h.p. 122 at 4,400 r.p.m. 3/4 speed or automatic transmission. Max. speed 103 m.p.h. Body design
under direction of Gene Bordinat.

MARLIN   U.S.A. 1966

2-door hardtop (fastback). V-8 water-cooled o.h.v. engine.
Bore and stroke 4.0 x 3.25. Displacement 327 cu. in. Max.
b.h.p. 274 at 4,700 r.p.m. 3/4 speeds or automatic transmission. Max. speed approx. 118 m.p.h.

MERCURY   U.S.A. 1966

Montclair, 2-door hardtop. V-8 water-cooled o.h.v. engine.
Bore and stroke 4.05 x 3.78. Displacement 390 cu. in.
Max. b.h.p. 250 at 4,400 r.p.m. 3 speeds or automatic
transmission. Max. speed approx. 116 m.p.h.

OLDSMOBILE   U.S.A. 1966

Tornado, coupé. V-8 4-stroke engine (super Rocket). Bore
and stroke 4.12 x 3.97 inches. Displacement 425 cu. in.
Max. b.h.p. 385 at 4,800 r.p.m. Max. speed 130 m.p.h.
Automatic transmission. Front wheel drive.

PLYMOUTH   U.S.A. 1966

VIP, 4-door hardtop. V-8 water-cooled o.h.v. engine.
Bore and stroke 4.25 x 3.37 inches. Displacement 383.0
cu. in. Max. b.h.p. 325 at 4,800 r.p.m. 3/4 speeds or automatic transmission. Max. speed approx. 122 m.p.h

WARTBURG   EAST GERMANY 1967

1000 Limousine Komfort, sedan. 3-cyl. water-cooled, 2-
stroke engine in line. Bore and stroke 73.5 x 78 mm.
Displacement 991 c.c. Max. b.h.p. 50 at 4,200 r.p.m.
4 speeds. Max. speed 81 m.p.h.

BMW GERMANY 1967

1600, coach. 4-cyl. water-cooled o.h.v. engine in line.
Bore and stroke 71 x 84 m.m. Displacement 1,573 c.c.
Max. b.h.p. 94 at 5700 r.p.m. 4 speeds. Max. speed 100
m.p.h.

FORD TAUNUS GERMANY 1967

15 MTS, sedan. V-4 cyl. water-cooled o.h.v. engine.
Bore and stroke 90 x 58.8 mm. Displacement 1,498 c.c.
Max. b.h.p. 83 at 5,000 r.p.m. 4 speeds. Max. speed
90 m.p.h.

OPEL GERMANY 1967

Rekord, coupé. 6-cyl. water-cooled o.h.v. engine in line.
Bore and stroke 82.5 x 69.8 mm. Displacement 2,239 c.c.
Max. b.h.p. 108 at 5,200 r.p.m. 4 speeds or automatic
transmission. Max. speed 106 m.p.h.

BENTLEY GREAT BRITAIN 1967

T, 2-door saloon. V-8 water-cooled o.h.v. engine (2
carburetors). Bore and stroke 104 x 91 mm. Displacement
6,230 c.c. Automatic transmission. Max. speed approx.
118 m.p.h. Body by Mulliner.

FORD CORTINA   **GREAT BRITAIN 1967**

1500 Super, sedan. 4-cyl. water-cooled o.h.v. engine in line. Bore and stroke 80.96 x 72.75 m.m. Displacement 1,498 c.c. Max. b.h.p. 65 at 4,800 r.p.m. 4 speeds or Borg-Warner automatic transmission. Max. speed 88 m.p.h.

HILLMAN   **GREAT BRITAIN 1967**

Hunter, sedan. 4-cyl. water-cooled o.h.v. engine in line. Bore and stroke 81.5 x 82.5 mm. Displacement 1,725 c.c. Max. b.h.p. 74 at 5,000 r.p.m. 4 speeds. Max. speed 90 m.p.h.

JENSEN   **GREAT BRITAIN 1967**

FF, sports coupé. V-8 water-cooled o.h.v. engine (Chrysler). Bore and stroke 108 x 86 m.m. Displacement 6,276 c.c. Max. b.h.p. 315 at 4,400 r.p.m. 4 speeds or automatic transmission. Max. speed approx. 140 m.p.h.

LOTUS   **GREAT BRITAIN 1967**

Europa, coupe. Renault 16 4-cyl. o.h.v. engine in line, water-cooled. Bore and stroke 76 x 81 mm. Displacement 1,470 c.c. Max. b.h.p. 78 (net) at 6,000 r.p.m. 4 speeds. Max. speed 115 m.p.h.

VAUXHALL　　　　　　　　　**GREAT BRITAIN 1967**

Viva SL 90, coach. 4-cyl. water-cooled o.h.v. engine in line. Bore and stroke 77.7 x 61 mm. Displacement 1,159 c.c. Max. b.h.p. 60 at 5,600 r.p.m. 4 speed. Max. speed 88 m.p.h.

FIAT　　　　　　　　　　**ITALY 1967**

124 Spider, cabriolet. 4-cyl. water-cooled o.h.v. engine (2 camshafts). Bore and stroke 80 x 71.5 mm. Displacement 1,438 c.c. Max. b.h.p. 90 at 6,500 r.p.m. 5 speeds. Max. speed 106 m.p.h. Body by Farina.

LANCIA　　　　　　　　　**ITALY 1967**

Fulvia Zagato, sports coupé. V-4 water-cooled d.o.h.c. engine. Bore and stroke 76 x 67 m.m. Displacement 1,216 c.c. Max. b.h.p. 80 at 6,000 r.p.m. 4 speeds. Max. speed 105 m.p.h. Body by Zagato.

DATSUN　　　　　　　　　**JAPAN 1967**

1000 Sunny de Luxe, coach. 4-cyl. water-cooled o.h.v. engine in line. Bore and stroke 73 x 59 mm. Displacement 998 c.c. Max. b.h.p. 56 at 6,000 r.p.m. 3 speeds. Max. speed 84 m.p.h.

TOYOPET   JAPAN 1967

1600 S, hardtop coupé. 4-cyl. water-cooled o.h.v. engine
in line (2 carburetors). Bore and stroke 80.5 x 78 mm.
Max. b.h.p. 95 at 5,800 r.p.m. 4 speeds. Max. speed
102 m.p.h.

DAF   THE NETHERLANDS 1967

44, Coach. 2-cyl. air-cooled o.h.v. engine with horizon-
tally opposed cylinders. Bore and stroke 85.5 x 73.5 m.m.
Displacement 844 c.c. Max. b.h.p. 30 at 5000 r.p.m.
Variomatic transmission. Max. speed 75 m.p.h.

VOLVO   SWEDEN 1967

144 S, sedan. 4-cyl. water-cooled o.h.v. engine in line
(2 carburetors). Bore and stroke 84.14 x 80 mm. Displacement 1,778 c.c. Max. b.h.p. 100 at 5,600 r.p.m.
4 speeds. Max. speed 103 m.p.h.

CADILLAC   U.S.A. 1967

Eldorado, sport coupe. V-8 water-cooled o.h.v. engine.
Bore and stroke 4.13 x 4.00 inches. Displacement 429
cu. in. Max. b.h.p. 340 at 4600 r.p.m. Automatic transmission. Max. speed approx. 125 m.p.h. Front wheel drive.

CHEVROLET U.S.A. 1967

Camaro, coupe. V-8 water-cooled o.h.v. engine. **Bore and stroke 4.00 x 3.25 inches. Displacement 327 cu. in. Max. b.h.p. 210 at 4,600 r.p.m. 3/4 speeds or Powerglide transmission. Max. speed approx. 122 m.p.h.**

DODGE U.S.A. 1967

Dart G.T., 2-door convertible. V-8 water-cooled engine. **Bore and stroke 3.62 x 3.31 inches. Displacement 273 cu. in. Max. b.h.p. 180 at 4200 r.p.m. 4 speeds or automatic transmission. Max. speed 107 m.p.h.**

PLYMOUTH U.S.A. 1967

Valiant Signet, sedan. 6-cyl. water-cooled **o.h.v. engine in line. Bore and stroke 3.40 x 3.12 inches. Displacement 170 cu. in. Max. b.h.p. 115 at 4400 rpm. 3 speeds or automatic transmission. Max. speed 90 m.p.h.**

RAMBLER U.S.A. 1967

Rogue, convertible. V-8 water-cooled o.h.v. engine. **Bore and stroke 3.75 x 3.28 inches. Displacement 290 cu. in. Max. b.h.p. 200 at 4600 r.p.m. 3/4 speeds or automatic transmission. Max. speed 100 m.p.h.**

CITROEN　　　　　　　　　　　　**FRANCE 1967**

Dyane, saloon. 2-cyl. air-cooled, horizontally opposed o.h.v. engine. 4-speed transmission. Capacity 425 c.c. Bore and stroke 66 x 62 mm. Max. output 18,5 b.h.p. (net) at 4750 r.p.m. Max. speed 100 km.h./62 m.p.h.

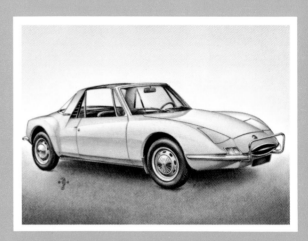

MATRA　　　　　　　　　　　　**FRANCE 1967**

M 530 A, coupé. Ford 17 M 4-cyl. water-cooled, o.h.v. engine in V. 4-speed transmission. Capacity 1699 c.c. Bore and stroke 90 x 66,8 mm. Max. output 73 b.h.p. (net) at 4800 r.p.m. Max. speed 172 km.h./112 m.p.h.

SIMCA　　　　　　　　　　　　**FRANCE 1967**

1100 GLS, coach. 4-cyl. transversely mounted, water-cooled o.h.v. engine in line. 4-speed transmission. Capacity 1118 c.c. Bore and stroke 74 x 65 mm. Max. output 56 b.h.p. (net) at 5800 r.p.m. Max. speed 141 km.h./88 m.p.h.

ISO　　　　　　　　　　　　**ITALY 1967**

Grifo Lusso GL 350, coupé. Chevrolet Corvette 8-cyl. water-cooled o.h.v. engine in V. 4-speed transmission, 5-speed optional extra. Capacity 5359 c.c. Bore and stroke 101,6 x 82,55 mm. Max. output 355 b.h.p. (SAE) at 5800 r.p.m. Max. speed 245 km.h./152 m.p.h.

242

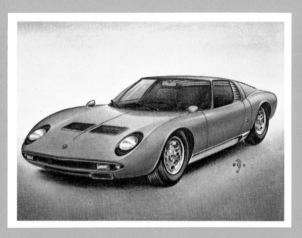

LAMBORGHINI   **ITALY 1967**

Miura P 400 coupé. Rear mounted 12-cyl. water-cooled,
o.h.v. engine in V. 5-speed transmission. Capacity 3929 c.c.
Bore and stroke 82 x 62 mm. Max. output 350 b.h.p. (net) at
7000 r.p.m. Max. speed 290 km.h./180 m.p.h.

MAZDA   **JAPAN 1967**

1500, saloon. 4-cyl. water-cooled, o.h.v. engine in line.
4-speed transmission. Capacity 1490 c.c. Bore and stroke
78 x 78 mm. Max. output 72 b.h.p. (net) at 5300 r.p.m. Max.
speed 150 km.h./93 m.p.h.

ANADOL   **TURKEY 1967**

A1, coach. Ford 12 M 4-cyl. water-cooled o.h.v. engine in V.
4-speed transmission. Capacity 1198 c.c. Bore and stroke
80,97 x 58,17 mm. Max. output 46 b.h.p. (net) at 4800 r.p.m.
Max. speed 127 km.h./m.p.h.

FORD   **U.S.A. 1967**

Thunderbird 4-door Hardtop Landau, saloon. 8-cyl. water-
cooled o.h.v. engine in V. Select Shift Automatic transmission. Capacity 7026 c.c. Bore and stroke 110,74 x 91,18 mm.
Max. output 365 b.h.p. (SAE) at 4600 r.p.m. Max. speed 200-
210 km.h./124-131 m.p.h.

HOLDEN   AUSTRALIA 1968

HK Premier V-8, saloon. 8-cyl. water-cooled, o.h.v. engine
in V. Powerglide automatic transmission. Capacity 5029 c.c.
Bore and stroke 98,42 x 82,55 mm. Max. output 213 b.h.p.
(SAE) at 4600 r.p.m. Max. speed 185 km.h./115 m.p.h.

OPEL   GERMANY 1968

Olympia, coupé. 4-cyl. water-cooled o.h.v. engine in line.
4-speed transmission. Capacity 1078 c.c. Bore and stroke
75 x 61 mm. Max. output 60 b.h.p. (net) at 5200 r.p.m. Max.
speed 140 km.h./88 m.p.h.

MERCEDES-BENZ   GERMANY 1968

250, saloon. 6-cyl. water-cooled o.h.v. engine in line. 4-speed
transmission. Capacity 2496 c.c. Bore and stroke 82 x 78,8
mm. Max. output 130 b.h.p. (net) at 5400 r.p.m. Max. speed
180 km.h./112 m.p.h.

NSU   GERMANY 1968

Ro, 80, saloon. Twin rotor Wankel engine, water-cooled.
3-speed, torque converter. Capacity 995 c.c. total. Each
497,5 c.c. Max. output 115 b.h.p. (net) at 5500 r.p.m. Max.
speed 100 km.h./62 m.p.h.

DAIMLER   GR. BRITAIN 1968

Limousine. Jaguar 420 6-cyl. water-cooled twin o.h.v. engine.
Borg Warner automatic transmission. Capacity 4235 c.c.
Bore and stroke 92,07 x 106 mm. Max. output 248 b.h.p. (SAE)
at 5500 r.p.m. Max. speed 177 km.h./110 m.p.h.

FORD   GR. BRITAIN 1968

Escort Twin Cam, coach. Cortina-Lotus 4-cyl. water-cooled
twin o.h.v. engine in line. 4-speed transmission. Capacity
1558 c.c. Bore and stroke 82,55 x 72,75 mm. Max. output
117 b.h.p. (SAE) at 6000 r.p.m. Max. speed 185 km.h./115
m.p.h.

SUNBEAM   GR. BRITAIN 1968

Rapier, coupé. 4-cyl. water-cooled o.h.v. engine in line.
4-speed transmission. Capacity 1725 c.c. Bore and stroke
81,5 x 82,55 mm. Max. output 88 b.h.p. (net) at 5200 r.p.m.
Max. speed 164 km.h./102 m.p.h.

VAUXHALL   GR. BRITAIN 1968

Ventora, saloon. Vauxhall Cresta 6-cyl. water-cooled o.h.v.
engine in line. 4-speed transmission. Capacity 3294 c.c.
Bore and stroke 92,08 x 82,55 mm. Max. output 124 b.h.p. (net)
at 4600 r.p.m. Max. speed 169 km.h./105 m.p.h.

ALFA ROMEO   ITALY 1968

1750, saloon. 4-cyl. water-cooled twin o.h.v. engine in line.
5-speed transmission. Capacity 1779 c.c. Bore and stroke
80 x 88,5 mm. Max. output 132 b.h.p. (SAE) at 5500 r.p.m.
Max. speed 180 km.h./112 m.p.h.

DE TOMASO   ITALY 1968

Mangusta, coupé, body by Ghia. Rear mounted Ford 8-cyl.
water-cooled o.h.v. engine in V. 5-speed transmission.
Capacity 4728 c.c. Bore and stroke 101,60 x 72,89 mm. Max.
output 306 b.h.p. (net) at 6200 r.p.m. Max. speed ± 250 km.h./
160 m.p.h.

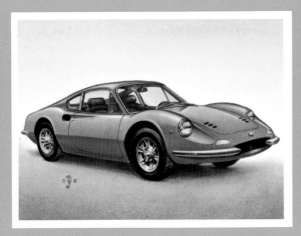

DINO   ITALY 1968

206 GT, coupé. 6-cyl. water-cooled, twin o.h.v. engine in V,
transversely rear mounted. 5-speed transmission. Capacity
1987 c.c. Bore and stroke 86 x 57 mm. Max. output 180 b.h.p.
(net) at 8000 r.p.m. Max. speed 235 km.h./146,5 m.p.h.

MASERATI   ITALY 1968

Ghibli, coupé, body by Ghia. 8-cyl. water-cooled, four o.h.v.
engine in V. 5-speed transmission. Capacity 4719 c.c. Bore
and stroke 94 x 85 mm. Max. output 330 b.h.p. (net) at 5500
r.p.m. Max. speed 280 km.h./175 m.p.h.

DATSUN JAPAN 1968

Bluebird 1600 SSS, saloon. 4-cyl. water-cooled, o.h.v. engine in line, twin horizontal carburetters. 4-speed transmission. Capacity 1595 c.c. Bore and stroke 83 x 73,3 mm. Max. output 109 b.h.p. (SAE) at 6000 r.p.m. Max. speed 165 km.h./ 103,5 m.p.h.

ISUZU JAPAN 1968

Florian, saloon. 4-cyl. water-cooled o.h.v. engine in line. 3- or 4-speed transmission. Capacity 1584 c.c. Bore and stroke 82 x 75 mm. Max. output 85 b.h.p. (net) at 5200 r.p.m. Max. speed 150 km.h./93 m.p.h.

MAZDA JAPAN 1968

1000 Coupé. 4-cyl. water-cooled, o.h.v. engine in line, twin carburetters. 4-speed transmission. Capacity 985 c.c. Bore and stroke 70 x 64 mm. Max. output 68 b.h.p. (SAE) at 6500 r.p.m. Max. speed 145 km.h./90 m.p.h.

SUBARU JAPAN 1968

1000 4-Door Sedan DeLuxe. 4-cyl. water-cooled, horizontally opposed o.h.v. engine. 4-speed transmission. Capacity 977 c.c. Bore and stroke 72 x 60 mm. Max. output 55 b.h.p. (net) at 6000 r.p.m. Max. speed 135 km.h./84 m.p.h.

TOYOTA   **JAPAN 1968**

Crown 2300, saloon. 6-cyl. water-cooled, o.h.v. engine in line. 3- or 4-speed transmission or automatic transmission. Capacity 2253 c.c. Bore and stroke 75 x 78 mm. Max. output 115 b.h.p. (SAE) at 5200 r.p.m. Max. speed 150-160 km.h./ 93-99 m.p.h.

DAF   **THE NETHERLANDS 1968**

55 Coupé. 4-cyl. water-cooled, o.h.v. engine in line. Vario-matic automatic transmission. Capacity 1108 c.c. Bore and stroke 70 x 72 mm. Max. output 45 b.h.p. (net) at 5000 r.p.m. Max. speed 138 km.h./84,3 m.p.h.

GAZ   **RUSSIA 1968**

Volga 24, saloon. 4-cyl. water-cooled o.h.v. engine in line. 4-speed transmission. Capacity 2445 c.c. Bore and stroke 92 x 92 mm. Max. output 98 b.h.p. (SAE) at 4500 r.p.m. Max. speed 145 km.h./90,1 m.p.h.

ZAZ   **RUSSIA 1968**

(export model: Yalta 1000 with Renault engine) 966, saloon. Rear mounted 4-cyl. air-cooled o.h.v. engine in V. 4-speed transmission. Capacity 1196 c.c. Bore and stroke 76 x 66 mm. Max. output 45 b.h.p. (SAE) at 4400 r.p.m. Max. speed 120 km.h./74,5 m.p.h.

ZIL   **RUSSIA 1968**

114, saloon. 8-cyl. water-cooled o.h.v. engine in V. Automatic transmission. Capacity 5980 c.c. Bore and stroke 100 x 95 mm. Max. output 230 b.h.p. (SAE) at 4200 r.p.m. Max. speed 160 km.h./99 m.p.h.

SEAT   **SPAIN 1968**

850, 4 Puertas, saloon. Rear mounted Fiat 850, 4-cyl. water-cooled o.h.v. engine in line. 4-speed transmission. Capacity 843 c.c. Bore and stroke 65 x 63,5 mm. Max. output 42 b.h.p. (SAE) at 5300 r.p.m. Max. speed 125 km.h./78 m.p.h.

MONTEVERDI   **SWITZERLAND 1968**

375 S, coupé. Chrysler 8 cyl. water-cooled, o.h.v. engine in V. 4-speed transmission. Capacity 7206 c.c. Bore and stroke 109,72 x 95,25 m.m. Max. output 380 b.h.p. (SAE) at 4600 r.p.m. Max. speed 250 km.h./155 m.p.h.

CHEVROLET   **U.S.A. 1968**

Corvette Sting Ray, coupé. 8-cyl. water-cooled o.h.v. engine in V. 3- or 4-speed transmission or Turbo Hydra-Matic automatic transmission. Capacity 5354 c.c. Bore and stroke 101,60 x 82,55 mm. Max. output 304 b.h.p. (SAE) at 5000 r.p.m. Max. speed 190-205 km.h./118-127 m.p.h.

JAVELIN AMC   U.S.A. 1968

SST, coupé. 8-cyl. water-cooled o.h.v. engine in V. 4-speed transmission. Capacity 4749 c.c. Bore and stroke 95,25 x 83,31 mm. Max. output 203 b.h.p. (SAE) at 4600 r.p.m. Max. speed ca. 180 km.h./112 m.p.h.

LINCOLN   U.S.A. 1968

Continental MK III. 8-cyl. water-cooled o.h.v. engine in V. Turbo Drive automatic transmission. Capacity 7536 c.c. Bore and stroke 110,74 x 97,79 mm. Max. output 370 b.h.p. (SAE) at 4600 r.p.m. Max. speed 200-210 km.h./124-131 m.p.h.

MERCURY   U.S.A. 1968

Cougar GTE Hardtop Coupé. 8-cyl. water-cooled o.h.v. engine in V. Select Shift Merc-O-Matic automatic transmission. Capacity 6964 c.c. Bore and stroke 107,44 x 96 mm. Max. output 395 b.h.p. (SAE) at 5600 r.p.m. Max. speed 200-210 km.h./124-131 m.p.h.

OLDSMOBILE   U.S.A. 1968

Cutlass Sedan Hardtop. 8-cyl. water-cooled o.h.v. engine in V. Jetaway Drive automatic transmission. Capacity 5736 c.c. Bore and stroke 103,05 x 85,98 mm. Max. output 253 b.h.p. (SAE) at 4400 r.p.m. Max. speed ca. 180 km.h./112 m.p.h.

PONTIAC   **U.S.A. 1968**

Le Mans 4-Door Hardtop. 3-speed transmission. Capacity 5799 c.c. Bore and stroke 98,43 x 95,25 mm. Max. output 269 b.h.p. (SAE) at 4600 r.p.m. Max. speed ca. 180-200 km.h./112-124 m.p.h.

RENAULT   **FRANCE 1969**

Type 6 saloon. 4-cyl. water-cooled, o.h.v. engine in line. 4-speed transmission. Capacity 845 c.c. Bore and stroke 58 x 80 mm. Max. output 34 b.h.p. (DIN) at 5000 r.p.m. Max. speed 117 km.h./75 m.p.h.

PEUGEOT   **FRANCE 1969**

Type 504 saloon. 4-cylinder, water-cooled o.h.v. engine in line. 4-speed transmission. Capacity 1796 c.c. Bore and stroke 84 x 81 mm. Max. output 76 b.h.p. (DIN) at 5500 r.p.m. Max. speed 156 km.h./98 m.p.h. Body by Pininfarina.

CITROEN   **FRANCE 1969**

Type Ami 8 saloon. 2-cyl., air-cooled, horizontally opposed, o.h.v. engine. 4-speed transmission. Capacity 602 c.c. Bore and stroke 74 x 70 mm. Max. output 35 b.h.p. (SAE) at 5750 r.p.m. Max. speed 123 km.h./79 m.p.h.

BMW   **GERMANY 1969**

Type 2500/2800, saloon. 6-cyl. water-cooled, o.h.v. engine in line. 4-speed transmission, ZF-Automatic gearbox optional. Capacity 2494 (2788) c.c. Bore and stroke 86 x 71,6 (86 x 80) mm. Max. output 150 (170) b.h.p. (DIN) at 6000 r.p.m. Max. speed 190 (200) km.h./118 (124) m.p.h.

FORD   **GERMANY 1969**

Type 20 M XL, 2-door hardtop. 6-cyl. water-cooled, o.h.v. engine in V. 4-speed transmission. Capacity 1998 c.c. Bore and stroke 84 x 60,1 mm. Max. output 90 b.h.p. (DIN) at 5000 r.p.m. Max. speed 160 km.h./100 m.p.h.

FORD   **GREAT BRITAIN 1969**

Type Capri 2000 GT. 4-cyl., water-cooled o.h.v. engine in V. 4-speed transmission; Borg-Warner automatic transmission optional. Capacity 1996 c.c. Bore and stroke 93,66 x 72,44 mm. Max. output 92,5 b.h.p. (DIN) at 5500 r.p.m. Max. speed 171 km.h./110 m.p.h.

JAGUAR   **GREAT BRITAIN 1969**

Type XJ6 4,2 Saloon. 6-cyl., water-cooled twin o.h.c. engine in line. 4-speed transmission; available with overdrive or Borg-Warner automatic transmission at extra cost. Capacity 4235 c.c. Bore and stroke 92,07 x 106 mm. Max. output 186 b.h.p. (DIN) at 4500 r.p.m. Max. speed 204 km.h./127 m.p.h.

FIAT ITALY 1969

Type 128 Coach. 4-cyl., water-cooled o.h.v. engine in line, transversely mounted; frontwheel drive. 4-speed transmission. Capacity 1116 c.c. Bore and stroke 80 x 55,5 mm. Max. output 55 b.h.p. (DIN) at 6000 r.p.m. Max. speed approx. 135 km.h./82 m.p.h.

ISO RIVOLTA ITALY 1969

Type Fidia 300 4-door saloon. 8-cyl., water-cooled o.h.v. engine in V (Chevrolet Corvette 327 engine). 4-speed transmission, 5-speed transmission available. Capacity 5359 c.c. Bore and stroke 101,6 x 82,55 mm. Max. output 355 b.h.p. (SAE) at 5500 r.p.m. Max. speed approx. 215 km.h./134 m.p.h. Body by Ghia.

VOLVO SWEDEN 1969

Type 164 saloon. 6-cyl., watercooled o.h.v. engine in line. 4-speed transmission, overdrive or automatic transmission optional. Capacity 2978 c.c. Bore and stroke 88,9 x 80 mm. Max. output 130 b.h.p. (DIN) at 5000 r.p.m. Max. speed approx. 180 km.h./122 m.p.h.

SAAB SWEDEN 1969

Type 99 2-door coach. 4-cyl., water-cooled o.h.v. engine in line. 4-speed transmission, Borg Warner automatic transmission optional. Bore and stroke 83,5 x 78 mm. Max. output 80 b.h.p. (DIN) at 5200 r.p.m. Max. speed 155 km.h./96 m.p.h. Fitted with Triumph engine; front wheel drive.

CHEVROLET U.S.A. 1969

Type Chevy Nova Sedan. 6-cyl., water-cooled o.h.v. engine in line. 3-speed transmission; automatic transmission „powerglide" optional. Capacity 3768 c.c. Bore and stroke 98,43 x 82,55 mm. Max. output 142 b.h.p. (SAE) at 4400 r.p.m. Max. speed approx. 160 km.h./99 m.p.h.

FORD U.S.A. 1969

Type Maverick Hardtop. 6-cyl., water-cooled o.h.v. engine in line. 3-speed transmission. Capacity 2788 c.c. Bore and stroke 88,9 x 74,67 mm. Max. output 105 b.h.p. (SAE) at 4200 r.p.m. Max. speed approx. 150 km.h./94 m.p.h.

OPEL GERMANY 1969

Diplomat E Sedan. 6-cyl. water cooled engine in line with high camshaft and petrol injection. Bore and stroke 92 x 69.8 m.m. Displacement 2784 c.c. Max. h.p. (DIN) 165 at 5600 r.p.m. 3-speed or automatic transmission. Max. speed ± 118 m.p.h.

TRIUMPH GREAT BRITAIN 1969

TR 6 sport cabriolet. 6-cyl. water cooled o.h.v. engine in line with petrol injection. Bore and stroke 74.7 x 95 m.m. Displacement 2498 c.c. Max. h.p. (DIN) 142 at 5500 r.p.m. 4-speed. Max. speed 188 km.h. = 117 m.p.h.

CHRYSLER　　　　　　　　　　　　　　　　**U.S.A. 1969**

New Yorker Sedan. V-8 water cooled o.h.v. engine. Bore and stroke 109.72 x 95.25 m.m. Displacement 7206 c.c. Max. b.h.p. (SAE) 355 at 4400 r.p.m. Automatic transmission. Max. speed ± 120 m.p.h.

AUTOBIANCHI　　　　　　　　　　　　　　　**ITALY 1970**

A112, coach. 4-cyl. transversely mounted water cooled o.h.v. engine in line, frontwheel drive. Bore and stroke 68 x 65 m.m. Displacement 903 c.c. Max. b.h.p. 44 (DIN) at 6000 r.p.m. 4-speed. Max. speed 84 m.p.h.

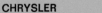

FORD　　　　　　　　　　　　　　　　　　**U.S.A. 1970**

Torino GT Sportsroof Coupé. 8-cyl. water cooled o.h.v. engine in V. Bore and stroke 101.6 x 88.9 m.m. Displacement 5749 c.c. Max. b.h.p. 253 (SAE) at 4600 r.p.m. 3-speed or 4-speed or automatic transmission. Max. speed approx 118 m.p.h.

CHEVROLET　　　　　　　　　　　　　　　**U.S.A. 1970**

Monte Carlo. V-8 cyl. water cooled o.h.v. engine. Bore and stroke 107.95 x 101.6 m.m. Displacement 7437 c.c. Max. b.h.p. 360 (SAE) at 4400 r.p.m. 3 or 4 speed or automatic transmission. Max. speed approx. 120 m.p.h.

INDEX